Producing Children

Rutgers Series in Childhood Studies

The Rutgers Series in Childhood Studies is dedicated to increasing our understanding of children and childhoods throughout the world, reflecting a perspective that highlights cultural dimensions of the human experience. The books in this series are intended for students, scholars, practitioners, and those who formulate policies that affect children's everyday lives and futures.

Series Board

For a complete list of titles in the series, please see the last page of the book.

Producing Children

Critical Studies in Childhood Creativity

EDITED BY PETER C. KUNZE AND
VICTORIA FORD SMITH

RUTGERS UNIVERSITY PRESS
NEW BRUNSWICK, CAMDEN, AND NEWARK, NEW JERSEY
LONDON AND OXFORD

Rutgers University Press is a department of Rutgers, The State University of New Jersey, one of the leading public research universities in the nation. By publishing worldwide, it furthers the University's mission of dedication to excellence in teaching, scholarship, research, and clinical care.

LIBRARY OF CONGRESS CATALOGING-IN-PUBLICATION DATA

Names: Kunze, Peter C. (Peter Christopher), editor. | Smith, Victoria Ford, editor.
Title: Producing children : critical studies in childhood creativity / edited by Peter C. Kunze and Victoria Ford Smith.
Description: New Brunswick, New Jersey : Rutgers University Press, [2025] | Series: Rutgers series in childhood studies | Includes bibliographical references and index.
Identifiers: LCCN 2024040200 | ISBN 9781978842311 (paperback) | ISBN 9781978842328 (hardcover) | ISBN 9781978842335 (epub) | ISBN 9781978842342 (pdf)
Subjects: LCSH: Creative ability in children. | Creation (Literary, artistic, etc.) | Child authors. | Child actors. | Child dancers.
Classification: LCC BF723.C7 P76 2025 | DDC 155.4/1335—dc23/eng/20241213
LC record available at https://lccn.loc.gov/2024040200

A British Cataloging-in-Publication record for this book is available from the British Library.

∞ The paper used in this publication meets the requirements of the American National Standard for Information Sciences—Permanence of Paper for Printed Library Materials, ANSI Z39.48-1992.

rutgersuniversitypress.org

CONTENTS

Producing Children

Introduction

PETER C. KUNZE AND VICTORIA FORD SMITH

"What Makes a Child an Art Prodigy?" asks the headline of a 2014 article in the *Atlantic* on seven-year-old Australian child artist Aelita Andre. Andre's paintings, the drop head continues, raise "the question of what separates true, precocious genius from mere youthful creativity with hype."[1] Below this hand-wringing: a picture of Andre herself in an art studio, her face and clothes splattered with paint, her feet bare, an arc of dynamic red paint curving from the brush in her hand onto a canvas on the floor. Propped against the walls are finished paintings—abstract compositions in red, yellow, blue, and pink—taller than the artist herself.

These headlines set up a troubled binary that has surrounded child artists since at least the nineteenth century. Andre is either a precocious genius or a scam, either a prodigy with miraculous creative instincts or a puppet of opportunistic parents and gallerists. The article that follows, by Jacoba Urist, perpetuates this uneasy back-and-forth. How, exactly, do we square our ideas of childhood—its purported naivete and innocence, its associations with dependence and immaturity—with our ideas of artistic genius and creative craft? Urist reflects on these contradictions as she walks to an Eighteenth Street gallery in Manhattan where Andre's paintings hang on the walls for her third solo exhibition. "Are her pieces only here, in one of the most influential art markets—and reportedly selling for five-figure sums—because she's young?" Urist asks. "Must a prodigy eventually break new ground? Be able to reflect on her work?"[2]

A few assumptions buzz beneath Urist's questions. First, she assumes that a young artist is not capable of the intention and critical reflection adult creators purportedly possess. Urist's curiosity about whether or not a painter should "be able to reflect on her work" implies that Andre does not, that she is innocent of the aesthetic or economic implications of her exhibit. And indeed, when Urist first describes Andre, she does so in a way that focuses almost entirely on her immaturity. She notes that the young painter "seems like a typical little girl in bright pink sneakers."[3] Urist brings her a Ring Pop and, amid questions about the artists who inspire her, asks her about her feelings regarding Disney princesses. In this respect, Urist's approach to Andre as an artist fits into a narrative of child art that stretches backward to the first radical experimentations of the modernists, when painters such as Picasso, Kandinsky, and Klee fetishized the unselfconscious, untrained drawings of kids, eager to mimic the child's "innocent eye"—a mimicry mediated, of course, through the adult artist's sophistication. Andre herself reinforces this narrative, explaining her process as one of natural ability and intuition rather than education or purposeful design. In interviews, she frequently recounts an origin story that presents her art as artless: she insists that she started painting at nine months old, when she crawled onto a canvas her father was working on. "Sometimes they say, 'Oh, a kid did it. It's not worth anything,'" she explains. "Critics say that I'm like Jackson Pollock. And they say it as a compliment, but I want to be known for my own style."[4]

Andre is savvy, perhaps, to direct her listeners away from the idea that she is simply parroting Pollock's paintings. The journalists, art collectors, and gallerists commenting on her work assume that if her work is not *entirely* her own, if it betrays even a modicum of influence or support from adults, it would not be nearly as interesting or impressive. Such interference would signify, at best, an out-of-control idealism on the part of her parents and, at worst, a nefarious use of a child for fame and profit. A *CBS This Morning* segment that aired in May 2012 covering the "controversy" surrounding Andre noted that her father, Michael Andre, answered this skepticism by filming his daughter creating paintings "from empty canvas to completion, to prove them wrong."[5] When Andre's mother, Nikka Kalashnikova, first showed her daughter's art to a gallery director, she identified her simply as "a female artist. After all, you never walk into a gallery and say, this artist is 24 or this one is 84. I wanted Aelita's work judged on its own merits." The exhibition Urist describes in her article includes paintings with titles such as *The Dome of the Dinosaur Spa* and *Rainbow Splash and the Fish Feather.* "Her mother," Urist notes, "is adamant that Aelita names each painting unassisted."[6]

Our point here is not to reveal Andre as either a genius or a joke. Instead, we are interested in media coverage of her art as evidence of a persistent cultural investment in children as both artless and artful, as both constructs of adult desire and creative agents. In short: we aim to acknowledge, understand, and complicate the stories we tell about child creators. Such children have always posed thorny questions, but our endeavor is even more vital at a moment when young people, empowered by digital platforms that in some ways democratize the creation and circulation of creative work, are both taking bolder control of their creations and finding themselves subject to more intense scrutiny from adults. How can we untangle the rhetorical and ideological knots that surround young creators? What can we make of those powerful cultural narratives of creativity, self-expression, and age that make some artists visible while obscuring others; elide the nuances and the value of collaboration, including partnerships between adults and children; and reinforce romanticized ideas of intention and craft? To return to Andre, what would it mean to acknowledge that her parents contributed somehow to her artwork—and to understand that contribution not as evidence that her fame is misplaced but instead as a reality of how the creative process works?

In response to those questions, this volume offers a series of case studies in child-produced culture that map a diversity of childhood creativity alongside approaches for studying it. Some of these children, like Andre, were the focus of public celebration or scrutiny; others did not reach celebrity status but were subject to similar questions about childhood and creative authority. Studying child-produced material challenges our received understandings of children's culture as culture by adults, for children, and about children. Traditionally, children's literature entails adults writing for child readers; this collection broadens that understanding to include work by children, for children (and, indeed, for adult readers as well). It expands upon "children's literature" as a cultural phenomenon that goes across and beyond genres, forms, and media. With the ongoing vibrancy of childhood studies as a multidisciplinary area of inquiry, studies of child-produced culture provide scholars with an exciting opportunity to complicate, enrich, and expand theorization of childhood creativity, children's culture, even children themselves. It also invites dialogue and collaboration across fields and disciplines invested in the critical understanding of children as embodied beings and childhood as simultaneously a stage of development and a discursive construct with social, political, economic, and cultural dimensions and influence.

Our intention here is to continue an ongoing conversation about childhood authorship and child-produced culture through new case studies and theoretical inquiries. Through close textual analysis, it also serves as an invitation for others from a range of contexts and disciplines to join us. Therefore, this collection's ambitions are neither dogmatic nor comprehensive, and our scope is far from exhaustive; for example, the case studies that follow privilege examples in the United States and United Kingdom. Indeed, we welcome debate, critique, and interventions that push the conversation forward, potentially reimagining and redirecting it in the process. By calling on the expertise of contributors in English, film and media studies, education, theater and performance studies, communication, and ethnomusicology, we hope to show shared affinities in how these disciplines discuss and study children and childhood while encouraging them to talk more with each other in the process of conducting and publishing their research. Child-produced culture is a global, transhistorical, cross-media phenomenon; therefore, it demands a rigorous multidisciplinary inquiry to examine its roots, expressions, and effects on and for the humanities and social sciences more broadly.

Questions and Theories

Scholars from a range of disciplines—sociology, anthropology, literary studies, education, and media studies, to name just a few—have long theorized the child as a participant in society and culture. While the central figures in those critical conversations vary from field to field, across disciplines that discussion has become invested in the possibilities of understanding children as more than passive recipients of culture, imagining them instead as savvy consumers, critical readers, creative cultural agents. In the process, scholars have wrestled with questions about embodied and constructed childhood, adult-child relationships, and child agency and power, complicating the perceived dynamics between child and adult to expand the definition of children's culture.

These investigations of the child's participation in culture have deployed a range of theoretical perspectives. For example, David Rudd draws on a Bakhtinian, dialogical approach to argue that "the child is necessarily both constructed and constructive," and "this hybrid border country is worthy of exploration."[7] That border country encompasses not only the messy meeting place of real children and our ideas about them, the space "between biological essentialism and cultural determinism," but also the intersections of adult and child. If, Rudd notes, "Children's literature consists of texts that consciously or unconsciously address particular constructions of the child," then "adults are as caught up in this discourse as children, engaging dialogically with it (writing/reading it), just as children themselves engage with many 'adult' discourses."[8] While social scientists such as Allison James have long wrestled with the challenges of theorizing children as social actors, Rudd's work anticipates the work of scholars in children's literature studies and childhood studies more generally that invites a serious consideration of children's agency, creative and otherwise—research on how children, while subject to adult discourses, nevertheless participate as consumers and creators of culture. Cultural historian Robin Bernstein, for example, offers a particularly influential argument, grounded in performance studies, that children are both scripted and scripting, subject to the demands of adults' expectations and able to play with and through them.[9] Marah Gubar engages critical frameworks from philosophy, history, literary studies, and education to suggest a "kinship model" of childhood, which holds that not only children but also adults are subject to powerful discourses that shape their behaviors, and their ability to respond to those discourses fluctuates over time, and not linearly—a position that rejects the assumption that adults enjoy unfettered agency while children are hopelessly passive.[10] Childhood studies scholar Rachel Conrad's work on child-authored poetry, perhaps closest to the concerns of this collection, reveals how an emphasis on what sociologists call the "becoming" rather than the "being" child—the young person understood in terms of their future rather than their present value—leads to the dismissal of child-produced culture. "Neglect of poetry written by youth and limits in theorizing youth agency," she argues, "are explainable in part by cultural beliefs and practices that obscure the possibility of valuing children's present knowledge, capabilities, intentions, and accomplishments."[11]

This critical turn toward the child as creator is not, of course, without its challenges, and a 2016 forum on child agency published in *Jeunesse* considers some of those obstacles in detail. That forum includes the work of scholars interested in finding pathways toward scholarly explorations of child agency amid the interference of adults' idealizations of childhood and despite the difficulties of locating, recovering, and documenting children's creative efforts. Gubar's essay on the kinship model is included here, as well as Richard Flynn's argument against "an overemphasis on children's alterity, in a model of children as helpless or even as victims, implying that children exercise little to no agency in participating in and creating their own culture." He prefers instead "models that focus on children as capable actors."[12] The optimism of theories such as Gubar's and Flynn's is balanced by those more skeptical of the scholarly project of excavating evidence of child agency. Sara L. Schwebel, for example, acknowledges that the "question of agency in connection with children's literature studies has been fruitful in that it has made scholars acutely aware of the adult influence evident in every aspect of children's books," but argues that "attempting to measure, quantify, or describe the agency of child readers . . . strikes [her] as unproductive" and that "pursuing the question of children's agency may lead to dead ends." Her study focuses largely on student responses to children's literature preserved in paper-based archives. "Most existing sources that document children's reading are opaque because they are produced within institutional settings," she argues. "When children write about books—as opposed to when they act out or play with books or when they write within them—they typically do so for adults."[13] That opacity, Schwebel suggests, is true of most material available to us that documents children's creative work.

Many of the scholars included in our collection interrogate Schwebel's concern about "adult influence" and the assumption that such interference makes even the description of children's agency too difficult to pursue. The essays that follow instead take up, like Conrad, a model of agency that recognizes the inevitability and affordance of adults' relationship to children's cultural production, rather than seeing that relationship as an obstacle. "Adults cannot 'grant' or 'give' children agency," Conrad explains, "but they can recognize, acknowledge, facilitate, preserve, ignore, obscure, erode, or obstruct the agency that children claim, practice, or express."[14] When we refer, then, to "child-produced culture," we are not assuming an entirely independent child creator, just as we do not assume an entirely independent *adult* creator when we examine any cultural artifact. The term "child-produced culture" presumes children have some kind of creative agency, but it also acknowledges that that agency may be shared, compromised, and hard if not impossible to fully distinguish from the contributions of adults: parents, collaborators, teachers, choreographers, and directors, for example. Our goal is in fact to *reject* a Romantic notion of singular genius, admitting the networked and interdependent nature of all creative endeavors.

Foundations and Inspirations

The study of child-produced culture is hardly a new area of inquiry, but rather one that has largely unfolded in separate fields that are not necessarily reading and talking with one another. In this brief section, we survey a range of contributions to the research on children's creative production that is by no means comprehensive but instead aims to identify some of the questions, approaches, and arguments that have shaped the contemporary critical study of child-produced culture across the humanities. Our volume is primarily interested in children—that is, people twelve years and younger—but in reviewing the literature on child-produced culture, we cannot ignore the important contributions of scholars who study cultural production by adolescents. Not only do such studies provide approaches and methods for studying children, but in many cases, they also examine children and youth interchangeably.

For example, a good deal of work has been done by literary studies scholars on writing by young people. We might loosely separate this research into two categories. The first would include juvenilia—a term usually used to refer to the early writings of authors who gained some acclaim as "adult" creators, such as Jane Austen or Charles Dickens. A cursory search of the *MLA International Bibliography* reveals that the overwhelming majority of this research focuses on writings produced in adolescence and, at least in the West, this area of study leans toward nineteenth-century writers, especially in the United Kingdom. As seen in Christine Alexander and Juliet McMaster's edited collection, *The Child Writer from Austen to Woolf*, the focus of much of this work, quite understandably, has been on tracing the early signs of authorial voice and demonstrating the artistic development of the writer into the major figure they would become in their adulthood.[15] As such, this juvenilia is often treated, at worst, as lesser-than and, at best, as evidence of the "becoming" artist—as creative efforts that provide a rounder portrait of the adult artist but which are not major works in their own right. Many studies of juvenilia celebrate nascence, promise, and precocity, but not artistic achievement in and of itself.

Happily, Alexander and McMaster's pioneering dedication to juvenilia and its worthiness of serious study has been expanded by scholars invested in the creative and scholarly importance of such work and to models of inquiry less sutured to future success. This second body of scholarship examines young people's writing without the looking-back quality one finds in some studies of juvenilia. Some of this scholarship concerns authors, such as Anne Frank, who were most productive creatively in their childhood or youth, but then either moved away from creative production or tragically died young.[16] Several, including Marjory Fleming or child poets of the 1920s such as Hilda Conkling and Nathalia Crane, became celebrities by virtue of their prodigious talent at an early age.[17] Daisy Ashford, author of the widely celebrated *The Young Visiters* (1919), fits within this category and is the subject of Katharine Slater's essay in this volume. While some of this work focuses on the idiosyncrasies of individual writers, many scholars turn to such juvenilia to retool our approaches to the cultural value of young people's writing. Laurie Langbauer's *The Juvenile Tradition: Young Writers and Prolepsis, 1750–1835*, for example, examines the work of both well-known writers, such as Robert Southey and

Felicia Hemans, and now-unknown young writers who, she argues, self-consciously performed juvenility through a proleptic envisioning of the future as having already happened. Her study reconsiders age as a critical category, arguing that it is a matter of self-conscious performance among these writers rather than merely a shared life stage.[18]

Two years later, in 2018, Lesley Peterson, David Owen, and Rob Breton founded the *Journal of Juvenilia Studies* with the goal of providing "a forum for a broad range of theoretical approaches and methodologies, in order to reflect and contribute to the international and interdisciplinary nature of the field of juvenilia studies."[19] The journal has featured the work of scholars looking to value all sorts of children's writing. For example, a 2021 special issue of the journal edited by Conrad focuses on "Juvenilia, Trauma and Intersectionality" and includes an essay by Caroline Lieffers on children's firsthand accounts of the bombing of Hiroshima collected by Asata Orata, a professor of education at Hiroshima University, and another essay on *Homes: A Refugee Story* (2018), a work of creative nonfiction produced through the collaboration of Abu Bakr al Rabeeah and his former teacher Winnie Yeung. These essays are evidence that scholars invested in juvenilia studies are both considering children's writing in its own right rather than as evidence of future literary fame, and abandoning Romantic models of authorship that would preclude adult influence. Such essays, in fact, not only acknowledge intergenerational creative production as far more common than children's solo efforts but also celebrate its possibilities and theoretical challenges. This methodology is in line with work by Gubar, Victoria Ford Smith, and Amy Fish, all of whom examine collaborations between adults and children to create original works of art.[20] Together, this work offers scholars generative microhistories into structures of feeling and developing understandings of authorship, childhood, and cultural production.

Studies of children's art, like studies of literary juvenilia, sometimes seem chronologically bound; such studies often cluster around explorations of the radical movements in visual art at the beginning of the twentieth century in the United States and Europe—movements that were shaped by a preoccupation with the naive artist and the child's "innocent eye." Often, such studies privilege the adult mimicking children's drawings, but there is a parallel critical tradition that recenters the child as a creator worthy of consideration in their own right (or at least alongside those they inspire). For example, art historian Jonathan Fineberg has curated exhibits and published studies about both the artists who collect and parrot children's art and the children creating that art. His book *The Innocent Eye: Children's Art and the Modern Artist*, for instance, examines the archives of child art collected by painters such as Paul Klee, Pablo Picasso, and Joan Miró to illuminate those adult artists' modes of representation; on the other hand, his edited collection *When We Were Young: New Perspectives on the Art of the Child* is more invested in foregrounding the creativity of the child artist or, to use the words of contributor Rudolf Arnheim, "beginning with the child."[21] Notably, Fineberg is invested in complicating the idealization of the child artist evident in the modernists and in some scholarship on children's art, recommending that scholars focus "on what we can understand about the cultural and social influences on children by acknowledging and analyzing our biases, rather than looking at the aesthetic development of children as a closed system of instinct and cognitive growth."[22] Scholars such as Smith and Joan Menefee have approached children's art in similar terms—both as evidence of adult's assumptions about children's creativity and naivete and as a record of children's creative agency.[23] The majority of studies of children's art, however, reside in studies of art education or psychology, focusing on method and curriculum or brain development, and many of the studies of contemporary or historical children's art that do consider children's drawings or paintings in their own right tend to focus on how the creative work of children documents historical events and, in particular, trauma and war.[24]

An equally exciting and robust area of inquiry has considered children as stage performers. Much of this recent work has been historical in nature, focusing on the Victorian stage in particular. Carolyn Steedman's *Strange Dislocations: Childhood and the Idea of Human Interiority 1780–1930*, for example, considers a range of child performers, both actors and acrobats, to make connections between how constructions of childhood inspire and emerge alongside modern understandings of the self.[25] Gubar has explored child performers on the British and American stages in her monograph and subsequent articles, pointing to the way that such attention complicates the fierce distinctions many scholars uncritically impose on children and adults as creative practitioners.[26] Gillian Arrighi and Victor Emeljanow's *Entertaining Children: The Participation of Youth in the Entertainment Industry* collection features a rich assemblage of articles on children as stage and screen performers, in both historical and contemporary settings.[27] In addition to a variety of national contexts, the collection also highlights the children as laborers working within the culture industries. In *Beyond Broadway: The Pleasure and Promise of Musical Theatre Across America*, Stacy Wolf examines the influence of Broadway musicals outside of the famed New York theater district, leading her to travel and observe such performances in dinner theaters, community theaters, and theater festivals.[28] For our purposes here, she includes two chapters of particular note on girls' summer camps and on schools producing adaptations of Disney shows for young performers. The former points to the ritualistic nature of theatrical production at a Jewish girls' summer camp in Maine, where the campers learn and stage a show within a matter of days. While the pacing can be grueling, these productions are staked in tradition and custom that build community and collectivity for the campers. Since the campers are only performing for each other, the ritual fosters unity among the girls that privileges the community over a faithful allegiance to the text. The Disney shows, by contrast, provide a way into theater for young performers. Even though the branding and commercialization of theater is not without its shortcomings, the shows' liberal and individualist messages nevertheless inspire joy, pleasure, and collectivity among the young performers. Wolf acknowledges the ideological limitations that come with producing such branded entertainments, but she also concedes that these shows remain empowering for the young performers who are able to take part in them.

Questions of play also have been central to childhood studies, as seen in Kyra Gaunt's *The Games Black Girls Play: Learning the Ropes from Double-Dutch to Hip-Hop*.[29] Focusing on the creativity of Black girls, Gaunt challenges us to look for children's self-expression beyond the traditional realms of cultural production. In so doing, Gaunt's ethnomusicological training demonstrates how we understand the interacting sonic, verbal, and physical dimensions central to generating children's culture. Her work also helps scholars move away from single children as subjects to communities of children, guided by established and shifting practices, values, and rules that structure their play. Relatedly, Bernstein provides novel ways of thinking through children's agency in relation to play and material culture by turning to performance studies. Introducing the term "scriptive things" to describe ways that objects tell us to utilize them, she has opened up new avenues of recovering children's agency throughout history and thinks through the relationship between ideas of childhood and present-day children.[30] Bernstein's subsequent essay in Anna Mae Duane's *The Children's Table: Childhood Studies and the Humanities*, for instance, encourages scholars to consider childhood itself as a performance to help negotiate the tension between childhood as a concept and stage of being and children as embodied beings living in the world.[31] Performance studies therefore offer scholars exciting ways of understanding agency beyond the stable print text, considering ephemeral, fluid, and even intangible expressions of childhood creativity.

Digital media reinvigorates the scholarly interest in children's creativity as an exciting site of critical investigation. Of course, historical studies, including those offered in this volume, demonstrate that children's creativity is hardly a contemporary phenomenon. If anything, it has been erased because of its ephemerality and devaluation, ignored or overlooked by archives and collectors as worthy of retention and preservation. Child creators take up digital technologies to digitize pre-digital modes and explore new opportunities for creative expression. Consequently, we may consider how digital media renders children's creativity more visible and more easily disseminated than earlier modes. At the same time, we should seek continuities as well as changes between developments in media, technology, and cultural production. One of the earliest studies to consider such connections blends what we might call analog and digital media: Mary Celeste Kearney's 2006 monograph, *Girls Make Media*, considers how girls, in particular, become media producers in their own right.[32] Kearney's study reveals an optimism in digital technology to inspire young people's creative expression, which in turn reflects a hope in the potential for web culture. That critical hope has since been tempered by the platformization (and attendant surveillance practices) brought about by search engines and social media companies, in particular, that monitor and monetize personal data.

Kearney's attention to children and youth culture noticeably examines both the heralded, even celebrity, as well as what we may call the everyday, child producer. In this manner, she anticipates Graeme Turner's observation that new media technologies, especially online, are not so much democratizing as demoticizing, rendering the everyday visible and central to digital culture.[33] In her consideration of zines, music, and film alongside websites, Kearney maps out how girls, so often narrowly defined by their consumer practices, become producers of their own culture on- and offline. Furthermore, she draws necessary attention to the intersectional dimension of cultural productions in terms of access and social barriers on young people's creative expression. Her interest, Kearney asserts, is specifically on girls as a population worthy of critical study and understanding on their own terms, not as future women.[34] Patricia G. Lange operates in a similar vein in an ethnographic study of children on the YouTube platform that she conducted over a period of two years. Engaging, even challenging, our presumptions about amateur or preprofessional media production, Lange shows how children develop the digital media literacies that empower the personal agency and creativity to produce "personally expressive media."[35] Finally, in his work on children and teen comedians on the now-defunct video app Vine, Peter C. Kunze argues that such efforts offer one extension of children's literature into the digital arena while also demonstrating how young creators have complicated discursive constructions of childhood and youth in the process.[36]

Over the past five years, in particular, interest in social media platforms and digital technologies more broadly have inspired a rich body of work on children creating online. Trevor Boffone's *Renegades: Digital Dance Cultures from Dubsmash to TikTok*, for example, examines young Black creators on social media and the ways their original creations are taken up, circulated, and even monetized by their white peers.[37] Boffone situates this cultural appropriation in a longer history of white appropriation of Black culture, and as a white scholar himself, he reflects on what it means to be not only an adult, but a white person, studying the cultural production of youth communities of color. Boffone turns to Marilyn Frye's concept of the "loving eye" to consider how researchers can become not only advocates but collaborators with the communities they study in their work.[38] He therefore uses his position as a white scholar writing for a prominent global press (in this case, Oxford University Press) to not only correct the whitewashing of digital dance culture but also to elevate the voices and cultural output of these young Black creators producing on the margins of the entertainment industries. Drawing on her ethnographic research in Richmond, Virginia, Ashleigh Greene Wade demonstrates the value of participant observation and cultural interpretation in understanding creativity among young people, specifically Black girls. Her generative theoretical framework, Black girl autopoetics, challenges scholars to include and look beyond artistry to consider how the creative practices of Black girls allow them to make themselves as well as their worlds. In so doing, scholars balance a focus on the individual with an investment in the collective to see how Black girls "invent and reinvent themselves, in turn, inventing and reinventing what it means to live, create, and preserve Black life."[39]

The social media celebrity status given to children—who often coproduce videos with their parents (who alternately serve as costars, creative collaborators, business partners, and talent managers)—has inspired studies by Crystal Abidin, Benjamin Burroughs, and Gavin Feller.[40] Rarely do these children rise to the level of acclaim we see traditional film and television celebrities achieve, but they do become recognizable market actors in an increasingly niche-oriented platform economy. For example, *Forbes* reported in early 2022 that two of the highest paid YouTubers were, in fact, children: seven-year-old lifestyle vlogger Nastya and ten-year-old toy reviewer Ryan Kaji.[41] Toy unboxing and reviewing videos especially have inspired a series of articles, due in large part to the way they raise intersecting concerns about children, childhood, marketing, merchandising, and promotional/influencer culture.[42] This body of work is important in part because of its de-Romanticization of child creators as original artists and its recontextualization of such efforts as labor in a highly lucrative, highly exploitative global market economy. The expression here, therefore, is not only personal artistic vision, but also the economic choices that young people make (alone or, more likely, with adult guidance and consultation) as market actors negotiating their clout as influencers and microcelebrities with both brands and platforms.

We offer this overview of work across fields to emphasize, on the one hand, the richness of available scholarship on children's cultural participation and, on the other, to bring to the fore some of the questions that can, and already do, unite this research and invite interdisciplinary engagement. These questions are embedded throughout the present collection as well. For example, scholars of child-produced culture across disciplines examine the assumptions that underpin whose childhood productions have been deemed worthy of attention—valued by the public, the scholarly press, the art world—and why. Literary studies scholars and historians have expanded conversations about child writing from the canonical to the everyday and the domestic, while elsewhere in the academy, those in media studies consider how new platforms have provided the tools of production to all sorts of children. The chapters in this collection are similarly concerned with the "who and why" question of child-produced culture, considering both the well-known child, as in Katharine Slater's essay on Daisy Ashford, and the private, domestic scene, as in Ivy Linton Stabell's chapter on family cookbooks.

The question of whose work is preserved and valued and why is also a political and ideological one, and scholars from the fields surveyed above are invested in thinking through how children's creative work, and how scholars' access to and interpretations of that work, is impacted by questions of race, class, and gender. The study of child-produced culture, then, can be the work of recovery and revaluation, in which previously dismissed or silenced child voices are acknowledged for the cultural contributions they have made and continue to make into the present. Brigitte Fielder's contribution on Phillis Wheatley and Scipio Moorhead is an important example of this type of work, as is Cristina Rhodes's chapter on Latina child activists.

Another question that transcends disciplinary boundaries concerns how we understand adults' roles in child-produced culture. Do adults offer interference, support, partnership? This power dynamic concerns art historians charting adults' valuation and appropriation of child art, theater studies scholars showing interest in how young people understand and perform within the structures of studio and stage that surround them, and historians of play examining how children negotiate adult-imagined toys and environments. Many of the scholars in our collection consider intergenerational elements of children's culture and argue for approaches to child-produced culture that take into account adult influence as part of, rather than antithetical to, children's creative work. See Gubar's celebration of the intergenerational pas de deux, Conrad's recognition of the generative partnerships between young poets and the adults supporting their work, and Kunze's meditation on the inevitable, and important, enmeshment of adult and child actors' decision-making in film.

Avenues and Approaches

As we hope we have shown, the study of childhood creativity is wide, and it is growing—encompassing individuals and communities, professional and amateur, permanent and ephemeral, commercial and anti-commercial. The study of child-produced culture requires scholars to adapt interdisciplinary and multi-methods approaches. The most prevalent strategy remains textual analysis, because it allows one to closely examine the efforts of the author firsthand. Rather than seeking broad generalizations, textual analysis allows scholars of childhood creativity to privilege the microsocial as well as the diversity of childhood creativity in its myriad expressions. Furthermore, as the research above has ably demonstrated, authorship is rarely singular. Indeed, children often have a variety of collaborators who take on varying degrees of contribution and intervention, and we must anticipate and negotiate the ways children's creativity may not necessarily be compromised but enriched by both intragenerational and intergenerational collaborations. This focus on the networked nature of authorship poses challenges but also invites opportunities for alternative approaches to agency, creativity, and authorship. For example, archival research may provide access to drafts complete with marginalia, editorial marks, correspondence, and other documentation of the creative process.

Ethnography's blending of participant observation and interviewing provides direct connection with creators to examine and understand creativity. (Trevor Boffone employs ethnography in his chapter here on TikTok, for example, and Smith corresponded with Arthur Tress, the photographer who is the subject of her chapter.) Children may not be fully aware of the rationale, values, and decision-making they are engaging in while creating, but we must admit that this fact is not unique to children. Artists of all ages, young and old, create without a sharp awareness of the reasoning behind, execution of, and effects of their work. Ethnography traditionally requires a level of long-term engagement and embeddedness that is not necessarily feasible for many scholars, but altering the methods accordingly and acknowledging those limitations can nevertheless provide valuable insights beyond textual analysis alone. But it also calls upon the researcher to think about the working relationship and power dynamic with the children. How do we study childhood creativity without privileging an adult perspective? How do we not speak for children, but instead amplify their own voices? As Allison James has argued, "We need to consider the ways in which children's interests are represented, by whom their voices are represented, and for what purposes. . . . What is the risk that children's voices may be employed simply to confirm established prejudices rather than to present new insights based on children's own perspectives as social actors?"[43] These questions are enduring, and the work ahead must take them up and continue to debate them for the vitality of the field.

Discourse analysis is also a crucial tool, especially in thinking about how we talk about the central concepts of childhood, creativity, artistry, authorship, and agency. Valuable work remains to be done on how child creators have been represented and discussed across different times, places, and venues. How are these discussions reflecting, shaping, even resisting parallel discourses of childhood in law and policy, education, medicine, arts, and culture? By interrogating these conversations, we can draw important connections between discourse, power, and lived experience that have material consequences for children's cultural production as well as their very lives.

Finally, methods for analyzing industry, such as political economy of communication, can help us to think through how child creators are not only artists but also laborers increasingly functioning with a globalized market economy. While these studies challenge us to navigate issues of scale, combining macrolevel analyses of industry structures with microsocial attention to cultural production and individual labor, this work helps us understand the cultural products, effects, and consequences of technological convergence, media conglomeration, neoliberal capitalism, and globalization for the youngest members of the population. In shifting our attention from the child as consumer to the child as producer, we assert children's creative expression in a context where it is often presumed powerless and moot. At the same time, however, we must be cautious of a utopian thinking that neglects the very real tensions and antagonisms children and all creators face, knowingly and unknowingly, amid these major political, economic, cultural, and social forces. Consequently, our critical analysis of creativity, agency, and child-produced culture must be theoretically informed, methodologically diverse, and interdisciplinary in order to better understand our contemporary moment and its historical precedents. As stated above, our case studies include both well-known child creators as well as those who never achieved celebrity status—indeed, some were unacknowledged or uncredited in their lifetimes. This combination of prominent and recovered child creators reaffirms the need for critical studies of childhood creativity to be wide reaching in their case studies to map out the diversity and depth of young people's self-expression. We sincerely hope that the chapters that follow model the richness and range of such a critical inquiry.

Chapter Summaries

In our attempts to be both multidisciplinary and multi-methods in scope, we invited scholars from a range of backgrounds to contribute studies of child-produced culture from across time, place, and media. However, all these chapters demonstrate an interest and investment in children's cultural production. For our purposes, we have organized the chapters into three general categories. Part I, "Authorship," is perhaps the most established approach to childhood creativity. Part II, "Performance and Play," examines children as artists and entertainers, bringing the visual and performing arts into the critical discussion. And finally, the scholars in part III, "Collaboration and Cocreation," analyze children as creative partners not only with other children but also with adults. Several of these chapters would be just at home in another section, but our focus here is to foreground frameworks and approaches over a historical or medial organization to draw commonalities across time, space, and media.

In what follows, each author takes children seriously as creators, craftspeople, and collaborators. Their analyses alternately revise received accounts, revive neglected artists, and direct necessary attention to emerging practices and modes of creative expression. While textual analysis is the primary method they employ for close study and appreciation of childhood study, select chapters use archival research, ethnography, and discourse analysis as well. The theoretical frameworks also vary, drawing from a range of traditions to center and complicate childhood creativity without resorting to a "children are geniuses, too" approach. In so doing, we hope to contribute to the ongoing conversation and theorization of childhood creativity while promoting a greater integration of approaches and inquiries taking place disparately in the fields represented herein.

Katharine Slater's chapter begins part I by drawing upon geographical approaches to literary criticism by focusing on the use of space and scale in Daisy Ashford's 1919 novel, *The Young Visiters*. Written when Ashford was only nine years old, the book demonstrates its author's handling of spatiality. Slater, in turn, argues that this use of space reflects the child author's manipulation of material realities. In so doing, it opens up metaphorical space for understanding children's creativity as a politicized engagement with the world around them.

Slater's focus on the child's voice continues in Rachel Conrad's essay on child-produced poetry by young Black and Latine poets in The Voice of the Children workshop. Led by June Jordan and Terri Bush in the late 1960s and 1970s, the workshop produced an important poetry volume, *THE VOICE of the Children*, featuring original compositions by the workshop's young participants. In elevating the artistry demonstrated in the collection, Conrad calls upon scholars to appreciate young people's writing as artful and well-crafted rather than as a cultural curiosity. She also reminds us of the contributions adults make to young people's creativity, viewing these collaborations not as contaminating but as cooperative exchanges.

Rounding off the first section, Brianna Anderson turns to graphic narrative as she explores environmental activism in the 1991 manga, *Secrets of the Earth.* Written and drawn by twelve-year-old Aika Tsubota, *Secrets* reveals how amateur cultural production can play an important role in understanding both childhood creativity and activist media. Tsubota tragically died in 1991, but her work continues to circulate online—as does her passionate advocacy for environmental issues. This case study ultimately attests to the authorial possibilities young people may find in established and emerging forms, but also how their young voices can transcend over time, even after they have matured or passed away.

The four chapters in part II turn their attention to performance and play. In doing so, they foreground questions of race, childhood, and creativity, in particular. The first of these essays, by Brigitte Fielder, considers the cultural afterlife of the 1773 frontispiece of Phillis Wheatley (Peters), itself based on an engraving by enslaved artist Scipio Moorhead. In the 1920s and 1930s, Fielder demonstrates, the story and image of Wheatley was taken up by Black children as both an inspiration and exemplar for their own creativity. This influence transcended writing to include performance, including a pageant play featuring young Black performers. Fielder's study considers the resonances of Wheatley's book of poems—reportedly published when she herself was only twenty—across African American literature with specific attention to its importance to young Black children's creative expression.

Maggie Morris Davis also explores the intersections of child creativity and race in 1930s America in her exploration of the ethnographic work of Ralph Ellison, author of *Invisible Man*, during his service to the Federal Writers' Project in the 1930s. Visiting playgrounds and speaking with children around Harlem, Ellison documented the children's play and language formation. Davis's archival research allows her to examine not only race but also class in understanding childhood expression, foregrounding how impoverished children must not be neglected in the historical and critical consideration of young people's cultural production. This intersectional exploration of race, class, and space underscores how ephemeral, everyday acts of personal expression are important cultural contributions in their own right.

Cristina Rhodes offers us a broader understanding of "performance" by examining the work of Latina child activists Sarai Gonzalez and Sophie Cruz to assert the role of creativity in youth activism as well as the possibilities for social change posed by cultural production. Turning her attention to the testimonio, a unique form of bearing witness within Latinx communities, Rhodes reminds us about how creative expression can be specific to one's culture and resonate within those communities in unique ways that warrant close contextualization and analysis. Childhood creativity manifests across different cultures, but not in the same ways and to the same effects. Testimonio allows young Latina girls to not only express themselves, but also to challenge the cultural expectations imposed on them in ways that may not be clear and obvious to observers outside of Latine communities.

In the last chapter of the section, Peter C. Kunze examines the child creator as a screen performer in recent world cinema. The critical study of child actors has a long history, privileging the efforts of white, cisgender stars working in Hollywood. Kunze moves beyond this elevation of the most famous and popular child actors to consider performances by nonprofessional, non-white, non-Hollywood performers. In focusing on the child performers as actors delivering crafted performances, Kunze asserts screen acting as a demonstration of children's creative expression while also acknowledging the impossibility of delineating decision-making by children and their adult collaborators. Rather than perceiving this challenge as an insurmountable obstacle, Kunze takes it as a reminder that a great deal of children's creativity is always already enmeshed with the influence and interactions of adult collaborators. His analysis sets up the final section, which explores child-adult collaborations in greater depth, while complicating the tendency to celebrate childhood creativity as individualized and prodigious.

The questions of adult-child power dynamics and collaboration central to Kunze's study also animate the four chapters in part III. Drawing on her extensive work in the archive, Ivy Linton Stabell opens the section with an essay on the family cookbook to make a case for considering more intimate and private collaborations. By turning to this household staple, she foregrounds the domestic and the everyday in the lived experiences of families in nineteenth-century America. These rich, eclectic volumes catalog the practices, traditions, and values that shaped families' lives, preserving them not only for subsequent generations but also for historians. Family cookbooks doubled as family chronicles for recording births, weddings, and deaths, and their essential polyphone speaks to the collaborative, networked authorship that crafted them over time. Linton Stabell's chapter, therefore, underscores the challenges of understanding creativity in the singular while also encouraging scholars to recuperate the quotidian in the expression of young people's creativity.

In Victoria Ford Smith's contribution, she turns to photographer Arthur Tress's *The Dream Collector*, a 1972 collection of photographs featuring child subjects acting out nightmares and dreams. Smith records the challenges and opportunities she encountered in researching the origins of the book—research that revealed multiple and conflicting accounts of the photographs' creation and, in particular, the nature of the creative relationship between adult photographer and child subject. Her chapter reflects on how childhood studies scholars might navigate the seeming opacity of many intergenerational collaborations, the difficulty they might encounter in trying to disentangle children's contributions from adults' creative authority, and why doing so is, ultimately, unnecessary.

Marah Gubar's chapter also deeply considers the dynamics of adult-child collaboration, furthering her influential work on the kinship model of adult/child relations with a consideration of dance. Taking up two archival dance performances she examined at Jacob's Pillow in Massachusetts's Berkshires, *Day on Earth* (1947) and *Lineage* (2000), she theorizes the pas de deux as a metaphor for intergenerational collaboration. Rather than emphasizing child and adult as dissimilar and oppositional, she calls for a greater understanding of the continuities and interconnectedness between both. Consequently, our attention turns not to singular expressions of creativity as individual genius, but to the generative nature of collaboration between and among individuals of various ages.

Trevor Boffone brings our collection to the present day through a discussion of adult-child collaborations on the social media platform TikTok. Much like Linton Stabell's essay opening the section, Boffone considers creative expression within families. He writes as a performer himself, collaborating with his young niece to create TikTok dances. As such, he embraces an autoethnographic approach that allows him to draw upon his own experiences while situating those collaborations within a self-reflexive critical framework as a trained scholar. Whereas a great deal of ethnographic work, including such work within childhood studies, wrestles with the issue of speaking for the young subjects under examination, Boffone foregrounds the need to approach one's subjects with self-awareness and compassion. His consequential analysis permits him to reveal not just the possible meanings within the cultural product, but the creativity demonstrated throughout the creation process itself.

In sum, these chapters offer no single answer or way forward. Such dogmatism was not our goal. Instead, we hope readers will find a range of questions and approaches for their own research. But what connects these essays is an insistence on a rigorous examination of the child as a creator and their place within critical studies of children's culture across various fields and disciplines, including literary studies, media studies, art history, and theater and performance studies. A more interdisciplinary dialogue can build affinities while also highlighting shared theoretical concerns and diverging critical approaches. We must reject any notion or presumption that children are merely passive consumers in the context of children's culture. At the same time, we must challenge attempts to elevate child creators as singular geniuses working in isolation. Just as this romanticized, Romantic vision has been challenged in studies of older creators, it must be treated with equal skepticism in understanding childhood creativity.

We believe that these essays, taken collectively, represent a productive intervention in childhood studies as well as the various disciplines the contributors represent. They also challenge many persistent myths: children as innocents and naïfs, children as passive consumers instead of active producers, and cultural production as the pursuit of singular geniuses. While we are hardly the first to make these observations, *Producing Children* affirms the need to actively resist them now and in the future. Our title is indebted to Mary Celeste Kearney's foundational work on girls' media production and, in particular, her use of "producing" to underscore how girls producing culture also produces girls and girlhood. As she writes in the introduction of *Girls Make Media*, entitled "Producing Girls," girl media producers "are helping to expand the experiences of contemporary girlhood and thus the spectrum of identities and activities in which all females can invest, for by engaging with the technologies and practices of media production, they are actively subverting the traditional sex/gender system that has kept female cultural practices confined to consumerism, beauty, and the domestic sphere for decades."[44] In that spirit, we must understand children not only as entities that have been socially, culturally, and politically created but also as agential beings who have actively resisted and refashioned those very constructions—not just now, but for centuries.

NOTES

1. Jacoba Urist, "What Makes a Child an Art Prodigy?" *Atlantic*, November 7, 2014, https://www.theatlantic.com/entertainment/archive/2014/11/what-makes-a-child-an-art-prodigy/382389.
2. Urist, "What Makes a Child."
3. Urist, "What Makes a Child."
4. Great Big Story, "This 12-Year-Old Has Taken the Art World by Storm," YouTube video, 2:47, September 3, 2019, https://www.youtube.com/watch?v=-9Sor27ylKc.
5. CBS News, "Controversy over Five-Year-Old Art Prodigy," YouTube video, 5:38, May 12, 2012, https://www.youtube.com/watch?v=4ZtvTH7-N4w.
6. Urist, "What Makes a Child."
7. David Rudd, "Theorising and Theories: The Conditions of Possibility of Children's Literature," in *International Companion Encyclopedia of Children's Literature*, vol. 1, ed. Peter Hunt (London: Routledge, 2004), 39.
8. Rudd, "Theorising," 39.
9. Robin Bernstein, "Toys Are Good for Us: Why We Should Embrace the Historical Integration of Children's Literature, Material Culture, and Play," *Children's Literature Association Quarterly* 38, no. 4 (Winter 2013): 458–463 and Bernstein, "Introduction: Playing Innocent: Childhood, Race, Performance," in *Racial Innocence: Performing American Childhood from Slavery to Civil Rights* (New York: NYU Press, 2011), 1–29.
10. Marah Gubar, "The Hermeneutics of Recuperation: What a Kinship-Model Approach to Children's Agency Could Do for Children's Literature and Childhood Studies," *Jeunesse* 8, no. 1 (Summer 2016): 291–310.
11. Rachel Conrad, *Time for Childhoods: Young Poets and Questions of Agency* (Amherst: University of Massachusetts Press, 2019), 4.
12. Richard Flynn, "What Are We Talking about When We Talk about Child Agency?" *Jeunesse* 8, no. 1 (Summer 2016): 255.
13. Sara L. Schwebel, "The Limits of Child Agency for Children's Literature Scholars," *Jeunesse* 8, no. 1 (Summer 2016): 288, 281, 282.
14. Conrad, *Time*, 9.

15. Christine Alexander and Juliet McMaster, eds., *The Child Writer from Austen to Woolf* (New York: Cambridge University Press: 2005).
16. For work on Anne Frank as a writer, see Jeffrey Shandler, "From Diary to Book: Text, Object, Structure," in *Anne Frank Unbound*, ed. Jeffrey Shandler and Barbara Kirshenblatt-Gimblett (Bloomington: Indiana University Press, 2012), 25–58 and Deborah E. Kaplan, "Anne Frank, Reviser," *Pedagogy* 18, no. 1 (January 2018): 87–107.
17. Katherine L. Carlson, "'We Can Feal Pangs as Well as You': Marjory Fleming and the Challenge of the Child Author," *Women's Writing* 18, no. 3 (August 2011): 367–384; David Sadler, "Innocent Hearts: The Child Authors of the 1920s," *Children's Literature Association Quarterly* 17, no. 4 (Winter 1992): 24–30; and Paul Bradley Bellew, "Girl Wonder: Nathalia Crane, Poetic Prodigy of the 1920s," *Journal of American Studies* 56, no. 1 (February 2022): 38–64.
18. Laurie Langbauer, *The Juvenile Tradition: Young Writers and Prolepsis, 1750–1835* (Oxford: Oxford University Press, 2016).
19. "About the Journal," *Journal of Juvenilia Studies*, accessed April 7, 2023, https://journalofjuveniliastudies.com/index.php/jjs/about.
20. Marah Gubar, *Artful Dodgers: Reconceiving the Golden Age of Children's Literature* (New York: Oxford University Press, 2009); Victoria Ford Smith, *Between Generations: Collaborative Authorship in the Golden Age of Children's Literature* (Jackson: University Press of Mississippi, 2017); and Amy Fish, "Agency in Absentia: Child Authorship under Racial Oppression in *The Me Nobody Knows*," *The Lion and the Unicorn* 44, no. 1 (January 2020): 56–77.
21. Jonathan Fineberg, *The Innocent Eye: Children's Art and the Modern Artist* (Princeton: Princeton University Press, 1997) and Fineberg, ed., *When We Were Young: New Perspectives on the Art of the Child* (Berkeley: University of California Press, 2006), 19.
22. Fineberg, *When We Were Young*, 15.
23. Victoria Ford Smith, "Exhibiting Children: The Young Artist as Construct and Creator," *Journal of Juvenilia Studies* 1, no. 1 (July 2018): 62–81 and Joan Menefee, "Art and Data: Children's Mark-Making and Modernity," *Children's Literature Association Quarterly* 36, no. 3 (September 2012): 225–244.
24. For examples of studies of child art focused on education or psychology, see Chris J. Boyatzis and Malcolm W. Watson's *Symbolic and Social Constraints on the Development of Children's Artistic Style* (San Francisco: Jossey-Bass, 2000) or Claire Golomb's *The Child's Creation of a Pictorial World* (Mahwah, NJ: L. Erlbaum Associates, 2003). For two examples of discussions of child art based in war and conflict, see Hana Volavkova, ed., *I Never Saw Another Butterfly: Children's Drawings and Poems from the Terezin Concentration Camp, 1942–1944* (New York: Schocken Books, 1994) and Yolanda Chávez Leyva, "'Behind Each Beautiful Painting Is a Child Longing to Be Free': Deep Visual Listening and Children's Art during Times of Crisis," *Global Studies of Childhood* 11, no. 2 (2021): 123–141.
25. Carolyn Steedman, *Strange Dislocations: Childhood and the Idea of Human Interiority 1780–1930* (Cambridge, MA: Harvard University Press, 1998).
26. See Gubar, *Artful Dodgers*, as well as Marah Gubar, "Entertaining Children of All Ages: Nineteenth-Century Popular Theater as Children's Theater," *American Quarterly* 66, no. 1 (March 2014): 1–34.
27. Gillian Arrighi and Victor Emeljanow, eds., *Entertaining Children: The Participation of Youth in the Entertainment Industry* (New York: Palgrave Macmillan, 2014).
28. Stacy Wolf, *Beyond Broadway: The Pleasure and Promise of Musical Theatre across America* (New York: Oxford University Press, 2020).

29. Kyra D. Gaunt, *The Games Black Girls Play: Learning the Ropes from Double-Dutch to Hip-Hop* (New York: New York University Press, 2006).
30. Robin Bernstein, *Racial Innocence: Performing American Childhood from Slavery to Civil Rights* (New York: New York University Press, 2011), 8–13.
31. Robin Bernstein, "Childhood as Performance," in *The Children's Table: Childhood Studies and the Humanities*, ed. Anna Mae Duane (Athens: University of Georgia Press, 2013), 204.
32. Mary Celeste Kearney, *Girls Make Media* (New York: Routledge, 2006).
33. Graeme Turner, *Ordinary People and the Media: The Demotic Turn* (Thousand Oaks, CA: SAGE, 2009).
34. Kearney, *Girls Make Media*, 304.
35. Patricia G. Lange, *Kids on YouTube: Technical Identities and Digital Literacies* (New York: Routledge, 2014), 16.
36. Peter C. Kunze, "Kidding Around: Children, Comedy, and Social Media," *Comedy Studies* 5, no. 1 (2014): 2–11.
37. Trevor Boffone, *Renegades: Digital Dance Cultures from Dubsmash to TikTok* (New York: Oxford University Press, 2021), 4–5.
38. Boffone, *Renegades*, xv.
39. Ashleigh Greene Wade, *Black Girl Autopoetics: Agency in Everyday Digital Practice* (Durham, NC: Duke University Press, 2024), 2.
40. Crystal Abidin, "Pre-School Stars on YouTube: Child Microcelebrities, Commercially Viable Biographies, and Interactions with Technology," in *The Routledge Companion to Digital Media and Children*, ed. Lelia Green, Donell Holloway, Kylie Stevenson, and Tama Leaver (New York: Routledge, 2022), 226–234, and Benjamin Burroughs and Gavin Feller, "The Emergence and Ethics of Child-Created Content as Media Industries," in *The Routledge Companion to Digital Media and Children*, ed. Lelia Green, Donell Holloway, Kylie Stevenson, and Tama Leaver (New York: Routledge, 2022), 217–225.
41. Abram Brown and Abigail Freeman, "The Highest-Paid YouTube Stars: MrBeast, Jake Paul And Markiplier Score Massive Paydays," *Forbes*, January 14, 2022, https://www.forbes.com/sites/abrambrown/2022/01/14/the-highest-paid-youtube-stars-mrbeast-jake-paul-and-markiplier-score-massive-paydays/?sh=2a459da81aa7.
42. See, for examples, David Craig and Stuart Cunningham, "Toy Unboxing: Living in a(n Unregulated) Material World," *Media International Australia* 163, no. 1 (May 2017): 77–86; Kyra Hunting, "Unwrapping Toy TV: Ryan's World and the Toy Review Genre's Impact on Children's Culture," in *The Marketing of Children's Toys: Critical Perspectives on Children's Consumer Culture*, ed. Rebecca C. Hains and Nancy A. Jennings (Cham, CH: Palgrave Macmillan, 2021), 105–124; and Jarrod Walczer, "Toy Unboxing Creator Communities," in *Creator Culture: An Introduction to Global Social Media Entertainment*, ed. Stuart Cunningham and David Craig (New York: New York University Press, 2021), 153–169.
43. Allison James, "Giving Voice to Children's Voices: Practices and Problems, Pitfalls and Potentials," *American Anthropologist* 109, no. 2 (June 2007): 262.
44. Kearney, *Girls Make Media*, 12. This introduction was based in part on Kearney's earlier essay, "Producing Girls: Rethinking the Study of Female Youth Culture," in *Delinquents & Debutantes: Twentieth-Century American Girls' Cultures*, ed. Sherrie A. Inness (New York: New York University Press, 1998), 285–310.

PART ONE

Authorship

1

Daisy Ashford and the Child Writer's Use of Scale

KATHARINE SLATER

Introduction; or, Size Matters

"As one of the poets says," Daisy Ashford writes in her 1919 novel, *The Young Visiters*, "great events from trivil [*sic*] causes springs."[1] The nine-year-old writer might have been describing her own book. A brilliant study in character, plot, and pacing, *The Young Visiters* oscillates between profound insights into and comical perceptions of late nineteenth-century British society. While the novel's perceptiveness and humor make it exceptionally readable, it is ultimately the unreconciled tension between the "great" and the "trivil [*sic*]" that makes *Visiters* a significant work in the larger canon of youth-authored literature. As a child writing about adults, Ashford attends to both the small and the large, her work deftly navigating social class, gender, and adult relationships through the metric of scale.

In *The Young Visiters*, physical size works to reinforce the distance between middle-class lives and upper-class aspirations. Ashford, I argue in this essay, shapes *Visiters* around the spatial and social tension between differently sized and differently leveled elements. Recognizing the centrality of scale to Ashford's novel allows us to consider how the child writer's representations are fundamentally bound up in her embodied and perceived relationships with the much larger world. If, as Juliet McMaster argues, child writers are "not trying to produce 'children's literature'" but have their "eye on the Canon," then relational size is necessarily inherent to the production, contexts, and receptions of their work.[2]

Origins and Public Response

The roots of *Visiters*, and Ashford herself, are relatively unremarkable. Born in 1881 to a middle-class English family, Ashford was the eldest of William and Emma Ashford's three daughters, encouraged from an early age by her parents in her love of storytelling. At the age of four, "she dictated the fictional biography of a

Jesuit priest who was a family friend," and wrote down *The Young Visiters* herself in 1890, five years later.[3] Three additional works followed, including *The Hangman's Daughter*, which the adult Ashford considered "the greatest literary achievement of my youth, for the reason that I put so much more effort into it than any of the others."[4] These years of fruitful production ended abruptly in 1895, as she aged out of early childhood and into adolescence. Although at the time Ashford aspired to become a published author, *The Hangman's Daughter* was the last book she ever wrote. To the adult Ashford, her child author self was "a Daisy Ashford of so long ago that she seems almost another person."[5]

Nearly three decades after Ashford first wrote *The Young Visiters*, she lent her recently rediscovered manuscript to amuse a friend, Margaret McKenzie, during the latter's illness.[6] McKenzie was delighted by the story of the bungling Alfred Salteena, a middle-class "elderly man of 42" training to become a gentleman in the hopes of winning the heart of the much younger Ethel Monticue, who is in turn infatuated with the wealthy Bernard Clark.[7] She took the handwritten notebook to Frank Swinnerton, an English novelist and editor working at the time as a reader for the publisher Chatto & Windus.[8] In 1919, Chatto & Windus published *The Young Visiters*, accompanied by J. M. Barrie's condescending preface, and the public responded with considerable enthusiasm. Selling 230,000 copies in the first two years of its publication, the book enjoyed tremendous success, which extended to multiple translations and its adaptation as a stage play.[9] For a few years, its cultural omnipresence in both the United States and Great Britain was such that critic Edmund Wilson, writing to his friend F. Scott Fitzgerald in 1920, could without context mock Fitzgerald's *This Side of Paradise* as a book that "ought to be a classic in a class with *The Young Visiters*."[10] Wilson's wry swipe at Fitzgerald's prose is in line with the contemporary perception of Ashford's work: a masterpiece of infantile frivolity. Both enormously popular and ridiculed for its "childishness," *Visiters* received a cultural response that simultaneously inflated and diminished Ashford's accomplishment.

Contemporaneous with *Visiters*'s immense popularity, however, were doubts about its authorship. Rumors quickly spread that it was "too precocious" to be the work of a child, and that Barrie himself must have been the author.[11] The accusation persisted for decades, despite clear evidence to the contrary in the form of Ashford's original 1890 manuscript: a small red notebook with "Daisy Ashford" and "Daisy" written in pencil on the front endsheet, as though the child Ashford were asserting her authorship long before it was ever contested.[12] That many readers believed *Visiters* the work of a celebrated adult writer is revealing, indicating far more about the adult readers in question than the child author. The Romantic view of childhood, popular in the late nineteenth and twentieth-century United States and Great Britain, constructs a racialized fantasy of childhood innocence that assumes white middle-class and wealthy girls are imbued with a kind of "holy ignorance."[13] And yet Ashford's keen perceptiveness challenges these assumptions, reflecting broader "competing conceptions of childhood . . . [where] the idea of the child as an innocent Other clashed most dramatically with an older vision of the child as . . . capable of working and playing alongside adults."[14] Daniela Caselli further complicates these competing views by noting tensions in critics' investigations of the child "within" adult author Djuna Barnes: "[The child is] made to reflect the author's prematurely lost innocence and her powerful seductiveness. On the other hand, the child is the trope adopted to dismiss some works as valueless."[15] The child figure, then, simultaneously compels as a symbol of the impossible Real—some supposed authentic core self—and a voice that can be condescended to or ignored. The public and critical reception of Ashford's writing reflects all of these positions: a deeply held belief in childhood innocence, a fascination with Ashford's "precociousness," a refusal to take her work seriously, and a perception of her as an author whose novel merited engagement alongside adult-written novels. Many contemporary readers, navigating these multiplicities, may have struggled to reconcile Ashford's age with her remarkable insights into adult relationships and sexuality, adult aspirations toward wealth, and adult feelings of personal inadequacy. How could a little child understand something so much larger than herself?

Spatializing Child Authorship

In her essay on child writers Opal Whiteley and Iris Vaughan, Juliet McMaster argues that children who write fiction conduct their research among adults in secret, "trading on [their] small size and inconspicuousness to become a witness to adult doings supposed to be beyond the child's ken."[16] McMaster's claims that children who "know so much" have "an exceptional receptivity" and ability to pay close attention are persuasive, acknowledging that children are active agents in their worlds.[17] But I am more interested in her insight that the "small size" of these child writers plays a central role in their observations. Notably, Ashford's novels are not interested whatsoever in the lives of children. As a child writing adult literature, then, she conceptualizes a physical vantage point not her own. Ashford's perspective of the adult world is fashioned not only by what information she receives or observes in others, but also by the angle and distance at which she receives or observes it. What she views is inherently scalar, dependent upon the way she perceives others from the viewing platform of her own small body. Studying adult behavior requires her to look up.

As Ashford's writings show us, space and place are innately part of the stratified structuring of human interaction, determining the way human beings understand and represent one another. At every level, from the smallest micro scale invisible to the naked eye, to the largest macro scale that encompasses all known materiality, spatiality is profoundly relevant "to all lived experience, and hence to all textual portrayals of it."[18] Literature is therefore inherently spatial in its concerns, a form that mediates between human perceptions of lived environments and textual representations of imagined locales. This centrality of geographies to textual interpretation extends to the work texts do themselves to make legible different forms of movement, mapping, speed, direction, or positionality. Because they are themselves sites, not just representations of sites, literary texts can function as "geographers": "[literature] generates norms, particular modes of readability, that produce a particular type of geography."[19] In short, literature *does* place, and literature *is* place.

Given that the relationship between geography and literature is mutually constitutive, scale is therefore one geographic dimension that participates in shaping the way texts communicate. Ashford, for example, sees the world at the scale a middle-class child body permits, "looking up" at both adult behavior and fantasies of wealth. There is no single definition of scale universally cited or used by geographers; in fact, geographers have consistently debated over whether scale can be considered an ontological reality. In the subfield of human geography, however, scale is typically understood as a socially constructed way of looking across processes that helps us perceive unequal development, or a metric that can give us a sense of power relationships between differently sized elements, materially, socially, and temporally.[20] The construction of scale "shapes the way different spaces are defined," while also having very real impacts on lived realities, a process that can change over the passage of time.[21] For instance, a child's physical world may be primarily limited to the micro level of home and school, but children's legal rights are also continually negotiated on national and global levels. A child's relationship to their scalar environments—local, national, and global—will also shift significantly as they grow into adulthood. Although conversations about scale are often historically focused on cartography, human geographers frequently use scale as a lens to consider at what levels, sizes, and distances various social processes occur, and to what extent scale impacts human agency and power. Scale produces insight into the ways human bodies and material objects exist not only in relation to their physical and scriptive functions, but also in relation to their immediate, local, regional, national, and global contexts.

The introduction of scale into conversations about child authorship has the potential to contribute to the ongoing debates over adult engagement with child writers. For decades, children's literature and childhood studies scholars have grappled with Jacqueline Rose's claim that the child is universally a projection or fantasy of adults, who can never really access or comprehend any sort of "real" child. Strict Rosian models have proved less resilient in the last fifteen years of scholarship, receiving important challenges and complications from Marah Gubar, Karen Sánchez-Eppler, Victoria Ford Smith, Katharine Capshaw, Juliet McMaster, Clementine Beauvais, and others engaging with child-produced material. Critical dialogue around child authorship now acknowledges the challenges of accessing unmediated child expression without denying the existence of actual children, with current debates framed around the complex divides of age, time, and space between child writers and adult readers. "Pursuing the question of children's agency may lead to dead ends," writes Sara L. Schwebel, noting the simultaneous fact of child-produced cultures and the way those cultures are shaped within adult-managed institutional settings.[22] An "authentic" and undiluted child author, then, cannot ever be satisfactorily untangled from the adult cultures within which they write and within which their work circulates.

The scant published scholarship on *The Young Visiters* puts the onus of interpretation on isolating the extent of Ashford's verifiable knowledge: What did the child author really know, and how did she come to know it?[23] Here, I purposefully leave behind questions about the child author's authentic voice, or adult interference into it, to explore Ashford's geographic formations of an adult space, and her authorial and embodied positioning as a child in relation to that space-making. How does the reliance of Ashford's worldview on size, distance, and proximity suggest a possible relationship to her child body? If spatial hierarchies are understood by geographers to be a product of social relations, then age must be considered alongside and within other sociospatial processes as a size-linked metric through which child writers navigate and represent the larger world.

The Young Visiters is not, conventionally speaking, a novel significantly focused on setting. As such, it may seem an odd choice to examine through the lens of scale. Ashford's novel is far more concerned with romance, yearning, social mores, and the seemingly intractable nature of late nineteenth-century British class systems than it is with geography. But to return to Marc Brosseau's claim that the text itself is a geographer—a thing that generates place and space in addition to representing it—I argue for approaching Ashford's novel as a work that jumps scale between differently sized bodies, emotional experiences, domestic spaces, and national spaces. *Visiters* paradoxically makes accessible this daunting world through an exploration of the complex verticalities of relationships, embodiments, and environments.[24] Adult doings and adult feelings are intelligible through the structures of hierarchical categorization and relational size, a framing that centers the child author's experience of navigating through "grown-up" spaces. This way of reading avoids the detective work of investigating Ashford's knowledge, instead uncovering how the spatiality of her novel reveals her ontological positioning as author: the child who gazes up at adulthood in the hopes of comprehending it.

Growing Up(ward) in *The Young Visiters*

From the opening paragraph, Ashford's novel appears intrigued by the distances created through age difference and size difference. Both are subtly bound up in the first descriptions of *Visiters*' co-protagonists:

> Mr Salteena was an elderly man of 42 and was fond of asking peaple [*sic*] to stay with him. He had quite a young girl staying with him of 17 named Ethel Monticue. Mr Salteena had dark short hair and mustache and wiskers [*sic*] which were very black and twisty. He was middle sized and he had very pale blue eyes. He had a pale brown suit but on Sundays he had a black one and

> he had a topper every day as he thorght [*sic*] it more becoming. Ethel Monticue had fair hair done on the top and blue eyes. She had a blue velvit [*sic*] frock which had grown rarther [*sic*] short in the sleeves.[25]

The body is an inherently scalar thing, frequently positioned by human geographers as the smallest scale in a global metric.[26] But the body's size and reach can only be understood in relation to other bodies, a reality *Visiters* seems to understand intuitively. That Mr. Salteena is an "elderly man of 42" may inspire laughter in adult readers for whom forty-two is proximate or past, but this description plainly stresses the substantial distance between Mr. Salteena and "quite a young girl" Ethel. The former is elderly in relation, not simply in isolation, and the deep social impropriety of this visit—an eligible young woman living unchaperoned with an unmarried single man—remains undiscussed but subtly acknowledged through the stark age gap. Significantly, the incompatibility of Mr. Salteena and Ethel extends beyond their ages to their bodies: the former is inadequately large, while the latter is growing over time. Mr. Salteena is only "middle sized," a reference to his height later contrasted with the impressively tall physique of Bernard Clark. The top hat he regularly wears elongates his body, with the effect of making Mr. Salteena appear larger than he actually is. This bit of physical description foreshadows the eventual trajectory of his character arc, in which he seeks to become a gentleman and secure the ambitious Ethel's affections. Both scaling efforts—the height augmentation and the class ascendence—are ultimately based in fantasy, an outcome contrasted by the reference to Ethel's dress as "grown rarther short in the sleeves." Presumably hinting at a growing body, this description signals not only Ethel's physical transition into marriageable adulthood, but also her eventual course toward what the novel views as a "greater" and "bigger" life. The expanding length and span of her frame is a material reality that Mr. Salteena cannot, and will not, achieve. Her eventual ascension to wealth and status is likewise unavailable to him.

I have previously stated that Ashford's fiction is not interested in children. While I stand by that claim, both Ethel and Mr. Salteena do present it with some important complications, as characters who occasionally embody and enact a subject position reminiscent of childhood. As adults who behave childishly, they occupy a liminal space between Ashford's child perspective and the adult representations her book seeks to portray.[27] Ethel's "child" status is somewhat different from Mr. Salteena's in that it is transitory, impacting her characterization largely in the novel's first half, before her eventual ascension to wealth, marriage, and implicit adulthood. Early in *Visiters*, Ethel runs in ways we associate with child movements, "throwing out her legs behind and her arms swinging in rithum [*sic*]."[28] At first, she appears uncertain of social customs a young woman of her class would presumably know: "Do we tip him asked Ethel quietly."[29] And while Mr. Salteena is much older than Ethel, his eventual education in "Socierty [*sic*] ways" positions him as concurrently unknowing and acquiring knowledge. He functions as a child figure aspiring toward but never fully reaching an adulthood conflated with social status:

> So [the groom] Procurio laid [clothing] out in neat array also a razer [*sic*] and brush for shaving. Then he opened a door saying This is the bath room shall I turn on hot or cold.
>
> I dont mind said Mr Salteena feeling very hot and ignorant.
>
> It is best for you to decide sir said Procurio firmly.
>
> Well I will try cold said Mr Salteena feeling it was more manly to say that.[30]

Here as elsewhere, Ashford succinctly captures Mr. Salteena's feelings of diminishment, both temporal and social, and the complex nuances of class-based power he appears incapable of navigating at this scale. To be decisive is to be knowledgeable. *Visiters* subtly mixes the entitlements of class status with the cultural awareness of adulthood, so Mr. Salteena's inability to know instinctively which is best, hot or cold water, is simultaneously reflective of his modest background and his struggle to understand the world around him. The aspect of age becomes clearly articulated through Mr. Salteena's choice of cold water, which he feels is "more manly" than the soft comforts of hot water. To be an adult—and, of course, to be a male adult in particular—requires choices that appear to demonstrate a resolute knowledge. Here, Mr. Salteena's scalar aspiration is simultaneously rooted in class ascension and the acquisition of "grown-up" information.

The contrast between the contracted bodies and actions of Ethel and Mr. Salteena and the elevated privileged life they both aim toward is most visible in the chapters that take place at Bernard Clark's home, Rickamere Hall. Bernard, "a tall man of 29" with "very nice long legs" and a "manly form," has a figure that matches his wealthy estate and surroundings.[31] Everything is maximized; the home has a "huge front door with tall pillers [*sic*]," and it is surrounded by "tall trees and big red flowers." The greeting butler has a "huge pale face," leading the visitors into a "very big" hall.[32] Given that *Visiters* is written in a roving third-person perspective, the descriptions of Bernard and his estate seem to reflect the co-protagonists' particular vantage point, gazing from a relatively small position. Size and social standing are synonymous: "You ourght [*sic*] to give a ball remarked Ethel you have such large compartments."[33] It is here that *Visiters* links the perspective of its child writer to a profound empathy for these two characters and their aspirational inadequacies. Like young children, who live in bodies that take up less space than the bodies of most adults, Mr. Salteena and Ethel are looking up, transfixed by an environment that appears at a considerable distance.

The Scalar Hierarchies of Class

Much of the novel is dedicated to Mr. Salteena's time at the Crystal Palace, where, under the instruction of the Earl of Clincham and Edward Procurio, he undertakes lessons in being "less mere," mixing with the aristocracy in hopes of becoming a gentleman.[34] The environment of the Crystal Palace is, like Bernard's estate, depicted in ways that emphasize its physical grandness in addition to its luxuriousness: as a "wondrous edifice."[35] It also marks Mr. Salteena's transition from smaller domestic spaces to an immense space emblematic of aspirational British nationalism, a scalar swing that implies that the effort to transcend one's class status requires the full absorption into the larger demands of the nation state.[36] Although its depiction in *Visiters* as a training site for would-be gentlemen is entirely fictional, the Crystal Palace was a very real structure in London, one that Ashford, who grew up not far outside the city, might well have visited herself. From the moment of its construction in 1851 for the first World's Fair, the Great Exhibition, the Crystal Palace reified a nationalist and colonialist worldview through its manifold displays and presentations, the majority of which extolled the virtues of the growing British Empire.[37] Following relocation in 1854 from Hyde Park to Sydenham Hill, an act that required its full reconstruction, the massive building remained a Matryoshka doll set in both size and chronology, "hosting numerous [artistic and cultural] replicas within itself and featuring a series of courts that drew from various periods of historic architecture and art."[38] Known as the "Palace of the People," it housed such a large variety of events—animal shows, social meetings, concerts, sport matches, and art exhibits—that its general purpose cannot be easily summarized, except as a site that shored up British identity through innumerable informational exchanges.

In Ashford's descriptions of the Palace, we see a similar juxtaposition of bigness containing small and smaller, the "wondrous edifice" guarded by "two huge men in gold braid." She writes: "Inside was a lovely fountain in the middle and all round were little stalls where you could buy sweets and lemonade also scent handkerchiefs and many dainty articles. There were a lot of peaple [*sic*] but nobody very noteable [*sic*]."[39] The rapid shift in the first sentence toward increasing smallness—the "little stalls," the sweets, the "dainty articles"—makes an enormous space accessible. Even the large numbers of people become scaled down in the reference to their social insignificance. For Mr. Salteena, dwarfed by his characterization as a child, his lack of knowledge, his class status, and now the realities of material scalar contrast, successful entrance into the daunting world of the Crystal Palace is viable only through Ashford's emphasis on other small things. The novel's interest in trivialities, its empathy and appreciation for the small, is evident in these careful attentions, which mirror the kindness it extends to the protagonist who will never entirely attain the elevated social standing he seeks.

That the Crystal Palace functions as an emblem of aspirational nationalism is reinforced through the building's relationship to imitation and artificiality, a connection that Ashford's novel implicitly reproduces. In its commitment to real-world replicas of art and culture, and in its complete reconstruction just a few years after it was first built, the Crystal Palace is a simulacrum that effectively transformed the geographies of British social life. The massive size of the Palace makes possible a "critical transformation," according to Aikaterini Antonopoulou: "The principle of the interior shifts scale, from the middle- or upper-class domestic interior . . . to the interior that contains in itself the outside world as a whole." By making "society an exhibit in itself" through the act of reproduction, the Palace employs its bigness toward an end goal of reconstructing an enclosed and artificial climate.[40] *Visiters* ignores most of the Palace's actual functions in favor of reinventing it as a living space for the British upper class, but the novel's interpretation nevertheless remains true to the building's discursive and geographical functions. In fiction, as in life, the Palace is a place large enough to contain the exhibit of society.

Both Ashford's Palace and the real-world Palace contain a succinct reproduction of British social distinctions in ways that depend on distance. The characters' conversations draw attention to the artificiality of class while also acknowledging the significant appeal of elevated social standing. Mr. Salteena's first meeting with the Earl of Clincham concisely captures this dynamic:

> Well my man said the good natured earl what I say is what dose [*sic*] it matter we cant all be of the Blood royal can we.
>
> No said Mr Salteena but I suppose you are.
>
> Lord Clincham waved a careless hand. A small portion flows in my viens [*sic*] he said but it dose [*sic*] not worry me at all and after all he added piously at the Day of Judgement what will be the odds.
>
> Mr Salteena heaved a sigh. I was thinking of this world he said.
>
> Oh I see said the Earl but my own idear [*sic*] is that these things are as piffle before the wind.
>
> Not being an earl I cant say answered our hero.[41]

Mr. Salteena is at the Palace to learn how to be a gentleman; effectively, he is gone away to school. This exchange stresses the great scalar distance between himself and the Earl: the "adult" or elevated standing that a title promises. Intriguingly, Mr. Salteena—looking to grow upward into wealth—is not defined here by ignorance, but by his own perceptions of class stratification. The Earl, in arguing that social rank "dose [not] matter," especially "at the Day of Judgement," ignores the extent to which social rank certainly does matter to those minimized by it, even in its artificiality. Like the larger building that contains him—another simulacrum—social rank is simultaneously something entirely fabricated *and* a material fact. Mr. Salteena understands this; he gently reminds the Earl that they are currently in "this world," and that although the Earl views class as "piffle before the wind," that perspective belongs to someone who, having great privilege and comfort, has no particular investment in interrogating it. *Visiters* demonstrates that children—both child writers and child-coded characters—are entirely capable of comprehending how a system might be simultaneously unfair and desirable. This complicated tension between unfairness and desirability might also be mapped onto Ashford's perspectives of adulthood, a state of being that, for the child writer, is simultaneously inaccessible and enthralling. Class stratification and age stratification, then, stand in for one another, a system that relies on a series of interconnected and differently sized containers: the domestic and the national, the aspirational and the wealthy, the child and the adult, the mildly agential and the powerful. *Visiters* understands that even when constituted at different levels, "what goes on at one scale significantly shapes what goes on at another."[42]

At the end of Ashford's novel, her characters all marry and procreate, with varying degrees of happiness. Ethel and Bernard, having returned from their honeymoon with a "son and hair [*sic*]," soon have six more children: "[Bernard] loved Ethel to the bitter end and so did she him and they had a nice house too."[43] And while Mr. Salteena secures a job "cantering after the royal barouche," a position that affords him social opportunities, the result is still the exchange of his labor for financial compensation, distinguishing him from Bernard and Ethel.[44] Marrying a maid who works in Buckingham Palace, and having ten children of his own, Mr. Salteena nevertheless grows "very morose as the years rolled by . . . dreaming of Ethel and wishing he could have marrid [*sic*] her. Still he was a pius [*sic*] man in his way and found relief in prayer."[45] Although the emphasis on size and distance is less severe than at the novel's beginning, Ashford still subtly underscores the role of hierarchies, as well as their absence. The description of Bernard and Ethel emphasizes mutuality; now having ascended to wealthy adulthood and a "nice house," Ethel no longer strives for something positioned above her. Mr. Salteena, on the other hand, is still looking up—toward Ethel, now happily situated in Rickamere Hall, and past Ethel, toward the comfort of religious belief. Like Ashford, he ends the novel as an outsider to an elevated space he cannot fully access but is nevertheless connected with through his fascination and his desire.

Conclusion; or, the Height of Perspective

In centering her book around class distinctions, by framing those distinctions as divisions between those with differing levels of agency, and by enacting this tension through size and distance, Daisy Ashford works through her own reality as a child looking up toward the lives of adults. Her novel is crucial support for Marah Gubar's call to view children's creative output through a model that acknowledges children's biological limitations and dependencies as well as their active cultural contributions.[46] Ashford's framing of (white, wealthy, British) adulthood is shaped in part by the scale of her (white, middle-class, British) child body, yes, but, importantly, that ontology does not constitute an absence of agency. Instead, it provides her with an angle from which she is able to see into and represent something much bigger than herself. If Gubar advises us to acknowledge the similarities between children and adults, there's an important link between *Visiters* and many adult-authored works of literature: their shared interest in exploring systems that greatly exceed the size of individual bodies. But it is Ashford's extensive employment of scale as a metric for understanding the world that sets her apart as a child writer. Her work demonstrates a keen awareness of the way levels, size, and distance contribute to structuring power. It offers us a way of theorizing child-generated texts in ways that allow for continuity with adult-written literature while acknowledging their simultaneous differences.

NOTES

1. Daisy Ashford, *The Young Visiters* (New York: George H. Doran, 1919), 76.
2. Juliet McMaster, "'Adults' Literature,' by Children," *Lion and the Unicorn* 25, no. 2 (2001): 281.
3. Caleb Crain, "B-Sides: Daisy Ashford's 'The Young Visiters,'" *Public Books*, last modified September 10, 2020, https://www.publicbooks.org/b-sides-daisy-ashfords-the-young-visiters/.
4. Daisy Ashford, foreword to *Daisy Ashford: Her Book* (New York: George H. Doran, 1920), 24.
5. Ashford, foreword, 26.
6. Jeffrey Mather, introduction to *The Young Visiters*, by Daisy Ashford (Edmonton: Juvenilia Press, 1997), x.
7. Ashford, *The Young Visiters*, 23.
8. "Clears Up Origin of 'Young Visiters,'" *New York Times*, November 27, 1923.
9. Juliet McMaster, "What Daisy Knew: The Epistemology of the Child Writer," in *The Child Writer from Austen to Woolf*, ed. Christine Alexander and Juliet McMaster (Cambridge: Cambridge University Press, 2010), 53.
10. William Goldhurst, *F. Scott Fitzgerald and His Contemporaries* (New York: World Publishing Company, 1963), 54.
11. "9-Year-Old's Book Is Termed No Hoax," *New York Times*, November 22, 1953.
12. Manuscript, *The Young Visiters*, by Daisy Ashford, Berg Collection, New York Public Library.
13. Robin Bernstein, *Racial Innocence: Performing American Childhood from Slavery to Civil Rights* (New York: New York University Press, 2011), 6. Contemporaries defended *Visiter*'s authorship by arguing that *only* a child could have written the novel. A childhood friend of Ashford's, Isabel Furbank, informed the *New York Times* that she did not think "that any grown-up person could produce quite that sort of thing" (*New York Times*, "Daisy Ashford a Very Real Young Lady," August 31, 1919, 74). Ernest Hunter Wright, identified then as a former English department chair at Colombia University, provided his professional opinion: "Neither Barrie nor any other author has ever been able to return so utterly to childhood as to produce a 'Young Visiters'" (*New York Times*, "9-Year-Old's Book Is Termed No Hoax," November 22, 1953, 57). This line of thinking denies the cultural debate at this time, disallowing for the possibilities of amorphous boundaries between childhood and adulthood, and reproducing the "holy ignorance" Bernstein identifies as central to a belief in childhood innocence. Both Furbank and Wright's statements rely on viewing children, and Ashford specifically, as fundamentally exiled from adult creative processes.
14. Marah Gubar, *Artful Dodgers: Reconceiving the Golden Age of Children's Literature* (New York: Oxford University Press, 2009), 9.
15. Daniella Caselli, "'Tendency to Precocity' and 'Childish Uncertainties' of a 'Virago at Fourteen': Djuna Barnes's 'The Diary of a Dangerous Child,'" *Yearbook of English Studies* 32 (2002): 191.

16. McMaster, "What Daisy Knew," 56.
17. McMaster, "What Daisy Knew," 60.
18. Elizabeth Jones, "What Literature is Spatial?," *Literary Geographies* 4, no. 1 (2018): 36.
19. Marc Brosseau, "Geography's Literature," *Progress in Human Geography* 18, no. 3 (1994): 349.
20. Andrew Herod, *Scale* (Abingdon, UK: Routledge, 2011), 28–29.
21. Michael Tavel Clarke and David Wittenberg, introduction to *Scale in Literature and Culture*, ed. Clarke and Wittenberg (London: Palgrave Macmillan, 2017), 11.
22. Sara L. Schwebel, "The Limits of Child Agency for Children's Literature Scholars," *Jeunesse* 8, no. 1 (Summer 2016): 281.
23. McMaster, "What Daisy Knew" and "'Adult's Literature,' by Children"; Mather, introduction to *The Young Visiters*; Clémentine Beauvais, "Is There a Text in This Child? Childness and the Child-Authored Text," *Children's Literature in Education* 50, no. 1 (2019): 60–75; and Pamela Pasak Sawallis, "Daisy Ashford: A Preliminary Checklist," *Bulletin of Bibliography* 50, no. 4 (1993): 255–262.
24. Geographers conceptualize scale through different visual metaphors. While the ladder and Russian Matryoshka dolls are familiar images, not all visual metaphors are vertical or hierarchical. Some, like concentric circles, spirals, or rhizomes, directly acknowledge that scale is not always enacted across levels. This essay prioritizes a traditional reading of scale as vertical in large part because Ashford's novel presents the adult world in ways that emphasize hierarchies: social, physical, and emotional.
25. Ashford, *The Young Visiters*, 23.
26. Herod, *Scale*, 86.
27. In each of her five published stories, Ashford's heroines are "young girls" in their late teenage years. Despite the use of that phrase, the narrative emphasis is universally on their readiness for marriage and the undertaking of adult women's roles. Arguably, "young girl" does more work to stress the social desirability of the characters, with youth and beauty conflated, than it does to reinforce their childishness.
28. Ashford, *The Young Visiters*, 27.
29. Ashford, *The Young Visiters*, 30.
30. Ashford, *The Young Visiters*, 60–61.
31. Ashford, *The Young Visiters*, 32, 92.
32. Ashford, *The Young Visiters*, 31–32.
33. Ashford, *The Young Visiters*, 37.
34. Ashford, *The Young Visiters*, 56.
35. Ashford, *The Young Visiters*, 49.
36. Paralleling Mr. Salteena's journey, Ethel leaves behind domestic spaces for more public ones, going to London with Bernard to enjoy the sights. Her scalar ascent into wealth and standing, however, depends less on an official education and more on her successful performance of desirable femininity, which earns her Bernard's effusive proposal of marriage. That performance is still implicitly aligned with Mr. Salteena's own efforts, as Ethel's entrance into heterosexual womanhood is also a project that affirms British nationalist goals through its ultimate emphasis on reproduction.
37. Alison Laurence, "A Discourse with Deep Time: The Extinct Animals of Crystal Palace Park as Heritage Artefacts," *Science Museum Group Journal* 11 (2019), http://journal.sciencemuseum.ac.uk/browse/issue-11/a-discourse-with-deep-time/.

38. Aikaterini Antonopoulou, "Large Scale Fakes: Living in Architectural Reproductions," in *Scale in Literature and Culture*, ed. Michael Tavel Clarke and David Wittenberg (London: Palgrave Macmillan, 2017), 187.
39. Ashford, *The Young Visiters*, 49.
40. Antonopoulou, "Large Scale Fakes," 192.
41. Ashford, *The Young Visiters*, 53–54.
42. Herod, *Scale*, 252.
43. Ashford, *The Young Visiters*, 103–104.
44. Ashford, *The Young Visiters*, 72.
45. Ashford, *The Young Visiters*, 104.
46. Marah Gubar, "The Hermeneutics of Recuperation: What a Kinship-Model Approach to Children's Agency Could Do for Children's Literature and Childhood Studies," *Jeunesse: Young People, Texts, Cultures* 8, no. 1 (2016): 291–310.

2

"I didn't die and felt the Earth"

Nature and the Urgency of Perception for Young Black Poets in *The Voice of the Children* Workshop

RACHEL CONRAD

I begin this discussion of youth-authored poetry with a poem by then thirteen-year-old Vanessa Howard from which the quotation in this chapter's title is taken; this poem deserves attention on its own terms and in relation to critical conversations about "nature poetry" and African American literature. Howard's line "I didn't die and felt the Earth," from her poem "The Question,"[1] contributes to her careful argument for the power and capacity of Blackness for an alive subject moving in and perceiving the world, or what we might term a phenomenology of perception in relation to Blackness.[2] In this chapter, I explore poems written by Howard and other young Black poets who were members of The Voice of the Children workshop launched and codirected by June Jordan and Terri Bush in Brooklyn, New York from the late 1960s to early 1970s to demonstrate that youth-authored poems, in addition to having value in and of themselves, can participate in literary-cultural projects, such as "what it means to write about nature."[3]

African Americans "have not been recognized in their poetic attempts to affix themselves to the landscape," writes Camille Dungy in the introduction to her edited anthology *Black Nature: Four Centuries of African American Nature Poetry*, and instead have been seen as "accidentally or invisibly or dangerously or temporarily or inappropriately on/in the landscape."[4] Dungy writes that African American poets help expand our sense of "what it means to write about nature" beyond Romantic and Transcendental conventions, in order to imagine the natural world either "aligned with or in opposition to the human world" and to "explore sources of connection to, but also alienation from, the land."[5] What can we learn by considering how young African American poets write about nature and what forms of connection or alienation they might create or depict? Lauret Savoy and Alison Deming, in introducing their anthology *Colors of Nature: Culture, Identity, and the Natural World*, refer to the fruitful and necessary "complication" of nature writing as a more inclusive enterprise inviting "a wealth of literature on nature from culturally and ethnically diverse voices."[6] Savoy and Deming write that the range of "distinct voices" included in their anthology of prose and poetry "help[s] us recognize how critical it is to think and write across threads of identity that are around and within us—those defined from within and those imposed from without—to understand more fully our place on Earth and connections with each other."[7] Considering youth among those "threads of identity" can add valuable perspectives to poetry that engages with nature and can help remake our sense of what nature poetry can be.

Not surprisingly, neither of these wonderful anthologies includes work by young writers, since poetry written by young people is not generally considered part of literary cultures. Occasionally, young poets gain a little visibility during cultural upticks of interest in youth-authored poetry which have afforded some opportunities for publication, audience, and community. Such writers and periods include young white British poets in the late eighteenth and early nineteenth century,[8] young white writers in the United States and United Kingdom in the 1920s,[9] young Black and Latinx writers in the United States during the 1960s and 1970s,[10] and contemporary youth slam poets.[11]

When poetry written by young poets does gain visibility, it is often with the assistance of adult allies, such as June Jordan and Terri Bush—a renowned Black poet (early in her career) and a white educator who together fostered and nurtured the long-term poetry workshop, The Voice of the Children, among Black and Latinx young people in Brooklyn beginning in late 1967.[12] The choices made by Jordan and Bush with the poetry anthology that was published in 1970, toward the end of the workshop's run, are notable: they referred to themselves as "collectors" rather than editors, selected a youth-authored poem as the foreword to the book, and positioned June Jordan's contextualizing discussion of the workshop as an afterword rather than an introduction—decisions which keep the young poets at the center of the project.[13] In her afterword, Jordan writes about the current educational and literary-cultural state of affairs that "our children have no voice—that we will listen to."[14] Jordan and Bush designed the Saturday workshop, which was initially under the auspices of the Teachers and Writers Collaborative, to be unlike school, since "for Black and Puerto Rican teenagers, school is mostly a burial ground for joy and promise. School is where these poets and writers are often termed 'verbally deficient,' or worse."[15] The workshop participants wrote according to their own priorities and artistic imperatives; as Jordan describes, "their writings have never been subjected to adult 'correction'" aside from spelling, since the young poets "want to avoid adult errors of understanding."[16] Jordan and Bush partnered with these young people—about forty over the course of the four years of the workshop, with roughly fifteen participants at any one time[17]—to support their artistic voices and help them find "peace and power."[18]

The Voice of the Children poets were mostly aged eleven to thirteen at the start of the workshop, which grew to encompass writers as old as sixteen or seventeen, and thus the name of the project is worth noting. The young writers decided on the name of the workshop themselves, as June Jordan recounts in "'The Voice of the Children' Saturday Workshop Diaries."[19] In choosing to include "children" in their project's name, these writers stressed their age status as children, as did June Jordan in writing about "the children" in her afterword to the anthology, where she writes that "everywhere they go, the voices of these children grow proud and more and more distinctive."[20] Jordan's use of the term "children" emphasizes their power and capability as "poets and writers," and she makes clear that for Black and Latinx youth in particular, their "voice" has typically not been "listen[ed] to."[21] As Jordan indicates regarding The Voice of the Children writers and their work, "they want people to receive the message, and no mistake about it."[22]

The young Black and Latinx poets in The Voice of the Children workshop wrote in the face of racist ideologies that threatened to constrain their language, perspectives, and identities. Vanessa Howard, in the prose poem that serves as the foreword to *THE VOICE of the Children* anthology, strongly critiques the use of the word "ghetto," which she writes "has become a definition meaning Black, garbage, slum areas."[23] Howard concludes "Ghetto" with these lines: "I think they put all Black people in a box marked 'ghetto' which leaves them having no identity. They should let Black people be seen for themselves, not as one reflection on all."[24] The directness of Howard's confrontation with anti-Black stereotypes and her incisive critique of their linkage between place and identity frames an important element running through many poems in *THE VOICE of the Children* anthology. These young poets wrote with an urgent drive to explore their conceptions of their worlds in relation to their complex identities in ways that deepen our understanding of poetic representations of identity and natural and human-built environments. In this chapter, I explore a selection of poems written by three of the young Black poets in *THE VOICE of the Children* anthology to discern the poets' strategies for representing nature, place, and identity and the complexity of their entanglements.

"They see the world around them": Vanessa Howard on Young Poets, Perception, and Experience

Vanessa Howard, one of the long-term participants in The Voice of the Children workshop, centers her poem "The Question" on a phenomenological argument for her Black speaker's capacity for and capaciousness of perspective, as set against the white anti-Black racism which drives its central question, "Must I be white to live in this humanity?"

> Must I lay down and die to feel the Earth?
> Must I sprout wings and fly to smell the air?
> Must I grow fins to swim to sea?
>
> Must I be white to live in this humanity?

I didn't die and felt the Earth.
I didn't sprout wings and I smelt the air.
I didn't grow fins and I swam the sea.

So Black is all I'm gonna be.[25]

At first glance, we can see the poem's structure as an argument: three lines beginning "Must I" and three lines beginning "I didn't" are stitched together by two lines interrogating race and being. These two lines are accentuated by constituting single-line stanzas and by carrying the poem's only end rhymes (aside from the repetition across the first and third stanzas) which connect these lines further to one another and to the final line of the other stanzas. Howard's opening set of rhetorical questions exposes the illogic of racism and its anti-humanism. Her title signals to us that these questions all lead to the central question—"Must I be white to live in this humanity?"—which rhetorically challenges the notion, forged through white anti-Black racism, that a Black person cannot "feel," "smell," "swim," or otherwise pursue a perceptually alive, rich, and embodied existence.

Howard engages throughout "The Question" in phenomenological thinking, which philosopher Maurice Merleau-Ponty describes in terms of a "demand for awareness" as "meaning comes into being" through philosophical thinking about experience.[26] In *Phenomenology of Perception*, Merleau-Ponty writes that "all my knowledge of the world . . . is gained from my own particular point of view" and way of being in the world.[27] Merleau-Ponty's phenomenology of perception is apt here since it encompasses the "primacy" of individual perception, which involves "render[ing] oneself present to something through the body."[28] Perception involves our unfolding embodied relationship to the world. "The phenomenological world," writes Merleau-Ponty, "is not the bringing to explicit expression of a pre-existing being, but the laying down of being."[29] In depicting this "laying down of being" in her poem "The Question," Howard challenges white supremacy and its setting of whiteness as default humanness: "Must I be white to live in this humanity?" While Howard's poem takes on anti-Black racism directly, it can also be in conversation with Kevin Quashie's recent argument for "black aliveness," for "the freeness of a black world where blackness can be of being."[30]

Howard's tone in "The Question"—in its seeming matter-of-factness—contains, controls, and deploys the outrageousness of racism's inhumanity, and the poem's undercurrent is a biting condemnation of white anti-Black racism. Of course, as a human being one does not need to "sprout wings" to "smell the air," or "grow fins" to "swim to sea." In the penultimate stanza, Howard has her speaker reverse the imperative "Must I" to anchor the lines with a string of first-person "I didn't" statements which offers consistent evidence that counters the premise of the central question. The poem's concluding line, while the shortest and least descriptive—"So Black is all I'm gonna be"—challenges the reader about how to read the word "all." Is it "all" as insufficiency or "all" as capaciousness, "all" as shaped by white anti-Black racism or "all" as all-encompassing Blackness? Michelle Wright uses the physics of space-time to discuss an expansive and inclusive notion of Blackness which she terms "the Multidimensionality of Blackness" and which includes "the *specific moment* in which Blackness is being imagined."[31] The final line of Howard's poem tests the reader to locate insufficiency and inadequacy in anti-humanist anti-Black racism itself and read "all" as the power, completeness, and brilliance of Blackness. Howard embraces the colloquialism of "gonna"—which challenges the grammar of white English—to nail the point.

Howard not only composed a rich body of poetry in *THE VOICE of the Children* anthology and in a solo volume of her poetry, *A Screaming Whisper*—published in 1972 when she was seventeen years old—but she also delineated a poetics of youth writing. When *Today's Girl* magazine invited Howard in 1971 to "tell her story," she negotiated the opportunity to discuss The Voice of the Children workshop and the value of poetry written by youth.[32] In Howard's essay "We Speak to be Heard," she describes children as "just as real and alive as anyone twenty-five or a hundred" and discusses how poetry both enabled and participated in the growth of the young writers in The Voice of the Children workshop: "In us, poetry was born while we were being born and born again, each time emerging as something different and new and constantly aware."[33] Because of the charged time in which they lived as Black and Latinx children in New York City during the civil rights era, the participants in The Voice of the Children workshop were able to capture adult attention in a way that happens only intermittently with young writers. Explaining their choice of name for their workshop and weekly magazine, Howard writes: "We called ourselves *The Voice of the Children*, for through writing we had a voice in a place where nothing was unimportant, and everyone was listening."[34] Howard discusses the import of their writing and sharing their work with public audiences through poetry readings: "We gave poetry readings in different places, speaking not only for ourselves, but for all children who had not yet found a means of being heard."[35] Thus, Howard sees the crucial need for and value of "speaking and . . . being heard" for all children, which writing and sharing one's works publicly helps fulfill.[36]

In her essay "We Speak to be Heard," Howard makes clear her contention that children's ideas and imaginations are typically "shushed quiet by an alien adult world" and that writing can validate children's perspectives and "strengthen" their minds.[37] She describes the young writers in The Voice of the Children as "just normal" and as readily perceiving the complexities of the world: "They see the world around them, they live in it, experience it and they have seen the dark and gloomy side of life."[38] As Howard herself approached age sixteen, she began to take on a mentoring role in relation to the younger children in the workshop ("working with other, younger children"), and encouraged them to write about their own experiences.[39] She describes her mentoring experiences in an interview in 1973 after her solo poetry volume *A Screaming Whisper* was published: "We'd put some jazz on the record player. Then we'd talk to the kids. We'd ask them what happened at school or at home. Now and then we'd say, 'Hey, that's interesting. Why not write about that?'"[40]

In these reflections a few years following "We Speak to be Heard," Howard views people's experiences across age as the wellspring for their writing. She believes that writers draw from the depth of their experiences regardless of age: "Kids—and older people, too—often think they have nothing to write about. Kids think that they're too young. That nothing has happened to them yet. But age has nothing to do with it. You could be 90 and hardly have lived at all. Or you could be a child and have lived through practically everything."[41] Thus, Howard's poetics of youth poetry simultaneously centers and decenters age in her argument for the value of experience. While her poem "The Question" does not invoke age, it condemns the illogic of white anti-Black racism and embraces the fullness of the perceptual power of its Black speaker.

"I'm like the birds whistling in the trees": Phillip Solomon's and Linda Curry's Strategic Uses of Nature and Perceptual Power

Vanessa Howard's discussion of the young writers in The Voice of the Children workshop who "see the world around them, . . . live in it, experience it and . . . have seen the dark and gloomy side of life" helps frame poems by Phillip Solomon and Linda Curry in *THE VOICE of the Children* anthology.[42] Phillip Solomon writes about the natural world to evoke the "fragile" and isolated nature of his speaker's subjectivity in an untitled poem:

> touch me not, for i am fragile
> I'm like the birds whistling in the trees,
> so content and happy where i am.
> leave me here, for if not here,
> I am dead.
> touch me not, for i am fragile.[43]

The identical opening and closing lines of Solomon's short poem are lyrical and writerly. The two halves of the line are balanced and make use of poetic rather than colloquial syntax in the first half—"touch me not" rather than "don't touch me"—and the lack of capitalization of "i" within these lines emphasizes a sense of fragility. The simile Solomon uses for his speaker is an unsurprising image of natural tranquility ("I'm like the birds whistling in the trees"), but he applies it in a startling way to evoke vulnerability in relation to his speaker's rootedness in place. He draws a stark all-or-nothing portrait of either being "like the birds whistling" and "happy where i am" or "if not here, / I am dead," which makes clear the high stakes involved. The poem enjoins the reader, through direct address, to "touch me not" and to "leave me here," a rhythmic echo that accentuates the poem's key repeated phrase. Ending the poem as it began—"touch me not, for i am fragile"—encapsulates this miniaturized portrait where the whistling birds are used to represent the fragility of not withstanding change and the isolation of someone in that "fragile" state who cannot be disturbed or "touch[ed]." At the same time, "I'm like the birds whistling in the trees" holds a power of perception, a beauty of being, that anchors the perceptual world of this poem and helps constitute its complexity.

Phillip Solomon writes a different kind of nature poem in "The Echo," which depicts a landscape of emotion as seen through a background of conflict and violence, which I read as racial conflict and racial violence, although it is worth noting that he chooses not to make this explicit. Here, Solomon again uses a trope of nature writing—in this case using a cave to enact a drama of a speaker's echoing voice—yet the drama is not solely one of individual emotion but also of cultural and political conflict. In this tightly constructed poem, the "echo" is depicted as an answering voice rather than a repeating voice, which establishes a heated conversational energy through response to the speaker's "shouting."

I walked through the cave and
　　　　shouted,
"Why is there hate?"
　　　　My echo came back, yes.

I walked through the cave,
　　　　as I shouted,
"Will it forever be the same?"
　　　　My echo came back, yes.

I walked through the cave,
　　　　shouting,
"Am I full of hate?"
　　　　My echo came back, yes.

Walking through the cave,
　　　　I shouted,
"Will the world ever find peace?"
　　　　No echo came back. . . . [44]

"Hate" is opposed to "peace," and the certainty of the existence of "hate" in the first three stanzas contrasts strongly with the unanswered question about the possibility of peace in the final stanza: "Will the world ever find peace?" The absence of echo reverberates in the final line, and the ellipses suggest the continuance of the reverberation. Here the natural world, the cave landscape, is a realistic echo of the extent and persistence of societal conflict.

Finally, Linda Curry depicts a bleak urban landscape as elemental and inextricable from human conflict, violence, and "pain" in an untitled poem:

the gray sky
　　　　　　the bare
　　　　　　　　street
　　　　　　　　what has life meant
　　　　　　　　to me

it has meant
brutality
pain
ignorance
pain
crying
pain
wars
pain
death
pain
life
pain

I saw the gray sky and the bare streets[45]

Curry builds her landscape from two environmental elements that frame the poem in its opening and closing lines—"the gray sky" and "the bare street" (which multiplies to "streets" by the end). Within the poem, she links her ideas through structural means by indenting and aligning columns of single words. The other elements of the poem are questioning "what has life meant / to me" and delineating the answers. The answers are almost consistently grim, and the dozen single-word replies include after each new element the refrain "pain" as a prayer or condemnation or sound of hurt. While the list of "brutality," "ignorance," "crying," "wars," and "death" ends with "life," "pain" still follows, underscoring the prevalence and pervasiveness of this "pain." Though not named explicitly, economic injustice, racial injustice, racist violence, and imperialist warfare are likely referents for the list. Curry's poem ends with its only complete sentence: "I saw the gray sky and the bare streets." Most of the words in this sentence have appeared within the poem already, yet they are now organized and linked explicitly as a finished statement through the first-person perspective of the speaker. Despite the long line of pain it delineates, the poem lands on the firm foundation of the speaker's perception of her surroundings. This perception and the completeness of its expression as a full sentence reflect the strength, insight, and capacity of Curry's poetic speaker, whose fortitude and clarity of vision anchor the poem.

Curry's final line returns us to the importance of the embodied perspective of these poets, the imagined subjectivities through which they construct their poetic worlds, and the complex and intersecting identities through which their perspectives are made. Together, the poems by Phillip Solomon and Linda Curry convey the clear-eyed, powerful perspectives of their speakers, in aligning with nature (Solomon, [touch me not]), viewing nature as a neutral mediator (Solomon, "The Echo"), or constructing the interaction of the natural and built environment as a platform for pain (Curry, [the gray sky]), while also referencing "fragil[ity]" and "hate," and "brutality" and "death." For readers of these poems written by young Black poets living in the turbulent late 1960s United States, considering the context of race, racism, and racial violence is warranted though is not the only interpretation. Creative work provides young writers a platform where they can choose whether and how to reference aspects of their identities and lives. Vanessa Howard more explicitly calls out white anti-Black racism in her indictment of its efforts to constrain ideas and realities regarding perception and embodiment ("The Question"), and in a rhetorical vein, Howard condemns the labeling of Black identity with the racist and reductionist term "ghetto" that flattens and distorts Black communities and environments ("Ghetto").

Even this small selection of poems from one project demonstrates different ways that these young poets, despite inhabiting the same urban space and time, work with complexities of nature, perception, and identity in pursuing their purpose and artistry. Dungy, in considering poetry written by Black adults, writes that "black poetry in America has recorded perspectives on the natural world as various as black perspectives on the nation," and young Black poets also inhabit vastly different subjectivities and imaginative worlds from one another, from which they construct their poems.[46] Young Black poets add crucial dimensions to "what it means to write about nature," and young poets add invaluably to our poetry and poetics more generally.[47]

As adult readers and critics, we would do well to try to discern young people's implicit or explicit conceptualizations of poetry. This also holds true in terms of particular literary-cultural projects, such as conceptualizations of nature in the poetic projects of the Brooklyn-based young Black poets involved with The Voice of the Children workshop. Vanessa Howard's essay "We Speak to be Heard" provides a glimpse of the depth of one young poet's theorizing about the individual and collective value for young people of writing poetry. Surely, poetry written by youth has an important role to play in introducing other young people to poetry, as well as adding to the poetic canon. How can this role be further recognized and mobilized so that young readers are regularly invited to hear or read the poetic artistry created by other youth, and see possibilities for their own poetic lives?

NOTES

1. Vanessa Howard, "The Question," in *THE VOICE of the Children*, collected by June Jordan and Terri Bush (New York: Holt, Rinehart and Winston, 1970), 45. Quotations from work by Vanessa Howard appear by permission of Vanessa Howard.
2. See discussion of Merleau-Ponty's ideas in *Phenomenology of Perception* (London: Routledge and Kegan Paul, 1962) later in this chapter.
3. Camille T. Dungy, "Introduction: The Nature of African American Poetry," in *Black Nature: Four Centuries of African American Nature Poetry*, ed. Camille T. Dungy (Athens: University of Georgia Press, 2009), xxvi.
4. Dungy, "Introduction," xxvii.

5. Dungy, "Introduction," xxvi, xxii.
6. Savoy and Deming, "Widening the Frame," 8, 6.
7. Savoy and Deming, "Widening the Frame," 11.
8. Katharine Kittredge, "Early Blossoms of Genius: Child Poets at the End of the Long Eighteenth Century," *Looking Glass: New Perspectives on Children's Literature* 15, no. 2 (2011), https://ojs.latrobe.edu.au/ojs/index.php/tlg/article/view/274; and Laurie Langbauer, *The Juvenile Tradition: Young Writers and Prolepsis, 1750–1835* (Oxford: Oxford University Press, 2016).
9. David Sadler, "Innocent Hearts: The Child Authors of the 1920s," *Children's Literature Association Quarterly* 17, no. 4 (1992): 24–30.
10. Katharine Capshaw, *Civil Rights Childhood: Picturing Liberation in African American Photobooks* (Minneapolis: University of Minnesota Press, 2014); Rachel Conrad and Cai Rodrigues-Sherley, "Kali Grosvenor, Aurelia Davidson, and the Agency of Young Black Poets," in *Literary Cultures and Twentieth-Century Childhoods*, ed. Rachel Conrad and L. Brown Kennedy (Cham, Switzerland: Palgrave Macmillan, 2020), 219–236; and Amy Fish, "Agency in Absentia: Child Authorship under Racial Oppression in *The Me Nobody Knows*," *Lion and the Unicorn* 44, no. 1 (2020): 56–77.
11. Gholnescar Muhammed and Lee Gonzalez, "Slam Poetry: An Artistic Resistance toward Identity, Agency, and Activism," *Equity and Excellence in Education* 49, no. 4 (2016): 440–453.
12. Participants in The Voice of the Children workshop began while students in junior high school, and some continued to participate through high school (Terri Bush, personal interview with author, New York, NY, June 6, 2017). The poets I discuss here were identified as age thirteen (Howard, "The Question," and Solomon, "The Echo"), fourteen (Solomon, [touch me not, for I am fragile]), or fifteen (Curry, [the gray sky]) in the anthology *THE VOICE of the Children* (collected by June Jordan and Terri Bush, New York: Holt, Rinehart and Winston, 1970).
13. See further discussion of Jordan and Bush's editorial choices in Rachel Conrad, *Time for Childhoods: Young Poets and Questions of Agency* (Amherst: University of Massachusetts Press, 2020).
14. June Jordan, afterword to *THE VOICE of the Children*, collected by June Jordan and Terri Bush (New York: Holt, Rinehart and Winston, 1970), 93.
15. Jordan, afterword, 95.
16. Jordan, afterword, 96. Spelling can be a matter of contention for young writers and their adult editors; see Capshaw's discussion of poet Kali Grosvenor.
17. Terri Bush, personal interview with author, New York, NY, June 6, 2017.
18. Jordan, afterword, 98.
19. June Jordan, "'The Voice of the Children' Saturday Workshop Diaries" in *Journal of a Living Experiment*, ed. Phillip Lopate (New York: Teachers and Writers Press, 1979), 134–157.
20. Jordan, afterword, 97. Jordan notes that as the project proceeded, the young writers gave poetry readings at a number of venues, and their poems were published in other collections and publications.
21. Jordan, afterword, 97, 93.
22. Jordan, afterword, 96.
23. Vanessa Howard, "Ghetto," in Jordan and Bush, *VOICE*, ix.
24. Howard, "Ghetto," ix.
25. Vanessa Howard, "The Question," in Jordan and Bush, *VOICE*, 45.

26. Maurice Merleau-Ponty, *Phenomenology of Perception* (London: Routledge and Kegan Paul, 1962), xxi.
27. Merleau-Ponty, *Phenomenology of Perception*, viii.
28. Maurice Merleau-Ponty, *The Primacy of Perception* (Evanston, IL: Northwestern University Press, 1964), 42.
29. Merleau-Ponty, *Phenomenology of Perception*, xx.
30. Kevin Quashie, *Black Aliveness, or a Poetics of Being* (Durham, NC: Duke University Press, 2021), 10.
31. Michelle M. Wright, *Physics of Blackness: Beyond the Middle Passage Epistemology* (Minneapolis: University of Minnesota Press, 2015), 30, 14.
32. "Vanessa Howard Speaks to be Heard," *Today's Girl* 1, no. 3 (Nov. 1971): 10.
33. Vanessa Howard, "We Speak to be Heard," *Today's Girl* 1, no. 3 (Nov. 1971): 10.
34. Howard, "We Speak," 10.
35. Howard, "We Speak," 11.
36. Howard, "We Speak," 11.
37. Howard, "We Speak," 10, 12.
38. Howard, "We Speak," 13.
39. Howard, "We Speak," 12.
40. "Vanessa Howard: Young Author of *A Screaming Whisper*," *Scholastic Scope* (29 Jan. 1973), 6.
41. "Vanessa Howard," 6.
42. Howard, "We Speak," 13.
43. Phillip Solomon, [touch me not], in Jordan and Bush, *VOICE*, 77.
44. Phillip Solomon, "The Echo," in Jordan and Bush, *VOICE*, 37.
45. Linda Curry, [The gray sky], in Jordan and Bush, *VOICE*, 80.
46. Dungy, "Introduction," xxviii.
47. Dungy, "Introduction," xxvi.

3

Representations of Youth Environmental Activism and Agency in Aika Tsubota's *Secrets of the Earth*

BRIANNA ANDERSON

In the face of an escalating global climate crisis and other ecological catastrophes of the late twentieth and twenty-first centuries, children and teenagers have increasingly emerged as highly visible, vocal environmental activists. Notably, many youths have engaged in high-profile, organized forms of advocacy on local, national, and even international scales. Teenagers Xiuhtezcatl Roske-Martinez and Greta Thunberg delivered speeches to the United Nations about the pressing need to address climate change in 2015 and 2019, respectively, and youth collectives have founded large-scale environmental organizations like SustainUS and Zero Hour. These impactful activist endeavors demonstrate young people's ability to exert agency and grapple intellectually and politically with ecological challenges. Alongside the heightened visibility of real-life activists, numerous depictions of youth environmental activists have appeared in children's culture and media in the last thirty years. For instance, Carole Lindstrom and Michaela Goade's Caldecott Medal-winning picture book *We Are Water Protectors* (2020) portrays a young heroine participating in Indigenous-led movements to protect waterways. Likewise, in September 2021, American Girl released Evette Peeters, a biracial doll advertised as "a nature lover who is full of crafty ideas for reusing and upcycling clothes."[1] The increasing prevalence of media representations of child activists points to a growing awareness of young people's capacity for and desire to participate in large-scale, organized environmental advocacy. Moreover, these fictional activists challenge traditional framings of youth in environmental media, which, as Clare Echterling contends, previously tended to "positio[n] the child or young adult as apolitical, capable of activism and change only within the boundaries of the private sphere and their own lives, and perhaps even incapable of grasping the temporal, geographical, political, economic, and cultural complexities wrapped up in climate change."[2] However, consumers and scholars have paid little attention to another significant form of youth activist media: texts created by children and teenagers to raise awareness of environmental issues and promote advocacy.

Twelve-year-old Aika Tsubota's manga *Secrets of the Earth* (1991) demonstrates how youth creators can use visual narratives to express their concerns about the environment and promote activism while navigating the classroom's constraints. The manga circulated widely in the 1990s and early 2000s, with the text's popularity stemming—at least partially—from its dramatic origin story. A paratextual note with no attributed author precedes the primary narrative and explains that Tsubota created the manga in 1991 "to fulfill an assignment from her homeroom to somehow present environmental issues so clearly that even first-graders can understand."[3] The night that she completed the project, the note continues, Tsubota suffered a fatal cerebral hemorrhage. As I will discuss, this tragic event has contributed to the girl's mythologization as a precocious eco-warrior in the paratextual discourse surrounding her work. After her death, Tsubota's parents self-published *Secrets of the Earth* to share at her elementary school in Hirata, Shimane, Japan. In 1992, the manga began to circulate transnationally when the Foundation for Global Peace and Environment (FGPE) published and distributed the original Japanese version and translated versions in Chinese, English, and Arabic. As of 2000, the manga had been translated into five additional languages, and FGPE and other environmental organizations had distributed more than four hundred thousand copies to children worldwide.[4] Though *Secret of the Earth*'s popularity has waned in the last two decades, Archive.org and several other websites offer free digital copies of the manga.

While Tsubota's death contributed to the manga's popularity, the text's appeal also comes from the narrative's mixture of whimsical characters and informative scientific facts, as well as its depiction of children as capable environmental advocates. The almost forty-page, handmade manga features two sixth-grade protagonists, Rumi and Eichi, who discover a book with the same title at their city library. When Rumi opens the book, an anthropomorphized Earth emerges from the pages. Tsubota depicts the planet as an angel-like figure dressed in blue robes with a globe for a head and small, humanlike hands and feet. Floating above the startled children's heads, the adorable Earth avatar announces, "I'm here to take you on a magical tour of the secrets of the Earth!"[5] Despite this fantastical beginning, the rest of the manga does not deliver the "magical tour" promised by the Earth. Instead, Tsubota presents a mostly realistic, nonfictional account as the anthropomorphic Earth narrates the planet's history, teaches Rumi and Eichi about scientific processes, and describes urgent environmental threats. The five-part narrative concludes with the now enlightened Rumi and Eichi suggesting ways children can help the environment and rallying their classmates to participate in advocacy.

Despite the manga's global influence, *Secrets of the Earth* has received virtually no critical attention from English-speaking scholars.[6] I argue that Tsubota's visual narrative is a revealing example of how visual narratives can empower children to advocate for the environment. Significantly, Japanese schools often banned manga in the 1990s due to the stigmatized medium's perceived lack of educational value; as a result, Tsubota's decision to create manga as a homework assignment can be interpreted as doubly progressive, both for its content and its form.[7] However, the manga's narrative structure and imagery also underscore how child creators navigate—and sometimes perpetuate—institutional power dynamics as they compose texts within an educational framework. As Christopher J. Jenks writes, "Power is a ubiquitous feature of classroom discourse, shaping in explicit and implicit ways how teachers and students make sense of each other and the ways in which they co-accomplish teaching and learning goals."[8] On the one hand, this institutional framework can facilitate students' creative expression by providing them with the materials, knowledge, and time needed to produce art. On the other hand, inherently unequal power dynamics between students and teachers can also hinder children's ability to exercise agency as they compose their creations. Thus, treating child-authored texts as valid objects of study, as Karen Sánchez-Eppler contends, "is not to pretend that children are fully independent actors, unhampered by the constraints of adult regulation and desire; but neither is it to see children as incapable of defining their own terms and grounds of power and meaning."[9] Analyzing *Secrets of the Earth,* I argue that the manga reveals how youth can use visual narratives to challenge, negotiate, and perpetuate institutional and social power hierarchies that contribute to environmental issues and hinder children's agency. Tsubota's creation reproduces troubling adult-child power dynamics—a predictable side effect of the project's origin as a homework assignment—though the text ultimately still offers empowering messages for young readers. Additionally, the manga's paratext provokes troubling questions about adults' perceptions of children's agency by presenting Tsubota as an exceptional environmental heroine.

"That's What You Think!": Exploring Pedagogical Power Dynamics

The tension between the narrative's dual roles as a mandatory homework assignment and a transgressive eco-advocacy text manifests in the first three of the manga's five chapters. These opening sections blend watercolor panels featuring the three main characters with illustrated figures visually conveying scientific information to young readers. Significantly, the Earth and the children's conversation occurs in a bookstore, not in a formal classroom setting (though this setting fades away after the opening panels, replaced by blank backgrounds). However, the manga perpetuates conventional school power hierarchies often associated with what Paulo Freire terms the "banking" education model. This form of pedagogy hinders students' creative thinking and critical engagement, Freire contends, because it consists of a "relationship involv[ing] a narrating Subject (the teacher) and patient, listening objects (the students)," who serve as empty receptacles that the teacher fills with knowledge.[10] In particular, Gerald LeTendre observes that 1990s Japanese middle schools framed education as a process of guidance, writing that the "*ideal* relationship between teacher and learner is that of guide and follower, master and disciple."[11] In Tsubota's manga, a one-page paratextual section titled "Main Characters" that precedes chapter 1 immediately establishes the Earth's role as an authoritative guide by noting that the anthropomorphic figure "knows all there is to know about our planet, Earth."[12]

The first three chapters of the manga reinforce this characterization of the Earth as an enlightened sage by framing the characters' conversation as a one-way flow of information from the lecturing planet to the listening students. Tsubota accompanies the Earth's informative dialogue with simplistic diagrams and explanatory text boxes. For example, chapter 2 includes an illustration titled "Creation of Organic Compounds From Sunlight" that provides a mostly accurate representation of the process of photosynthesis. However, Tsubota adds a creative flourish by depicting miniature, gnomelike figures who funnel the particles into machines to produce oxygen and water (see Figure 3.1).[13] While Tsubota's visual anthropomorphization of nature gives the manga a somewhat fantastical quality, the Earth's straightforward narration of environmental processes and the inclusion of educational figures mean that the manga most closely resembles the science textbooks that children encounter in K–12 classrooms. Myra Zarnowski and Susan Turkel argue that these textbooks often fail to properly educate young readers about "science as a way of thinking and learning. . . . They consist, instead, of facts, facts, and more facts, without providing any insight into how those facts were obtained, interpreted, or defended in the broader scientific community."[14] Textbooks that emphasize facts over process perpetuate the banking model of pedagogy by centering the voices of authority figures—the writers and teachers—and by mystifying the development of scientific knowledge.

Similarly, *Secrets of the Earth* presents its environmental knowledge as a compilation of facts delivered by the omnipotent Earth, not as an evolving process children can question or participate in. Throughout these explicitly educational opening sections, the planet frequently asks Rumi and Eichi questions such as "Did everything make sense?" or "Do you want to learn about that next?"[15] However, these shallow inquiries merely gauge Rumi and Eichi's understanding of and interest in the provided environmental information. The Earth does not encourage the children to participate in their own scientific inquiry or seek environmental knowledge from other sources. As a result, while the Earth does effectively teach the reader facts about nature, the manga—like the science textbooks that Zarnowski and Turkel criticize—does not invite the child characters or the implied young readers to participate in "critical engagement," which Joe Sutliff Sanders defines as "a sharing of authority between books and children, allowing for a form of active dialogue between text and reader rather than the reader's passive receipt of information from the authoritative text."[16] Texts that foster critical engagement empower children to seek gaps in narratives, question how biases and dominant power structures influence knowledge production, and participate in critical inquiry. Of course, what counts as "good" pedagogy is culturally situated, and Sanders primarily

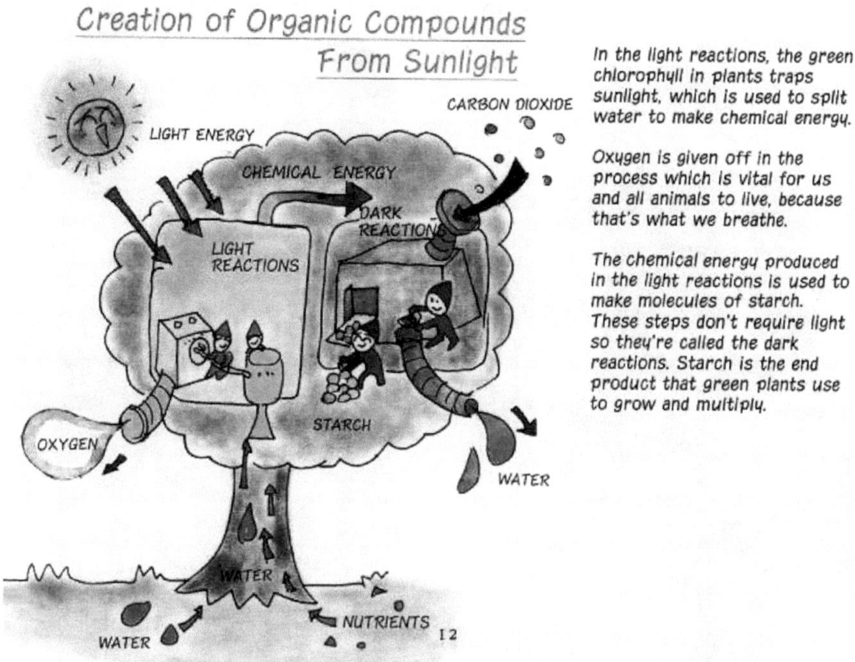

FIGURE 3.1 An illustration of the carbon cycle in Tsubota's *Secrets of the Earth* (12).

analyzes Western texts. Still, the opening chapters of *Secrets of the Earth* model a more conservative form of pedagogy than later sections by presenting the teacher-figure Earth's narration as a series of indisputable environmental facts for children to "bank," or absorb, not as a starting place for young readers to engage with nature and science critically. Tsubota's inclusion of gnomes in the diagrams *could* potentially offer one opportunity for critical engagement by inviting readers to question the accuracy of the Earth's environmental knowledge. However, these fantastical figures seem more likely to confuse or misinform young readers than provoke deeper engagement with the text.

In addition to framing the Earth as an authoritative teacher, these didactic opening chapters depict Rumi and Eichi as eager, though largely passive, pupils. Tsubota repeatedly uses the manga's visual and verbal narratives to emphasize the sixth graders' ignorance. For instance, in chapter 2, the Earth begins its discussion of plants by introducing the children to photosynthesis. Question marks surround Eichi's body as he declares, "Photo-what? Never heard of it!" Two panels later, an alarmed-looking Rumi exclaims, "Whoa! Light reactions? Dark reactions? You lost me!" (see Figure 3.2).[17] The panels juxtapose the robed Earth's sage-like gestures—a raised pointer finger, outspread hands—and declarative statements with the children's bewildered poses and erratic speech, further emphasizing the knowledge divide between the teacher and student figures. On the following page, after the Earth uses a diagram and textual narration to educate the children about

FIGURE 3.2 Tsubota uses the visual and textual narratives to contrast the Earth's wisdom with the children's confused ignorance in *Secrets of the Earth* (12). Like most traditional manga, this story should be read from right to left.

photosynthesis, a wide-eyed Rumi clasps her hands together and says, "Wow! First soil and now plants. . . . I never knew any of this!"[18] This pattern repeats throughout the manga's first three chapters: the children express their ignorance on an environmental subject, the Earth enlightens them, and they react by expressing their amazement and excitement—but not by asking additional questions or thinking critically about the information they have received. Read generously, Tsubota's characterization of Rumi and Eichi as uneducated but enthusiastic pupils could make learning about the environment seem less daunting or tedious for young readers. Viewed through this lens, the children's frequent exclamations as they listen to the Earth—"Nature works in wondrous ways!", "Nature is incredible!", and so on—do not merely draw attention to their lack of knowledge but also encourage the implied audience to feel passionate and concerned about the environment.[19]

However, the first three chapters' binary portrayal of the main characters as either an enlightened instructor or passive students also demonstrates how youth-created comics navigate—and sometimes re-create—dominant institutional power structures. While the manga's emphasis on the children's ignorance seems intended to promote the learning process as exciting, Tsubota complicates this message by depicting the Earth repeatedly chastising the children for their lack of knowledge. In chapter 2, Eichi dismisses the importance of soil, saying, "It's just the brown stuff we walk on every day. What's to know?" Staring out of the panel as though it expects the reader to share its exasperation, the Earth responds, "Golly, I thought you'd at least know a little . . ."[20] In the following chapter, when the planet asks the children if they have heard about acid rain, a smirking Eichi shrugs and declares, "But that's over in Europe. . . . It's not our problem!" Suddenly furious, the Earth shouts, "That's what you think!!" (see Figure 3.3).[21] The jagged edges of the speech bubble and the panel's red background visually reflect the character's anger. These troubling exchanges reinforce the Earth's authority and superior knowledge by casting the planet as a scolding teacher who must correct the misinformation promoted by the children. Together with the Earth's role as the primary deliverer of environmental knowledge, these moments promote what Nathalie op de Beeck describes as a "top-down approach" to environmental pedagogy. She writes, "Most pedagogical work, mainstream and scholarly, envisions adult gatekeepers—naturalists, scientists, authors, parents, teachers—guiding children in a process of coming to appreciate nature."[22] This approach divests Rumi and Eichi of agency by placing the responsibility for their environmental education solely on the Earth, not the children themselves. Moreover, the Earth's negative reactions to Rumi and Eichi's uneducated responses indicate that children should feel ashamed or inferior for failing to comprehend and feel concern for the environment. Troublingly, then, the manga's unflattering representation of the two young characters perpetuates harmful stereotypes by suggesting that children lack the intellectual and affective capacities to care about and understand environmental processes and crises—or, at the very least, that children will only care about these concepts if a (pseudo-)adult educator delivers knowledge to them.

FIGURE 3.3 The Earth corrects Eichi's ignorance about acid rain in *Secrets of the Earth* (20).

Of course, it is important to note that Tsubota—like her fictional child characters—was a sixth-grade student when she created *Secrets of the Earth*, and the manga's informative textual and visual representations of nature demonstrate that youth *can* effectively grasp the complexities and urgency of environmental issues. As a result, the manga's portrayal of Rumi and Eichi presumably reflects the institutional framework of the classroom as Tsubota strives to mimic adult-authored educational texts rather than the girl's own beliefs about the intellectual capabilities of herself and her peers. The assignment inherently frames young children as ignorant and incapable of grasping complex ideas by requiring the student creators to render scientific concepts and environmental issues so simplistically that "even" a first grader could understand them. The teacher likely created this instruction as a well-intentioned effort to have students create projects that present environmental knowledge in an accessible format. However, by explicitly requiring students to oversimplify concepts for the implied young reader, the assignment—and, by extension, Tsubota's manga—perpetuates an "ideology of oppression" by, as Freire writes, "projecting an absolute ignorance onto others" and by presenting environmental information as "a gift bestowed by those who consider themselves knowledgeable upon those whom they consider to know nothing."[23] In other words, the assignment enables the student creators to exercise agency by creating media that conveys environmental information, but it also forecloses the target younger audience's critical engagement with this knowledge by framing them as empty receptacles who can only understand simplistic concepts. Shaped by this institutional framework, Tsubota's manga reduces children to passive recipients of scientific facts dictated by an authority figure rather than agents who actively seek knowledge.

However, Tsubota's anthropomorphization of the Earth does complicate the characters' seemingly oppressive teacher-student dynamic. Throughout the first three chapters, the planet is an authoritative educator but physically resembles a child more than a human adult. Tsubota draws the Earth at roughly the same height as Rumi and Eichi, and the planet's bare feet, large, globular skull, and wide eyes all point to its apparent physical immaturity. These infantile characteristics amplify the inherent childlikeness of anthropomorphized beings in children's literature. Lisa Rowe Fraustino contends that such beings "occupy the same liminal space as children themselves. Like liminal child characters, anthropomorphized characters are hybrid, in-between; they are not Real, not really animals or tree or trains and not really people, either."[24] Tsubota's Earth occupies this hazy in-between space, functioning as either a childish teacher figure or a teacher-like child figure and physically blending the features of a globe with a human body. The manga's opening frame narrative also emphasizes the Earth's hybridity: the planet appears from and, at the conclusion of the manga, returns to the pages of Rumi's copy of *Secrets of the Earth*, traversing the boundary between the fictional world of the intertextual book and the "real" world inhabited by Rumi and Eichi. As indeterminate beings, both the Earth and the children exist as not-adult semi-citizens who live in society's margins (literally, in the case of the book-inhabiting planet).

The anthropomorphic Earth's liminal status shapes the manga's environmental message in several significant ways that demonstrate how comics can foster children's agency and challenge existing power structures. By visually drawing parallels between the anthropomorphized Earth and the child characters—and therefore, between the Earth and the implied young reader—Tsubota invites the audience to view the planet as a living, feeling, and vulnerable entity. This affective connection may cause the audience to experience greater feelings of urgency while reading the manga, particularly chapter 3, "Our Planet Today!!," which centers on late twentieth-century environmental issues. Second, Tsubota somewhat resists the oppressive banking model of education portrayed in the manga by casting a border-straddling adult/child, planet/human figure as the narrative's primary source of information, not an identifiable human adult. By depicting the Earth as a childish entity who nevertheless assumes an educator role typically associated with adults, Tsubota implies that the manga's target child audience can also attain the same level of environmental awareness and even act as teachers themselves by sharing their knowledge with others, as Tsubota did by creating the manga. Thus, while the manga's characters initially reinforce stereotypical adult/child and teacher/student power hierarchies, the anthropomorphized Earth unsettles these binaries by suggesting that all age groups have the ability—and responsibility—to grapple with and disseminate knowledge of environmental issues. These contradictions and reversals underscore the inherent messiness of child-created texts—particularly texts produced as homework assignments—which inevitably fluctuate between competing, adult-influenced ideologies and motivations.

"There's Only One Limited Planet Earth": Modeling Youth Environmental Activism

The manga's final sections also disrupt the oppressive pedagogies depicted in the textbook-like opening chapters by highlighting Rumi and Eichi's newfound agency and teaching readers how they can help the environment. Chapter 3 centers on the Earth's voice as the planet lectures the children about various environmental threats, but the section concludes with Eichi saying, "You've been telling us how the Earth is threatened. . . . I just happened to think, isn't there anything we can do to help?" Winking and pointing out of the panel at the reader, the Earth responds, "Let's put our heads together, and think of ways to save the Earth!"[25] This moment serves as a pivotal turning point in the narrative. For the first time, one of the children critically engages with the manga's educational material by asking a question and steering the conversation. Instead of directly answering, the Earth encourages critical engagement by asking the children and, tacitly, the implied young reader, to work "together" to think of solutions. The planet's invitation for youth collaboration is a drastic departure from the didactic opening sections, reframing children from passive, uneducated recipients of knowledge to budding activists capable of imagining and implementing new "ways to save the Earth." Like Tsubota's depiction of the Earth as a liminal being, the manga's acknowledgment of children's ability to advocate for the environment also destabilizes binary divisions between "adult" and "child" by suggesting that people of all ages—even those who do not initially possess in-depth knowledge of nature, like Rumi and Eichi at the beginning of the narrative—can take part in activism.

Furthermore, the last two chapters position children as capable agents by depicting Rumi and Eichi learning about and participating in environmental activism. In chapter 4, "Working Together to Protect the Earth!!," the Earth teaches the children about steps they can take to combat the frightening environmental issues introduced earlier, such as the destruction of the Amazon rainforest and oil spills. The Earth describes four forms of organized environmental activism: international cooperation nongovernmental organizations (NGOs), public awareness groups, citizens' movements, and individuals.[26] On the following page, the planet briefly summarizes six international treaties, demonstrating how "governments around the world are also helping to protect the Earth."[27] An illustration accompanies each of the textual descriptions of the treaties, providing visual callbacks to earlier panels. For example, the Ramsar Convention on Wetlands of International Importance appears alongside an illustration of birds swimming in a pristine blue pond; one of the birds grasps a fish in its beak. Below this illustration, the United Nations Convention on the Law of the Sea features an image of a smiling young girl sitting on the bank of the ocean (see Figure 3.4). These images serve as utopic reimaginings of the polluted waters and dead or poisoned wildlife portrayed in chapter 3 during the Earth's discussion of oil spills. Similarly, Tsubota's entry for the Convention on International Trade in Endangered Species[28] features an illustration of a group of placid-looking animals against a background of lush green trees.[29] The drawing mirrors an earlier illustration of a herd of frightened animals fleeing across a barren landscape after humans have destroyed their rainforest habitat. By contrasting illustrations of ravaged and idyllic nature across the manga, Tsubota suggests that international cooperation and legislation can help prevent future environmental crises and protect nature from harmful human actions. While the manga does not imply that children can directly participate in the creation of international treaties, the Earth's overview of various types of environmental activism

FIGURE 3.4 The Earth teaches the children about international treaties focused on environmental issues in *Secrets of the Earth* (29).

informs readers about how they can help influence legislation, such as by joining a public awareness group.

In addition to portraying political and organized forms of activism, the final pages of chapter 4 also instruct children about individual, everyday actions they can undertake to help address environmental issues. Initially, this section of the manga appears to conform to the apolitical, conservative model of eco-activism criticized by Echterling. The Earth informs Rumi and Eichi about strategies they can use to conserve water at home, such as purchasing a water-saving shower head and shutting off the water when brushing their teeth.[30] Obviously, these individual, simple efforts will not address serious environmental issues like water waste as effectively or publicly as passing an international treaty or participating in a citizens' movement. By promoting these small actions *after* highlighting organized activism and political interventions, however, Tsubota depicts environmentalism as a broad spectrum of activities that take place on local and global scales, individually and collectively, and publicly and privately. This framework provides a more accurate representation of environmental activism than children's literature that merely advocates recycling, and the manga's promotion of at-home activities also invites young readers to participate in the forms of advocacy most accessible to them.

Most importantly, the manga concludes with Rumi and Eichi transcending the Earth's teachings to participate in environmental activism on their terms. After the planet educates them about ways to conserve water, the children begin to think of everyday ways to help protect the environment, such as recycling newspapers and avoiding plastic bags. The Earth praises their initiative, saying, "You're coming up with one good idea after another!" Two panels later, the planet returns to its book in a cloud of smoke, remarking, "If your eyes are opened, it's time for me to say good-bye!"[31] The Earth's departure signals that Rumi and Eichi have matured from uneducated students to empowered activists who take ownership of their relationship with the environment by participating in local advocacy. Chapter 5, "What Happened After That," further emphasizes children's ability to assume roles as capable environmental activists. Rumi and Eichi join forces with two other unnamed children to collect discarded aluminum cans. When their companions question the main characters' sudden interest in gathering recyclables, Eichi declares, "There's only one limited planet Earth . . . so we should recycle everything that can be recycled!"[32] This exchange shows that Eichi has superseded the Earth as an educator by teaching his peers about the importance of environmental activism, albeit in a less authoritarian manner than the planet. The narrative concludes with the four smiling children taking their cans to a nearby recycling station as Rumi remarks, "We'll collect paper next time around!"[33] The optimistic ending emphasizes the importance of collective action and provides a realistic model of local, youth-centered activism that readers could easily imitate in their communities. The noticeable absence of any adults (or pseudo-adults, in the Earth's case) in the conclusion also highlights the children's agency by demonstrating their ability to build coalitions and share environmental information without the aid of adults and outside of institutional spaces such as the classroom. However, the placement of these empowering chapters at the manga's conclusion somewhat lessens their effectiveness, particularly given the stark contrast between these sections and the instructional opening chapters. Children who read the narrative linearly must first navigate through chapters 1 through 3, which overwhelmingly portray young people as powerless, incapable of critically engaging with environmental knowledge, and even contemptuous of nature. Chapters 4 and 5 counter this negative representation by depicting Rumi and Eichi as increasingly empowered agents undertaking activism without adult guidance. However, these smaller final chapters, which only total eight pages, complicate but do not cancel out the almost thirty pages of disempowering narrative that precedes them.

"A Comic Book Hero": The Afterlife of Aika Tsubota

The manga's conflicting representations of children also manifest in the paratexts surrounding the primary narrative. In a one-page afterword, Tsubota explains her motivations for creating the manga. She writes, "Regarding the environment, the most important thing is for people to stop thinking they can't do anything just because they are only one individual. If everybody thought that way, planet Earth really would be doomed! If everybody pitches in, I know we can turn this world into a beautiful place!"[34] This optimistic paratext reinforces the primary narrative's concluding message by emphasizing both the importance of individual responsibility and collective action and urging "everybody," regardless of their age or education level, to feel empowered to engage in environmental activism. By contrast, paratextual materials about *Secrets of the Earth* published by adult authors consistently portray Tsubota as an exceptional and even saintly environmental prodigy. For instance, Janice Wilson's *Our Earth: How Kids are Saving the Planet* (2010) includes a short profile on Tsubota that describes the girl's creation of the manga and early death, stating, "Aika Tsubota had always felt one with the universe, one with Earth, and all life."[35] The text does not include any citations or direct quotes from Tsubota to support this claim. Similarly, Garth Sundem's *Real Kids, Real Stories, Real Change: Courageous Actions around the World* (2014) repeatedly emphasizes Tsubota's prowess as an artist and environmental activist. He labels the girl as a "Comic Book Hero" and narrates her creation of *Secrets of the Earth*, writing, "She checked out dozens of books from the library to learn more about the environment. She sculpted each page until it was perfect. . . . Did she know this book would be her last?"[36] On the next page, Sundem declares, "Finally Aika was finished with *Secrets of the Earth* and she handed it in to her teacher. It was a masterpiece."[37] Sundem romanticizes Tsubota as a child genius who engaged in extensive research and obsessed over her "masterpiece" until she perfected it. Additionally, by speculating that Tsubota may have known that the manga "would be her last" creation, Sundem suggests that the girl had unnatural foresight about her sudden death. These paratextual profiles depict the girl as an admirable Other by emphasizing the ways that Tsubota did not behave like a regular child, even as they praise her youth activism. As Cathryn Halverson observes, "The unnatural fact of a child having written a text that speaks to adults makes for an uneasy sense that this child writer is not a real child at all."[38] Similarly, Sidney I. Dobrin and Kenneth Kidd observe that environmental children's literature often presumes that young people "have a privileged relationship to nature, thanks largely to the legacy of romantic Victorian literature, which emphasized—often to the point of absurdity—the child's proximity to the natural world and consequent purity."[39] Rather than suggesting that all children can engage in activism, as Tsubota does, Wilson and Sundem depict the girl as a Romantic environmental martyr with an uncanny connection to nature and the universe. Of course, Wilson and Sundem's posthumous glorifying biographies of Tsubota do not cancel out or erase the child creator's agency, especially given that the adults published these works separately from the primary text and two decades after Tsubota's death. However, their idolization of the girl reveals how adult discourses often present youth environmentalists as exceptional or unnatural rather than as an empowering influence for all young people to engage in activism.

Ultimately, then, *Secrets of the Earth* reveals societal tensions surrounding the ways adults view children's capabilities to engage in environmental activism and the impact these ideas have on children's perceptions of their own abilities. The manga confronts readers with troubling questions about children's capacity to exercise creative and political agency in adult spaces, the power of institutions to restrict children's imagination, and the difficulties of motivating meaningful activism in the face of daunting challenges like climate change and pollution. Is *Secrets of the Earth* a "good" or "bad" example of child-produced activist literature? Is Tsubota an empowered creator, or does her dual status as a child and a student inevitably disempower her? And how much responsibility should children have to fix environmental catastrophes created by adults and corporations? As Gerry Canavan observes, "The need for narratives that empower children to understand themselves as potential actors with agency and responsibility is clear. At the same time, a privileging of children's agency that would lead us to conclude that children have agency . . . that could meaningfully intervene in a timely manner against the grinding but intensifying slow violence of the ecological crisis—seems deeply mistaken, to say the least."[40] *Secrets* empowers youth to participate in activism, but in doing so, the manga reinforces larger narratives that unfairly displace the responsibility for saving the planet onto child saviors.

Of course, readers who approach amateurish, child-produced texts like *Secrets* with the expectation of encountering wholly empowering and implausibly precocious narratives that inspire large-scale, meaningful social change will likely be disappointed. Instead, these narratives reveal the nuances and limitations of child agency and youth-authored media. Both inside and outside of the classroom, youth must navigate complicated and often unspoken cultural and institutional forces, and the texts they produce are always marked, to varying degrees, by adult presence and mediation—and yet their narratives are still engaging, influential, and provocative, despite and *because of* these influences. Furthermore, Tsubota's manga demonstrates how youth-created narratives can simultaneously reengrave and resist adult-child power dynamics inherent in the institutionalized space of the classroom. While *Secrets* does somewhat mimic oppressive adult teaching methods, the text also productively illuminates how the comics medium allows child creators to craft empowering visual narratives that they could not have produced through more conventional forms of environmental education, such as conducting a science experiment, taking notes from a teacher's lecture, or writing a report. In this way, *Secrets* indicates that youth-produced manga can serve as powerful eco-educational tools that help children exercise agency and reflect young people's efforts to imagine and produce more sustainable and equal futures.

NOTES

1. "Evette Peeters Doll & Book," American Girl, https://www.americangirl.com/shop/p/evette-doll-and-book-hcj68. Accessed February 14, 2022.
2. Clare Echterling, "How to Save the World and Other Lessons from Children's Environmental Literature," *Children's Literature in Education* 47, no. 4 (December 2016): 285–286.
3. Aika Tsubota, *Secrets of the Earth* (Japan: SAVE THE SEA Campaign Committee, 1993).
4. "Aika's Legacy: A Comic Book for the Earth," *Earth Island Journal* (June 2000).
5. Tsubota, *Secrets*, 7.
6. However, numerous Japanese news articles and at least one Japanese-language scholarly article do engage with Tsubota's manga. For instance, see Mitsuyuki Imamura, "Classification of 'Environmental Picture Books' and the Significance of the Processes of 'Environmental Picture Books,'" *Japanese Journal of Environmental Education* 17, no. 1 (2007): 23–35.
7. Kate Allen and John E. Ingulsrud, "Manga Literacy: Popular Culture and the Reading Habits of Japanese College Students," *Journal of Adolescent & Adult Literacy* 46, no. 8 (2003): 877.
8. Christopher J. Jenks, *Researching Classroom Discourse: A Student Guide* (New York: Routledge, 2021), 93.
9. Karen Sánchez-Eppler, *Dependent States: The Child's Part in Nineteenth-Century American Culture* (Chicago: University of Chicago Press, 2005), 291.
10. Paulo Freire, *Pedagogy of the Oppressed* (New York: Bloomsbury, 2012), 71.
11. Gerald LeTendre, "Guiding Them On: Teaching, Hierarchy, and Social Organization in Japanese Middle Schools," *Journal of Japanese Studies* 20, no. 1 (Winter 1994), 57.
12. Tsubota, *Secrets*, 6.
13. Tsubota, *Secrets*, 12.
14. Myra Zarnowski and Susan Turkel, "How Nonfiction Reveals the Nature of Science," *Children's Literature in Education* 44, no. 4 (2013), 295–296.
15. Tsubota, *Secrets*, 11, 13.
16. Joe Sutliff Sanders, *A Literature of Questions: Nonfiction for the Critical Child* (Minneapolis: University of Minnesota Press, 2018), 13.

17. Tsubota, *Secrets*, 12.
18. Tsubota, *Secrets*, 13.
19. Tsubota, *Secrets*, 15, 17.
20. Tsubota, *Secrets*, 10.
21. Tsubota, *Secrets*, 20.
22. Nathalie op de Beeck, "Children's Ecoliterature and the New Nature Study," *Children's Literature in Education* 49, no. 1 (2018): 81.
23. Freire, *Pedagogy*, 72.
24. Lisa Rowe Fraustino, "The Rights and Wrongs of Anthropomorphism in Picture Books," in *Ethics and Children's Literature*, ed. Claudia Mills (New York: Routledge, 2016), 158.
25. Tsubota, *Secrets*, 27.
26. Tsubota, *Secrets*, 28.
27. Tsubota, *Secrets*, 29.
28. The translated manga uses "on" instead of "in." I've corrected the spelling to reflect the proper name of the convention.
29. Tsubota, *Secrets*, 29.
30. Tsubota, *Secrets*, 30.
31. Tsubota, *Secrets*, 32–33.
32. Tsubota, *Secrets*, 34.
33. Tsubota, *Secrets*, 35.
34. Tsubota, *Secrets*, 36.
35. Janet Wilson, *Our Earth: How Kids are Saving the Planet* (Toronto: Second Story Press, 2010), n.p.
36. Garth Sundem, *Real Kids, Real Stories, Real Change; Courageous Actions around the World* (Minneapolis: Free Spirit Publishing, 2014), 29.
37. Sundem, *Real Kids*, 30.
38. Cathryn Halverson, "Reading Little Girls' Texts in the 1920s: Searching for the 'Spirit of Childhood,'" *Children's Literature in Education* 30, no. 4 (1999): 246.
39. Sidney I. Dobrin and Kenneth Kidd, "Introduction: Into the Wild," in *Wild Things: Children's Culture and Ecocriticism*, ed. Sidney I. Dobrin and Kenneth Kidd (Detroit, MI: Wayne State University Press, 2004), 6.
40. Gerry Canavan. "Unless Someone like You Cares a Whole Awful Lot: Apocalypse as Children's Entertainment," *Science Fiction and Television* 10, no. 1 (2017): 84.

PART TWO

Performance and Play

4

Phillis Wheatley's Image and the Creative Black Child

BRIGITTE FIELDER

As the *Massachusetts Gazette* advertised, Phillis Wheatley's 1773 *Poems on Various Subjects, Religious and Moral*, was "adorned with an elegant Frontispiece, representing the Author."[1] The engraving of Wheatley was unusual. Scholars including Vincent Carretta, Lena Hill, and Megan Walsh have noted the rarity of frontispiece portraits for living writers in the eighteenth century. This point was compounded, of course, by Wheatley's gender, age, race, and enslaved status, as well as by the possibility that this image of the enslaved author was based on the art of another young, enslaved artist, Scipio Moorhead. In the portrait, young Phillis sits at a writing table, upon which we also see a book. Her pen hovers over lines already written, her face resting on her left hand. Her eyes glance away from the page, upward into some distance not visible to us. The author pauses in her composition, contemplative. We do not here observe the act of writing but a moment of thought, care, craft, and potential. The frontispiece imagines her in some prior moment that produced the manuscript. In this way, the portrait is retrospective, looking backward on a rare moment of enslaved labor (see Figure 4.1). But this portrait, engraved and printed and circulated far beyond the original creators' scope, is also future glancing, toward the subsequent generations who would receive Wheatley's image as a creative Black child. This chapter presents Wheatley's image as one framed for the inspiration of other creative Black children, showing ultimately how this is an image of, by, and for Black children.

This illustration of Wheatley evokes the creative Black child in its subject and its creator. The poet known as Phillis Wheatley or Phillis Wheatley Peters was born in the Senegambia region of West Africa around 1753 or 1754.[2] She was kidnapped by enslavers at the age of seven or eight and sold to the Wheatley family in Boston, whose last name she bore until her marriage to John Peters in 1778. The enslaver Wheatleys named the small girl who would also bear their surname after the ship that carried her and ninety-four other humans (only seventy-five of whom would survive the journey) to a life of captivity and forced labor in North America. As an

FIGURE 4.1 Phillis Wheatley, engraving on paper, 1773. National Portrait Gallery, Smithsonian Institution.

enslaved child working for this family, young Phillis learned to speak and read English, and to write. Her first published poem appeared in a Rhode Island newspaper in 1767, when she was about thirteen or fourteen years old. The enslaved teenager continued to write and publish poetry in the years leading up to her foundational collection, published in London when she was only nineteen or twenty. Scipio Moorhead was also a creative Black child. He may have had instruction in visual art from one of his enslavers, Sarah Parsons Moorhead, who taught lessons, and possibly also from other Black members of the community, which included the enslaved engraver Pompey Fleet.[3] This essay posits Moorhead's image of Wheatley, i.e., a child's creation. Reading available records from Boston enslavers, literary historian Eric Slauter estimates that Scipio Moorhead was younger than Wheatley, possibly as young as twelve years old, when her collection was published bearing a possible rendering of his portrait of her.[4]

Moorhead's image of Wheatley as writer appears in the front matter of a book that would include the names of the several white men who would attest to her authorship. In a way, the engraving provides another kind of evidence for the text. It brings Moorhead's image of Wheatley, preserved in youth, paused in thought, authorial, to future readers of her poetry—including child readers who might be inspired themselves to creative production. Later repetitions of Wheatley's image would overwhelmingly be based on Moorhead's portrait, translated via this frontispiece. In this way, Moorhead's imagining of Wheatley would become *the* iconic image of her, accompanying textual descriptions that similarly preserved her in youth. Although Wheatley was only thirty or thirty-one years old when she died in 1784, she was by then a free, married woman, somewhat removed from the popular imagining we have preserved.

While there is a danger of rendering Black people (and especially enslaved Black people) as perpetual children in the popular U.S. imaginary, the fact of Wheatley's childhood authorship complicates this. She is known not only as a Black woman writer, but specifically as a child creative—someone whose literary acumen was surprising to white adults particularly because of the various intersectional positions of oppression she occupied. That an enslaved Black girl could write such poetry made Wheatley a figure of curiosity, skepticism, dismissal, wonder, and celebration for her various readers. I focus on the last of these understandings of Wheatley, as this was the primary mode in which she has been received by the African American writers who would circulate her image from Moorhead's moment of creation to the present. I show how the reception of this Black child figure has especially been framed for other Black children, circulating in the early African American press, African American educational materials, and African American children's literature.

I here trace Phillis Wheatley's image from its publication as the frontispiece to her poetry collection to nineteenth, twentieth, and twenty-first-century iterations in African American literature as broadly "picturing" gifted Black youth. Reading these repetitions and reverberations of Wheatley's image across time, I argue, shows how imaging and imagining Wheatley became a practice for celebrating and fostering creativity among Black children beyond the poet herself.[5] Wheatley's (and Moorhead's) examples celebrate not only Black creativity or genius, but Black childhood. Doing so, they highlight the particular conditions of this exceptional person's creative production while also de-exceptionalizing Black creativity more generally, employing Wheatley's iconic image to promote, facilitate, and celebrate future Black creativity. De-exceptionalizing Wheatley is crucial to countering the ways Black figures like her have been presented as exceptions to—rather than as representative of—Black ability. We might take the lyrics of Nina Simone's iconic late twentieth-century song about gifted Black children as an important reminder about both Wheatley and Black children, more generally:

> In the whole world you know
> There's a million boys and girls
> Who are young, gifted and black
> And that's a fact.[6]

I cite this truth to emphasize Wheatley's place among many creative Black children—those she knew, like Moorhead; those she inspired via the various literary venues I discuss here; and those whose gifts may only be known to those closest to them. May we recognize and celebrate them all by remembering that Wheatley is only one example of the Creative Black Child.

"Thy various works, imperial queen, we see": Picturing Phillis Wheatley

African American and visual studies scholar Jasmine Nichole Cobb has discussed how Black people employed various forms of visuality to "picture freedom" in the early twentieth century.[7] I have noted, similarly, how photographs of Black children reproduced throughout issues of the early twentieth-century children's periodical *The Brownies' Book*, allowed readers to "picture Black childhood" in the early twentieth century.[8] With Wheatley's portrait, we might understand a similar sort of "picturing." U.S. literature and culture scholar Betsy Erkkila recognizes that it is the image of Wheatley, not the accompanying description, that comprehends her as "a black woman reading, thinking, and writing," allowing viewers to understand her beyond her enslavement.[9] Scholars of Wheatley's poetry have attended to how the image accompanying Wheatley's collection draws attention to her embodiment—the Black body of an enslaved teenage girl being a key point of interest for her work. Mary Balkun, for example, describes Wheatley's poetry as directing attention away from her body and toward her "unbodied mind," while Robert Kendrick and Lena Hill attend to Wheatley's emphasis on embodiment in her poetry.[10] Scholars such as Lucia Hodgson and Camille Owens have also shown how Wheatley becomes a key figure for picturing childhood more generally, in its rhetorical figuring and construction in early America.[11]

We can also consider the resonances of Wheatley's image beyond the scope of the 1773 volume, as the image of Wheatley as author would signify not only as paratextual material for her poetry but elsewhere as an image for Black authorship and for creative Black childhood. In this way, picturing Wheatley was a project employed for the encouragement, uplift, and support of Black children. One example of this is another image of Wheatley, taken after her frontispiece engraving, that appeared in *The Freedman's Third Reader*, published by the American Tract Society in 1866 (see Figure 4.2). Wheatley again appears at her table, with her pen and paper, at the beginning of a children's reading lesson. The brief biography accompanying the illustration begins, of course, with her childhood, telling young readers that "Phillis Wheatley, whose likeness is on this page, was brought to this country from Africa in the year 1761. She was then between seven and eight years old."[12] Thus the image (whatever we might perceive Wheatley's age here) is overlayed with this image of a child kidnapped in her youth. The "modest appearance and pleasant face" the essay describes as having prompted her purchase by the Wheatleys is echoed in this image.[13] The lesson goes on to describe Wheatley's own youthful education and creativity, as "Phillis early showed great eagerness for learning, and was often found trying to make letters upon the wall with a piece of chalk or charcoal. . . . She soon learned to write also; and, in four years from the time of her being stolen from Africa, this negro girl wrote interesting letters on various subjects."[14] These images of Wheatley writing and learning are framed with the key terms for this lesson, which include words such as "pleas-ant," "learn-ing," "ea-ger-ness," and "in-ter-est-ing" as well as "chalk" and "char-coal," the instruments of Wheatley's early creative expression, each word syllabicated so as to facilitate readers' attempts to write them.

Another example, from the African American press, facilitated readers' visualization of Wheatley without even reproducing her image. William J. Wilson's "Afric-American Picture Gallery," a seven-part sketch serialized in the *Anglo-African Magazine* in 1859, describes (but does not visually illustrate) the various contents of an art gallery dedicated to celebrating Black icons. Wilson's imagined gallery includes "A HEAD OF PHILLIS WHEATLEY," which he writes is "a constant charm and study," reading her features as "perfection of beauty in the female face."[15] In their discussion of recovering Wilson's text, nineteenth-century U.S. literature scholars John Ernest, Rian Bowie, Leif Eckstrom, and Britt Rusert note that Wilson's imagining of Wheatley (like other images of Wheatley from the 1850s), was likely inspired by a reproduction of the 1773 frontispiece included in an 1834 edition of *Memoir and Poems of Phillis Wheatley*.[16] In a way, this is an imagined extension of Moorhead's work. Ernest, Bowie, Eckstrom, and Rusert describe the media shift Wilson makes from engraved portrait to sculpture, writing that "ultimately these ekphrastic descriptions require the reader's imaginative capacities, thereby transforming frontispieces and other images into three-dimensional sculptural busts. And so fantasy also becomes central to Wilson's transformation and arrangement of print sources on the walls of his virtual gallery."[17] Wilson also, importantly,

THIRD READER. 75

LESSON XXXIX.

bought	**pleas-ant**	**daugh-ter**	**ap-pear-ance**
chalk	**char-coal**	**learn-ing**	**ea-ger-ness**
health	**six-teen**	**al-though**	**in-ter-est-ing**

PHILLIS WHEATLEY.

PHILLIS WHEATLEY, whose likeness is on this page, was brought to this country from Africa in the year 1761. She was then between seven and eight years old. She was bought by Mrs. John Wheatley, a Boston lady, who chose her from a crowd of robust negroes, although she looked feeble and slender, because of her modest appearance and pleasant face.

FIGURE 4.2 Phillis Wheatley, Lesson XXXIX, *The Freedman's Third Reader* (Boston: American Tract Society, 1866), 75.

Courtesy of the American Antiquarian Society.

describes Wheatley's likeness as "an index of healthy intellectual powers, combined with an active temperament, over which has fallen a slight tinge of religious pensiveness."[18] His imagining is a kind of repetition and revision of this earlier image of the author not just in the act of writing but in deep thought.[19] To imagine the extension of Wheatley's portrait into other media is a projection of the Black artist known for rendering her image into a speculative future.

I introduce Wilson's ekphrastic projection of Wheatley's image to illustrate the blending of visual and literary renderings that have allowed and continue to allow us to "picture" Wheatley. As Laura Wasowicz notes, the image of Wheatley included in *The Freedman's Third Reader* in 1866 "could very well be the first image of Wheatley seen by many nineteenth-century African American children and youth on both sides of the Mason-Dixon line."[20] As with Wilson's example, this picturing of Wheatley extends beyond the literal reproduction of her portrait (even while versions of this portrait did continue to circulate alongside writing by and about Wheatley, as I will discuss later). By "picturing" I mean also to evoke the various imaginings of Wheatley's image, imaginings that have overwhelmingly figured her specifically as a child author. Just as the engraved frontispiece's copy of Moorhead's creation provided a once-removed rendition of the creative Black child, we can trace later reverberations of this initial image beyond the visual, to later discussions of Wheatley. Coupling the locus of her most famous literary work with the only extant image of her created during her lifetime, this image is one of youthful creation, repeated and recirculated in ways that coupled and blurred distinctions between visual and literary aesthetic forms.

Picturing Wheatley was also always a project of dialectic conversation, first articulated by Wheatley herself. Elsewhere I have discussed Wheatley as not only a child author but a writer who, within a larger context of early Black writers, addressed children.[21] Responding to Moorhead's work, Wheatley praises another creative Black child. Her poem "To S. M., a Young *African* Painter, on Seeing his Works" lauds the artistry of this "wond'rous youth," writing that seeing his "beauties" "doth give my soul delight." Moreover, Wheatley couples her and Moorhead's creative media, writing that "still may the painter's and the poet's fire / To aid thy pencil, and thy verse conspire!" Their relationship as creative children is one of reciprocal support. She encourages further creative work: "May the muse inspire each future song!" While Wheatley's poem is characteristically concerned with Moorhead's otherworldly future, we might also take the poem as gesturing beyond the worldly scope of both artists.

That none of Scipio Moorhead's art is known to have been preserved is a shame. This absence is a result of the structural violence of attempted erasure with which white people obscured Black lives. But Wheatley's poetry, like Wilson's imagined art gallery, provides glimpses into Moorhead's work, from the perspective of someone well poised to understand an enslaved Black child's art. As Black feminist poet and theorist June Jordan notes, Wheatley is deliberately "addressing her Brother Artist not as so-and-so's Boy, but as 'Scipio Moorhead, A Young

African Painter.'"[22] This address is a result of these children's friendship and creative co-inspiration. Wheatley scholar David Waldstreicher argues that "the occasion to sit for Scipio Moorhead . . . meant much more to Wheatley than joining the club of colonists with the means to have their likeness taken. . . . Encouraging him, she argues for what was possible when Africans received encouragement and credit."[23] Wheatley's poem is an opportunity to understand these children in conversation, registering the fact that her poetry and the accompanying image of her is not only a product of young gifted and Black people, but one for them as well. Little is known about Moorhead's life, but in these afterimages of his work, we see the residue of a Black child whose creativity could not be entirely suppressed, even in enslavement.

"And all attest how potent is thine hand": Imagining Wheatley in the Early Black Press

Even without an accompanying image, Wheatley's name would appear throughout early African American periodicals, from the early nineteenth century into the early twentieth, as a means of "picturing" this icon of Black literature. Such discussions named her specifically as an enslaved child and connected her example to Black children of the era. Mentions of Wheatley throughout the early Black press attend to Wheatley specifically as a gifted child. An 1855 letter to the editor in *Frederick Douglass' Paper* reprints stanzas from four of her poems, lauding a book that "contains some rare gems of thought, and displays a remarkable knowledge of history and literature, for one whose advantages had been so limited."[24] The brief biographical information it gives is exclusively about Wheatley's youth, leading up to the publication of her collection. Emphasizing her quickness to learn speaking, reading, and writing in English, the author provides a meritocratic account of Wheatley's recognition. A key example to this point is that "as to her writing, her own curiosity led her to it, and this she learned in so short a time, that in 1765, when she was only eleven years of age, she wrote a letter to the Rev. Mr. Lecom, the Indian Minister, while in England."[25] As I show here, it is not uncommon to emphasize both Black intellectual ability and Wheatley's particular genius and ingenuity.

Wheatley's childhood is central to these picturings of her. An 1882 essay by "Everett" in the *Christian Recorder* compares Wheatley's "perseverance" to that of white Scottish mathematician and scientist Mary Somerville.[26] This example of a white woman mathematician and scientist makes clear how sexism produces barriers to education which thereby require additional efforts to obtain. Black women, however, faced barriers based on both gender and race. Everett also compares Wheatley to formerly enslaved activist and orator Sojourner Truth, "a woman without education who today still preserves and is building a monument whose top will reach the highest heaven."[27] Like others, this account emphasizes Wheatley's education as an enslaved child, writing that "born as she was in Africa, taken away from her parents while young, she studied day and night that she might gain knowledge."[28] Briefly noting Wheatley's life after emancipation, the piece nevertheless preserves her in childhood, as "that slave girl, set free."[29] Although Wheatley was twenty years old when Susanna Wheatley finally freed her in 1773 and a married woman at the time of her death, her earlier moments of childhood literary production are overwhelmingly prioritized in biographies. This move is a fraught one, given mythologies of slavery as paternalist stewardship and histories of characterizing Black people (and white women) as children to justify their disenfranchisement and other forms of white patriarchal control. But imagining Wheatley's youth is essential for recognizing her as an enslaved child writer. Picturing Wheatley not only involves recounting or celebrating this exceptional child's life and work but also positing dreamlike speculations about how she might also inspire Black futures.

Early African American periodical discussions of Wheatley date back to the first known African American newspaper, *Freedom's Journal*, which published a letter to its editor Samuel Cornish in November of 1827. The piece takes Wheatley as an example refuting racist ideas about "African inferiority," describing this as produced and perpetuated by the system that denies Black children equal access to formal education. The writer laments the idea, common even among white liberals, "that a little reading and writing are enough for our children." This critique of Northern racism and educational disparities appears amid a description of Boston's architectural beauty and culminates with a connection to Wheatley and her legacy. Alongside the call to support Black children's education, the writer notes that "Boston is the place where that sweet poetess of nature, Phillis Wheatley, first tuned her lyre under the inspiration of the Muses."[30] This celebration of Wheatley also decries the absence of a stone marker at the poet's burial place, proposing a monument to Wheatley, and "if our brethren here, do not feel able or willing to erect a monument, let a general contribution be made by us through the Union—let us evince to the world that we are not insensible to the fame and renown which her writings have conferred upon us—that we are proud of them."[31]

The letter does not give a description of what such a monument might look like, though one familiar with Black Boston memorials in our present moment might imagine something like Meredith Bergmann's 2003 statue of Wheatley at the Boston Women's Memorial. This memorial is clearly based on the author's engraved image. Here she does not sit but leans upon the block bearing her name. There is no book or pen, though the latter is suggested by the positioning of her gently closed hand. One might say that she appears older than she does in the engraving, but her glance is the same: directed upward, inward. Wheatley appears not just writing but thinking. Coupling Wheatley's potential memorialization with the intellectual potential of other Black children, this writer to *Freedom's Journal* pictures Wheatley in a similar way to Bergmann's memorial, as a writer and thinker who might serve as an inspirational model for others—particularly Black children.

As Wheatley became iconic among early African American authors, the reverberations of her image—both literal and otherwise—were framed sometimes for adults but often for Black children. I now turn to two examples of picturing Wheatley as a figure both of and for gifted Black childhood. The first is a brief biography appearing in the August 1920 *Brownies' Book*, a Black children's periodical, where Wheatley's inclusion served as inspiration for readers and for potential Black child writers. The second is a literal staging, in Mary Church Terrell's 1932 "Historical Pageant-Play Based on the life of Phyllis [*sic*] Wheatley," in which Black children themselves staged Black creativity via Wheatley. Both examples employed Wheatley's image as iconic and exemplary, but also as an inspiration to encourage creativity among others.

"How bright their forms! how deck'd with pomp by thee!": Imagining Wheatley in *The Brownies' Book*

Discussions of Wheatley in the early Black press were also directed at Black child audiences. Osceola F. Gordon, writing to the *Christian Recorder* in 1887, discusses Wheatley in direct conversation with Black women and girls, writing, "Young ladies, remember Miss Phillis Wheatley, the colored poetess, whose ambition for reading and studying should be emulated by every colored woman."[32] Gordon's interpolation of Black girls and women is in keeping with early African American newspapers' capacious address to diverse Black audiences. Readers of early Black newspapers included free and enslaved people, men and women, readers and those who had the paper read to them, adults and children.

One early twentieth-century piece allows us to consider the stakes of these repetitions and revisions of Wheatley's image for considering a future of Black authorship, in *The Brownies' Book*. *The Brownies' Book* was not the first African American children's periodical, but it is the first for which current researchers have a complete run. Created by W.E.B. Du Bois, Augustus Granville Dill, and Jessie Redmon Fauset, it emerged from *The Crisis*, the official magazine of the NAACP, and ran for two years, from January 1920 to December 1921. Its dedication, written by Fauset, reads

> To Children, who with eager look
> Scanned vainly library shelf and nook,
> For history or Song or Story
> That told of Colored Peoples' glory—
> We dedicate *The Brownies' Book*[33]

The magazine included an array of material, from poetry and short stories to international and domestic news, a "Grown-Ups' Corner" for older readers, and images of and information about some of its young readers. It also included short biographies of important figures of Black history. "The Story of Phillis Wheatley: A True Story" appeared in the August 1920 issue (see Figure 4.3). Beginning with speculation about young Phillis's happy childhood in Africa and her subsequent kidnapping, it goes on to discuss the injustice of her enslavement, her relatively privileged position as an enslaved girl who had access to literacy instruction, her literary accomplishments, and her death in poverty.[34] Wheatley's portrait accompanied her story, on the opposite page, visualizing Black thought, writing ability, and potential in the image of an enslaved girl.

What precedes and follows the story gives texture to this context for Wheatley's image.[35] "The Story of Phillis Wheatley" appears on the pages just before Blanche Lynn Patterson's "The Heritage," in which a girl named Julia complains, "I love my books as much as ever, but I'm tired of working myself to death to stay in school. . . . Two years more of slaving is more than I can stand."[36] Mother Mason, who offers encouragement, also chastises her for this analogy. "Two years ain't nothin' in comparison with three hundred years that yo'r fo'parents spent in endless drudg'ry without no hope of reward," she says, "You young folks have ev'r chance that yo'r parents didn't have. You owe it to them never to quit till you have showed that you can use the opportunities you have."[37] Julia reconsiders, deciding to continue her studies, now noting "that I am not struggling alone, and that I have my whole race to work for," Mother Mason adding "two generations' hopes to fulfill."[38] "The Story of Phillis Wheatley" begins on the next page.

Just two pages after its conclusion, we see the familiar images of Black children that the magazine regularly produced, the "Little People of the Month," along with brief information about its young readers. This was followed by "The Jury," which recounted some of these readers' correspondence with the magazine. In this column, Audre Wright of Washington, DC had written, "It is surprising to know how many high school girls know nothing or very little about our own Negro heroines such as Harriet Tubman, Frances Ellen Watkins Harper and Sojourner Truth. I believe if you could give us a short sketch of their lives every month or suggest certain books that we could read pertaining to them it would be greatly appreciated by those who wish to know more about their own race women."[39] "The Story of Phillis Wheatley" is one answer to this call.

In *The Brownies' Book*, the image of Wheatley as writer and thinker is juxtaposed with images of these early twentieth-century Black children. In "The Jury," other children write brief accounts of their educational experiences. Seven-year-old Natica Marshall of Brooklyn, New York writes, "When I grow up I am going to be a teacher."[40] Several children express their love of reading. Thirteen-year-old Thelma Powell of Columbus, Ohio, writes "I would very much like to write for THE BROWNIES' BOOK. Would you kindly send me some advice and information on the subject, as I am very, very interested?"[41] Readers encountered these children's voices alongside images of Black children who were their contemporaries and with the image of Wheatley, who read and wrote and thought as an enslaved Black child over one hundred years earlier. This juxtaposition situates these children not as newcomers to the legacy of Black literature but within its long history and poised to position themselves within it. The presence of Wheatley as a creative Black child within that legacy frames Black children's aspirations not as distant future but as already possible.

THE STORY OF PHILLIS WHEATLEY

A TRUE STORY

SOMEWHERE in Africa nearly 175 years ago a band of children were playing on the sea-coast. They were youngsters of seven and eight who were so engrossed in their childish games that they did not notice the appearance of a boat with a number of white men in it. When they did become aware of this it was far too late, for the men had stolen up to them and seizing several had rushed off to the boat in which they were carried to a ship anchored not far away.

Only a few of the children escaped but the rest were borne off to America where they were to be sold as slaves. For these white men were slavers and the waiting ship was a slave-vessel.

Among the children who were captured and led off to such a cruel fate was a little girl of six or seven years. She was a slender, delicate little thing who had never gone far from her mother's side. Picture then her fear and anguish when she found herself torn away from everything and everybody whom she had ever known, on her way to a strange land full of queer looking people who were going to subject her to she knew not what experiences and hardships.

After a long and stormy voyage, during which the little girl was very seasick, she arrived, thin and wretched, with only a piece of carpet about her fragile body, in Boston where she was offered in the streets for sale. This was in 1761.

Of course the best thing that could have happened to this little child of misfortune would have been to be left with her mother in Africa. As that could not be, it is pleasant to realize that the next best lot was hers. A well-to-do tailor, John Wheatley by name, happened to be in that neighborhod that day. He had long been looking for a slave girl to be a special servant for his wife and his twin children, Mary and Nathaniel. He spied the wretched little African maiden, and despite her thinness and her miserable appearance, or maybe on account of it, it occurred to him that this was just the kind of child to whom to give a home. So he bought her for a few dollars and took her to his house to live.

The Wheatley family was a kind one. They received the little stranger gladly, named her Phillis Wheatley and proceeded to make her acquainted with the strange new world to which she had come and to the part which she was to play in it. In particular little Mary Wheatley became very fond of her slave playfellow and between her and Phillis there seems to have developed a strong attachment. At first Phillis' place in the house was simply that of servant, though partly because of her extreme youth and the considerateness of the Wheatleys it seems likely that her duties were not very arduous. But before long, owing to what was considered a remarkable tendency in a slave child of such tender years, her lot became very tolerable indeed.

This was what happened. One day Mary Wheatley came across Phillis busily engaged in making letters on the wall with a piece of charcoal. Phillis had already shown herself apt at picking up the spoken language but that she should display an interest in writing was a new idea to the Wheatleys and gave them much pleasure. From that day on Mary constituted herself Phillis' teacher. They progressed from letters to words and from words to complete sentences. And behold the keys to

FIGURE 4.3 "The Story of Phillis Wheatley: A True Story," *The Brownies' Book*, August 1920, 251.

Library of Congress, Rare Book and Special Collections Division.

"Thy wond'rous acts in beauteous order stand": Staging Wheatley as "Historical Pageant-Play"

Wheatley would continue to be a figure for Black education, celebrated not only on the page but also on the stage. About a decade after Wheatley appeared in *The Brownies' Book*, early Black feminist activist and educator Mary Church Terrell wrote a children's pageant play centered on the poet. Wanting to include Black history in celebrations planned for the 1932 bicentenary of George Washington's birth, Terrell used the occasion of Wheatley's 1776 poem "To His Excellency George Washington" (and Washington's favorable response) as an opportunity to stage Wheatley's life for the public. Terrell's Wheatley pageant was staged by public schools in Baltimore, Maryland and Washington, DC in the early 1930s. Katharine Capshaw situates this pageant among others by Black writers—including W.E.B. Du Bois and Alice Dunbar-Nelson—during the New Negro Renaissance and the age of U.S. pageantry and the Black "little theater" movement that made the nation's capital a prominent place for Black children's drama.[42] Capshaw describes the pageant's role in reimagining history, writing that "through tableaux, writers signpost features of a collective black identity; and more to the point, the pageantry format confers on images from black history multiple levels of authority, that of the classroom, textbook, and print culture as well as that of the theater, the communal, and the oral tradition."[43] These plays staged history, and Terrell thereby placed Wheatley's life and writing within that history.

Terrell's play was, in part, an odd attempt to recuperate Washington, an enslaver, for Black children, arguing that "he was broad-minded, generous-hearted and just enough to give credit where credit was due to make written acknowledgement of the talent of an African girl and to pay homage to her while she was still being held as a slave."[44] Highlighting Wheatley's creative genius as undeniable even to a notorious enslaver, Terrell stresses the poet's laudability and the inherent value of her work. Still, the Washington bicentennial served more as an excuse for introducing one of his Black contemporaries, as African American activists responded to the attempted erasure of Black history from this and other national celebrations. With Wheatley at the center of Terrell's play, this was not a usual U.S. history; it staged a history of and for Black children.[45]

In the pageant program for a May 1933 performance at Booker T. Washington Junior High School in Baltimore, Terrell cited racial disparities among historical figures in children's education, noting, "I felt that if they saw the life story of this remarkable African girl pictured before their very eyes, it would make a deep impression upon them, would increase their pride in their racial group and thus strengthen their self-respect."[46] Capshaw shows how "dramatists spotlighted black childhood . . . by placing the child onstage and challenging audiences to witness through childhood the building of a new black nation."[47] The portrayal of Wheatley served as an example to Black child audiences, an "attempt to transform the child's vision of black history" into one that included people like them—Black children.[48]

Explaining her intentions for the pageant, Terrell writes, "I wanted to increase the colored youth's respect for his African ancestors by showing the native ability and the brilliant literary success of an African girl stolen from her native land and sold as a slave in this country, when she was but a small child."[49] Terrell's writing on Wheatley dwells in her youth. Her prologue continually refers to Wheatley as a "girl," solidifying her in childhood, as would be echoed by schoolchildren's portrayals of her.[50] In this, Terrell emphasizes not only Wheatley's literary accomplishment but the years leading up to her book's publication. She represents Wheatley as a precocious and eager girl, staging an enslaved child's trauma and her intellectual and creative aptitude. This emphasis echoed Terrell's 1928 essay, "Phillis Wheatley, An African Genius," which similarly repeats "young," "girl," "child," and "little" to describe the poet, conjuring an image of Black childhood despite the absence of an accompanying illustration of Wheatley.[51] The pageant play multiplied the figure of the girl poet with its other Black youth performers.[52]

Young actors' renditions of Wheatley onstage were also mirrored by the image of Wheatley that appeared in promotional materials for some productions. The program for a June 1932 performance at Lincoln Congregational Temple in Washington, DC included an illustration designed after Moorhead's frontispiece (see Figure 4.4). These events included an address by Terrell, a reading of Wheatley's poetry by Miss Sara Magowan, an organ selection by Miss Mary L. Europe, and various choral performances and other remarks. Beyond the image of young Wheatley via this children's performance, the program for this production reveals further interest in Wheatley's image for promoting early twentieth-century Black children's creativity. The program acknowledgments includes a note of thanks to African American illustrator "Mr. Elton Fax for charcoal portraits of Phillis Wheatley used as prizes in Essay Contest."[53] Like Wilson's imagined bust of Wheatley, I do not know what these illustrations looked like. I cannot definitively trace these to the program image because I have not (yet) located a Wheatley portrait attributed to Fax, who was known especially as a cartoonist and illustrator of children's books. But it would be unsurprising if they, too, followed the iconic frontispiece. Fax's drawings were rewards for an essay prize—a fitting memento. Clearly, someone thought young writers might like to have an image of the young poet herself. This icon would serve not only as a reminder of the prize and this occasion but also as an image for inspiration and encouragement for their future creative endeavors.

Terrell's oldest daughter, born in 1898, was named Phyllis, after the eighteenth-century poet. Phyllis Terrell would follow in her mother's footsteps as a Black woman activist for suffrage and civil rights. Phyllis Terrell was not a child writer, but she too was a gifted, creative child. Writing about her and Terrell's niece, Mary Church, who they also raised, Alison Parker notes that the parents "decided to cultivate their musical talents," the family even singing together at home.[54] Ultimately Phyllis Terrell earned a music degree from Howard University and taught music in DC public schools, herself becoming an educator and encourager of

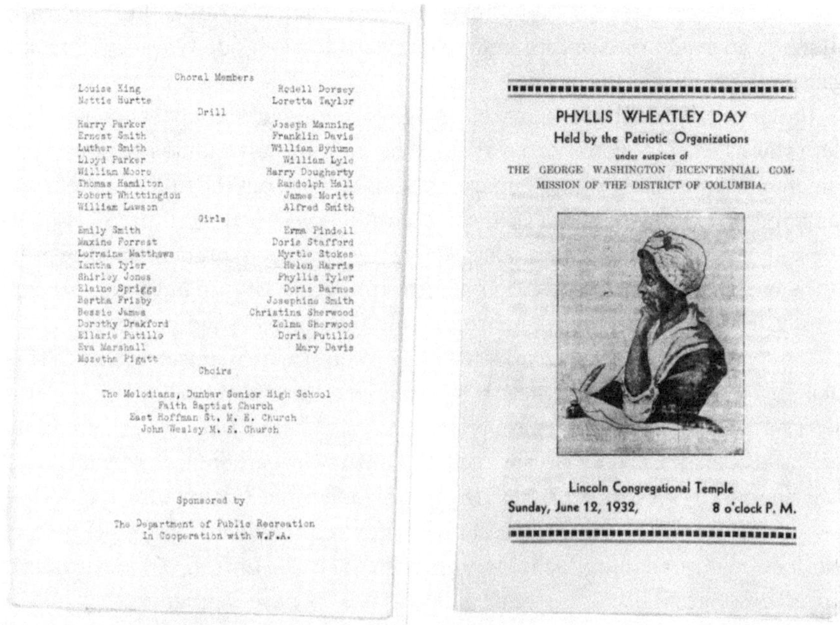

Choral Members

Louise King — Rodell Dorsey
Nettie Hurtte — Loretta Taylor

Drill

Harry Parker — Joseph Manning
Ernest Smith — Franklin Davis
Luther Smith — William Bydume
Lloyd Parker — William Lyle
William Moore — Harry Dougherty
Thomas Hamilton — Randolph Hall
Robert Whittingdon — James Moritt
William Lawson — Alfred Smith

Girls

Emily Smith — Erma Pindell
Maxine Forrest — Doris Stafford
Lorraine Matthews — Myrtle Stokes
Iantha Tyler — Helen Harris
Shirley Jones — Phyllis Tyler
Elaine Spriggs — Doris Barnes
Bertha Frisby — Josephine Smith
Bessie James — Christina Sherwood
Dorothy Drakford — Zelma Sherwood
Ellarie Putillo — Doris Putillo
Eva Marshall — Mary Davis
Mozetha Pigatt

Choirs

The Melodians, Dunbar Senior High School
Faith Baptist Church
East Hoffman St. M. E. Church
John Wesley M. E. Church

Sponsored by

The Department of Public Recreation
In Cooperation with W.P.A.

PHYLLIS WHEATLEY DAY
Held by the Patriotic Organizations
under auspices of
THE GEORGE WASHINGTON BICENTENNIAL COMMISSION OF THE DISTRICT OF COLUMBIA.

Lincoln Congregational Temple
Sunday, June 12, 1932, 8 o'clock P. M.

FIGURE 4.4 "Phyllis Wheatley Day" Program, Lincoln Congregational Temple [Washington, DC], June 12, 1932.

Mary Church Terrell Papers, Library of Congress, Manuscript Division.

creative Black children. She lived into the late twentieth century, passing away in 1989. As with Wheatley's tribute to Moorhead, imagining Terrell's musician daughter named after the poet suggests that inspiration for young Black creativity might translate across forms. I end my discussion by briefly contextualizing these representations within the longer history of circulating Wheatley's biography and image in more recent African American children's literature. This history illustrates how Wheatley's representation would position her to inspire a future of Black childhood creativity.

"Imagination! who can sing thy force?": Wheatley's Continued Resonance

Images inspired by Wheatley's portrait would continue to circulate in African American children's literature into the twenty-first century—both by Black writers, as with Jacquelyn McLendon's 2002 *Phillis Wheatley: A Revolutionary Poet*, Afua Cooper's 2009 *My Name is Phillis Wheatley: A Story of Slavery and Freedom*, and Bunmi Oyinsan and Natalia Cano's *Phillis Wheatley: The Girl Who Wrote Her Way to Freedom* and by white writers, as with Kathryn Lasky and Paul Lee's 2003 *A Voice of Her Own: The Story of Phillis Wheatley, Slave Poet.* Considering the circulation of not only Wheatley's poetry and biography but also the image of a reading, writing, thinking

Black child we can, perhaps, better imagine other reading, writing, thinking Black children who would receive this recirculated portrait alongside Wheatley's literary legacy in the centuries to come.

Children may see the recognizable image of this iconic Black poet and not only relate themselves to words by or about Wheatley, but also fantasize about the moment pictured there. Via this image, they might flesh out the fullness of Wheatley's mind or body, as William J. Wilson did in his imagined picture gallery or as later sculptors of her image have done. Seeing this image, children might even project the young, enslaved poet's gaze not into a physical distance but toward themselves, into the Black futures of her readership that were beyond her scope.

Contemporary African American writers often situate themselves within this Black future, acknowledging their places in a long lineage of Black writing. Zetta Elliott's 2020 children's poetry collection, *Say Her Name: Poems to Empower*, illustrated by Loveis Wise, does this by including poetry by earlier Black women poets alongside Elliott's poetic tributes. In her introduction, (which also memorializes victims of police violence and celebrates Black women and girls), Elliott describes poems meant to "echo" writers such as Lucille Clifton, Nikki Giovanni, Audre Lorde, and Phillis Wheatley. Elliot writes, "I have deliberately 'sampled' some of their verses in order to place my poems in conversation with the poet-elders who showed me what was possible."[55] But even while she acknowledges Wheatley as her chronological "elder," Elliott emphasizes Wheatley's childhood in her explanatory notes, describing her as "an enslaved eighteenth-century teen poet and the first Black person to publish a book of poetry in the United States."[56] Coupling childhood and literary significance in this line, Elliott presents Wheatley explicitly as a child poet of vast literary significance. Even in this brief biography, Elliott's attention to and recognition of Black girls is clear.

The collection includes Wheatley's "On Being Brought from Africa to America," which inspired Elliott's poem "On Being Builders of a New World." The latter of these follows the style and form of Wheatley's poem, also connecting Wheatley to later Black thinkers and writers, echoing Dr. Martin Luther King Jr. in the lines "A riot's the language of the unheard" and Langston Hughes with "Our race besieged, has had its dreams deferred."[57] Wheatley is here situated within a long history of African American thought, and she is recognized among adult thinkers and creatives.

The last lines of the poem allude most clearly to Wheatley: "Remember, *Brothers*, Sisters' lives count too; / As equals we could build this world anew."[58] Elliott's feminist turn is characteristic of the collection, but I am also interested in how the juxtaposition of these poems takes us from Wheatley's iconic, individual experience of kidnapping and captivity to a call for communal creation. The shift from "On Being Brought" to "On Being Builders" merges the image of Wheatley as an enslaved child and as a creative one. She was "brought"—kidnapped from her home and family and held enslaved—but she was also a "builder," a poet through whose foundational work "Africa lives on." Elliot takes Wheatley's form to encourage readers to recall the murdered, to refuse to let Black names and language and dreams die in obscurity, and to engage (collectively) in building a better future. An illustration of a single bird (perhaps a dove) appears underneath Wheatley's poem. The previous poem, "Runaway" helps to frame Wheatley's and this image. Considering Wheatley alongside this icon of freedom, flight, and hope, the collection gestures beyond her captivity.

Under "On Being Builders," we see an image of the earth, with blue oceans, white clouds. In place of the continents there are groups of hands—holding, touching, gesturing—in various shades of green. The image is not of a person or even groups of people, but of a deindividualized collective, engaged in the work of creating. Even if readers picture Wheatley as an enslaved child or as a poet, Elliott and Wise leave readers with an image of a different scale and scope. Might this, too, be an image of Wheatley, taken from afar? As she contemplates the transatlantic voyage, what mercy, redemption, or refinement might we understand as we take our gaze outward from this creative Black child toward this broader view of Black, creative "builders"? Elliott's and Wise's rendering pictures Wheatley by expanding their child reader's view toward other possibilities for their own creativity and future world-making.

NOTES

1. Advertisement, *Massachusetts Gazette*, April 16, 1773.
2. For the purposes of this essay, I have deliberately chosen to refer to Wheatley by the name under which she wrote as an enslaved child and was first published, rather than using her married name, Peters. I do this because her published name is the one that has become iconic alongside her image and I wish to recognize the ways that this naming, too, preserves her in childhood. Because the name originally given to her by her own family is unknown to current researchers—wrenched from this child through the process of her kidnapping and enslavement—available choices for naming her at all are fraught. For further discussion on naming Wheatley, see Tara Bynum, Brigitte Fielder, and Cassander Smith's discussion in their introduction to a special journal issue on Wheatley, "Dear Sister: Phillis Wheatley's Futures," *Early American Literature* 37.3 (Fall 2022): 668–669.
3. See Eric Slauter, "Looking for Scipio Moorhead: An 'African Painter' in Revolutionary North America," in *Slave Portraiture in the Atlantic World*, ed. Agnes Lugo-Ortiz and Angela Rosenthal (Cambridge: Cambridge University Press, 2013), 97.
4. Slauter, "Looking for Scipio Moorhead," 92, 98.
5. Imagination is therefore key to my discussion. The quoted lines in this essay's section headings are taken from Wheatley's poem "On Imagination," included in her *Poems on Various Subjects, Religious and Moral* (London: Archibald Bell, 1773).
6. Nina Simone, vocalist and composer, "To Be Young, Gifted and Black," lyrics by Weldon Irvine, recorded October 26, 1969, track 7 on *Black Gold*, RCA, 1970, sound recording.
7. See Jasmine Nichole Cobb, *Picture Freedom: Remaking Black Visuality in the Early Nineteenth Century* (New York: New York University Press, 2015).
8. I discuss Wheatley's image and biography in *The Brownies' Book* below.
9. Betsy Erkkila, *Mixed Bloods and Other Crosses: Rethinking American Literature from the Revolution to the Culture Wars* (Philadelphia: University of Pennsylvania Press, 2005), 78.

10. See Mary Balkun, "To 'pursue th' unbodied mind': Phillis Wheatley and the Raced Body in Early America," in *New Essays on Phillis Wheatley*, ed. John C. Shields and Eric D. Lamore (Knoxville: University of Tennessee Press, 2011), 387–388; Robert Kendrick, "Other Questions: Phillis Wheatley and the Ethics of Interpretation," *Cultural Critique* 38 (1997), 47; and Lena Hill, *Visualizing Blackness and the Creation of the African American Literary Tradition* (Cambridge: Cambridge University Press, 2014), 28–29.
11. See Lucia Hodgson, "Infant Muse: Phillis Wheatley and the Revolutionary Rhetoric of Childhood," *Early American Literature* 49, no.3 (2014): 663–682 and Camille Owens, "'I, Young in Life': Phillis Wheatley and the Invention of American Childhood," *Early American Literature* 57, no. 3 (Fall 2022): 727–749.
12. Lesson XXXIX, *The Freedman's Third Reader* (Boston: American Tract Society), 75.
13. Lesson XXXIX, 75.
14. Lesson XXXIX, 76.
15. Ethiop [William J. Wilson], "Afric-American Picture Gallery," *Anglo-African Magazine* 1, no.7 (July 1859): 217–218.
16. John Ernest, Rian Bowie, Leif Eckstrom, and Britt Rusert, "Visionary History: Recovering William J. Wilson's 'Afric-American Picture Gallery,'" in *Against a Sharp White Background: Infrastructures of African American Print*, ed. Brigitte Fielder and Jonathan Senchyne (Madison: University of Wisconsin Press, 2019), 233.
17. Ernest et al., "Visionary History," 233.
18. Ethiop [Wilson], "Afric-American Picture Gallery."
19. This repetition and revision is in keeping with other Black cultural reiterations, similar to what playwright Suzan-Lori Parks refers to as a "Rep & Rev" jazz aesthetic. See *The America Play* (New York: Theatre Communications Group, 1995), 8–9.
20. Laura Wasowicz, "Nuggets from the Field: The Roots of African American Children's Literature, 1780–1866," in *Who Writes for Black Children?: African American Children's Literature Before 1900*, ed. Katharine Capshaw and Anna Mae Duane (Minneapolis: University of Minnesota Press, 2017), 217.
21. Brigitte Fielder, "Early Black Futures," in *African American Literature: In Transition, 1750–2015*, vol. 1, 1750–1800, ed. Rhondda Thomas (Cambridge: Cambridge University Press, 2022), 228–254. Courtney Weikle-Mills discusses eighteenth-century Black poet Jupiter Hammon's similar direct address to Wheatley as early African American children's literature in "Free the Children: Jupiter Hammon and the Origin of African American Children's Literature," in *Who Writes for Black Children?: African American Children's Literature Before 1900*, ed. Katharine Capshaw and Anna Mae Duane (Minneapolis: University of Minnesota Press, 2017), 22–40.
22. June Jordan, "The Difficult Miracle of Black Poetry in America or Something like a Sonnet for Phillis Wheatley," in *Some of Us Did Not Die* (New York: Basic/Civitas Books, 2002), 182.
23. David Waldstreicher, *The Odyssey of Phillis Wheatley* (New York: Farrar, Straus and Giroux, 2023), 185–186.
24. H.N.G., letter to the editor, "Poems by Phillis Wheatley," *Frederick Douglass' Paper*, August 31, 1855.
25. H.N.G., letter.
26. Everett, "What are the Elements of True Womanhood?" *Christian Recorder*, March 9, 1882. The name "Everett" appears in italics and seems to be a pseudonym. I am grateful to Nafissa Thompson-Spires and Derrick Spires for helping me obtain access to this issue of the *Christian Recorder*.

27. Everett, "Elements of Womanhood?"
28. Everett, "Elements of Womanhood?"
29. Everett, "Elements of Womanhood?"
30. "Letter, No. V," letter to the editor, *Freedom's Journal*, November 2, 1827.
31. "Letter, No. V." *Freedom's Journal* reprinted Wheatley's poems "Hymn to Morning" and "Hymn to Humanity" in its November 9, 1827, issue.
32. Osceola F. Gordon, "Alabama's Appreciation of Literature," *Christian Recorder*, June 16, 1887.
33. Jessie Fauset, dedication to *The Brownies' Book* 1, no. 1 (January 1920): 32.
34. "The Story of Phillis Wheatley: A True Story," *The Brownies' Book* 1, no. 8 (August 1920): 251–253.
35. Although I compare this to the image of a girl enslaved in the North, Katharine Capshaw (Smith) describes how Patterson's piece celebrates Black Southern legacies for educational achievement. See Katharine Capshaw Smith *Children's Literature of the Harlem Renaissance* (Bloomington: Indiana University Press, 2004), 40.
36. Blanche Lynn Patterson, "The Heritage," *The Brownies' Book* 1, no. 8 (August 1920): 249–250.
37. Patterson, "The Heritage," 250.
38. Patterson, 250.
39. "The Jury," *The Brownies' Book* 1, no. 8 (August 1920): 256.
40. "The Jury," 256.
41. "The Jury," 256.
42. Katharine Capshaw Smith, *Children's Literature of the Harlem Renaissance* (Bloomington: Indiana University Press, 2004), 54–58.
43. Capshaw Smith, *Children's Literature*, 66.
44. Mary Church Terrell, *A Colored Woman in a White World* [1940] (Salem, NH: Ayer Company Publishers, 1992), 412.
45. Terrell's and other Black leaders' participation in the Washington bicentennial was not uncontroversial. Black historian and activist Carter G. Woodson, for example, critiqued the event's segregated planning in "George Washington Bi-Centennial Commission Has Colored Sideshow," *Afro-American*, December 12, 1931. On this controversy, see Lurana Donnels O'Malley, "'Why I Wrote the Phyllis Wheatley Pageant-Play': Mary Church Terrell's Bicentennial Activism," *Theatre History Studies* 37, no. 1 (2018): 229–232.
46. See Mary Church Terrell, "Forward," program notes for "Phillis Wheatley, A Pageant" performance at Booker T. Washington Junior High School in the school auditorium, May 26 and 27, 1933, 8:15 P.M., image 60 of Mary Church Terrell Papers: Subject File, -1962; Phillis Wheatley Pageant, 1932 to 1933, Manuscript/Mixed Material, Library of Congress, https://www.loc.gov/item/mss425490319/.
47. Capshaw Smith, *Children's Literature*, 53.
48. Capshaw Smith, *Children's Literature*, 54.
49. Terrell, "Forward." Terrell repeats this explanation in Mary Church Terrell, typescript, "Why I Wrote the Phyllis Wheatley Pageant-Play," Mary Church Terrell Papers 102, Box 6, Folder 156, Manuscript Division, Moorland-Spingarn Research Center, Howard University. Cited in O'Malley, "'Why I Wrote,'" 226.
50. Mary Church Terrell, prologue to "Phyllis Wheatley Pageant-Play," image 4 of Mary Church Terrell Papers: Subject File, -1962; Phillis Wheatley Pageant, 1932 to 1933, Manuscript/Mixed Material, Library of Congress, https://www.loc.gov/item/mss425490319/.

51. Mary Church Terrell, "Phillis Wheatley, an African Genius," *Star of the West* 19, no. 7 (October 1928): 221–223.
52. See O'Malley, "Why I Wrote," 227. O'Malley also discusses the significance of Black youth playing the part of white historical figures such as George Washington. See O'Malley, 237–238.
53. Mary Church Terrell, acknowledgments in program notes for "Phillis Wheatley, A Pageant" performance at Booker T. Washington Junior High School, image 65 of Mary Church Terrell Papers: Subject File, -1962; Phillis Wheatley Pageant, 1932 to 1933, Manuscript/Mixed Material, Library of Congress, https://www.loc.gov/item/mss425490319/.
54. Alison Parker, *Unceasing Militant: The Life of Mary Church Terrell* (Chapel Hill: University of North Carolina Press, 2020).
55. Zetta Elliott, introduction to *Say Her Name: Poems to Empower*, illust. Loveis Wise (New York: Jump at the Sun, 2020), 3.
56. Zetta Elliott, notes to *Say Her Name*, 79.
57. Zetta Elliott, "On Being Builders of a New World," in *Say Her Name*, 50.
58. Elliott, "On Being Builders," 50.

5

"When he saw the pencil put to paper"

The Meaning-Making of Children's Language in Depression-Era Harlem

MAGGIE E. MORRIS DAVIS

Saturated with suffering made sharper by black-and-white film, documentary photographs from the Depression era present complicated constructions of young people in poverty. Framed to give the reader access to the child's everyday context, the details within these photographs clearly mark lack. Strikingly, the bodies of children seem to most often be at rest, as though they have been asked to pause or have chosen to be still in the presence of a camera and the adult accompanying it as they wait for what is next.

Aaron Siskind's *Most Crowded Block in the World* collection contains a sequence of photographs taken in the late 1930s of a group of children in Harlem playing on and around a tidily stacked pile of planked lumber. Within this series it is notable that only three photographs follow the aforementioned pattern of depicting a child in poverty. In Figure 5.1, for example, we see a child at rest, sitting on a jutting plank. The look on the boy's face suggests bright sun coming from behind Siskind. Holes in the child's overalls show his knees, and the leather of his shoes is worn through.

Yet the overwhelming majority of the photos in Siskind's sequence represent children's bodies in motion: crouched down and playing in discarded wooden shipping boxes, laughing and talking with other children, sword fighting with sticks while balancing atop a single plank stretched between stacks, jumping down from piles of lumber into another child's outstretched arms. Figure 5.2, for example, features the same overalled child. He is joined in the frame by a child in the middle of saying something—body leaning forward, right hand gesturing for emphasis—that is making the child at the left laugh. This child's shrugged shoulders, smile, and balled fists suggest his active participation in the exchange, too.

These photographs of children in motion build a compelling counternarrative about childhood in Harlem in the Depression era. Not static and listless during

FIGURE 5.1 "[Boy sitting in front of pile of wood planks], 1938–1939 from The Most Crowded Block" (1968.0333.0249). Copyright Virginia Museum of Fine Arts.

Courtesy of the George Eastman Museum.

the widespread suffering of the 1930s, these children were working, playing, talking, arguing, laughing, creating, watching, learning. This is not to suggest that children were not affected in profound ways by the brutal economic and cultural contexts in which they lived; an idyllic childhood is not, after all, a prerequisite for play. Instead, this is to suggest that these photographs, taken together, offer an accessible metaphor for what we can learn of children in the archive. Framed by adult photographers, children in these photographs still move within, with, and against such frames. And, as Siskind's photographs suggest, such movement was accompanied by talk. This chapter will focus on what Harlem children said while in motion, their language of play. This language offers a rich entry point into the cultural production of children in this era. By focusing on an understudied

FIGURE 5.2 "[Two boys sitting in front of a pile of wood planks], 1938–1939 from The Most Crowded Block" (1968.0333.0251). Copyright Virginia Museum of Fine Arts.

Courtesy of the George Eastman Museum.

archive of children's language, Ralph Ellison's ethnographic notes from his time as a Federal Writers' Project field worker in Harlem, I hope to demonstrate how children actively made meaning through their language choices during play.

"The jungles and doggerels of childhood": Using Play Studies as an Entry Point

Franklin D. Roosevelt's controversial New Deal programs were designed to get Americans back to work. One such program, the Works Progress Administration (WPA), included a group of public works projects framed around the arts such as the Federal Writers' Project (FWP) and its sister projects in theater, art, and music.[1]

Ellison joined the FWP in New York City in 1938, and in 1939 he began working in the Living Lore Unit.[2] The Living Lore Unit reflected the theories of Benjamin A. Botkin (named the Project's national folklore editor in 1938), a shift that marked the Project's turn to redefining folklore as the study of "living culture."[3] Botkin's insistence that folklore "constantly has to get back to the spoken word to be renewed" pushed against previous folklorists' understanding of the primacy of the past to argue for careful attention to the contexts in which "living speech" cataloged the lore born of a specific moment, including in urban contexts.[4]

Botkin's shift in emphasis within the study of folklore anticipated where the field was headed. And his emphasis on revaluing the everyday mirrored trends in other social science fields in their approach to the study of play. Published in the same year that Ellison arrived in New York City, for example, sociologist Elizabeth F. Boettiger's *Children's Play Indoors and Out* delineates the ways adults are obligated to "supply the conditions, [and] set the stage" for generative play for the white, middle-class children described but not explicitly stated as the focus of her research.[5] Boettiger's book is representative of the larger shift in research in the 1920s–1930s from seeing play as "frivolous and useless" to seeing it as a generative form of socialization into the work of adulthood.[6] Building on this shift, rhetorics of "progress" and functionality have dominated play studies across the twentieth century.[7] Yet contemporary scholarship about play has turned away from seeing children's play as only a scaffolded placeholder on the way to the work of adulthood and instead has turned back toward childhood as a separate site of inquiry. Demarking childhood as worthy of theorization insists on the capacity of children. Play, then, provides a frame for meaning-making as it requires the child to critically read and interact with their community and, therefore, also themself. Thomas S. Henricks's 2015 *Play and the Human Condition*, for example, argues that play is a "sense-making activity" and that "people play in order to learn who they are, how they are situated, and what they can do."[8] This "rebellion against the forms and forces of the world" is a process of self-realization that requires the player to be cognizant of what is as well as what they hope to negotiate as an alternative.[9]

Play studies serves as an entry point for critically reading children's folklore gathered under the FWP because it invites us to analyze the ways in which these children actively made political and cultural meaning through their language choices during play, both in the scripts they took up and their revisions to those scripts, as well as in their performances of those scripts for an adult audience.

"Simultaneously scripted and scripting": The Meaning-Making of the Language of Play

The archival record suggests that Ralph Ellison's method of recording children's folklore, to which I will soon turn, was not standard among FWP field workers. When reading across the children's folklore collected across the nation, however, other patterns emerge.[10] The most obvious pattern is that the same rhymes are frequently repeated, sometimes with slight variations that, even in their archival cataloging, have been attributed to regional contexts and differences in dialects. This parallels seminal mid-twentieth-century studies by Iona and Peter Opie, renowned folklorists of children's games, songs, and rhymes in Britain. It is imperative to note that the work of the Opies often erased differences of class and race and ability in their efforts to represent "the child population as a whole." From their preface to *Lore and Language*, for example, we read the following:

> The study does not, however, except incidentally, include the lore current among children in the private, fee-charging establishments. And it does not, despite the sections on tortures and pranks after nightfall, set out to include the lore and language of the delinquent. We are concerned here merely with the fun-loving but father-fearing specimen who is typical of the vast majority. It seems necessary to say this because there continues to be such a spate of books about children who are socially deprived or mentally handicapped, or who are in trouble with the police, that a book about the ordinary child is rather extraordinary. (xiv)

The Opies's effort to establish a norm dismisses what they frame as opposite poles of childhood experience. One extreme is wealth, "children in private, fee-charging establishments," though it is the second pole that receives the most attention for its lack and aberrancy: "delinquents," "socially deprived," "mentally handicapped."

Thus, in the Opies's supposedly normed sample, the commonality of the "ritual and phraseology" of children's lore was unexpected, and yet they contributed "variations, even apparently creative ones," to "mishearing or misunderstanding."[11] "[Occurring] more often by accident than design" they said, for the Opies children's lore came from an "unselfconscious culture . . . unnoticed by the sophisticated world."[12] This well-intended yet deficit thinking both celebrates—and, in doing so, makes visible the lore of children—and simultaneously trivializes children as agential language users. "Language is still new to them," they wrote, "and they find difficulty in expressing themselves."[13]

What becomes possible, though, if we read children's lore and rhymes assuming a purposefulness to children's language? Furthermore, what happens when the language of children whose lived experiences differ from what is centered as "ordinary" are not excluded from the record but instead carefully listened to? Looking at variations in the enactment of these scripts as within the realm of possibility of children's design and choice suggests what Rachel Conrad invites us to consider in her book *Time for Childhoods*: "Cultural conceptions of youth that neglect appreciating young people's lives in the present" overlook the ways children's agency is "an active practice" in which the "ideas, desires, and strategies that children envision, rehearse, practice, or enact" can manifest in everyday practices that might not be highly visible to adults.[14] Here I also enter into conversation with Marah Gubar's kinship model, which both acknowledges what Karen

Sánchez-Eppler and others have claimed—that children "begin life . . . immersed in discourses not of their own making that ineluctably affect how [they] conceive of [them]selves and the world around [them]"—and insists that children are "simultaneously scripted and scripting."[15] My efforts to read in this way are attempts to answer Gubar's call for new methodologies that tend to a "hermeneutics of recuperation" that prompt us, in these texts, to examine the performance of these rhymes and the revisions to and the enactment of the language therein.[16] And this, of course, requires that we consider their use during and through play.

Many childhood studies scholars have argued for the value of examining the material culture of children as a means of expanding the archive with which to study the lives of children, cultural constructions of childhood, and the ways children actively participate in creating culture. Robin Bernstein's *Racial Innocence: Performing American Childhood from Slavery to Civil Rights*, for example, argues that

> Children do not passively receive culture. Rather, children expertly field the co-scripts of narratives and material culture and then collectively forge a third prompt: play itself. The three prompts then entangle to script future play, which continues to change as children collectively exercise agency.[17]

Similarly, in her argument to tend to the "stuff they leave behind," Sánchez-Eppler notes that "looking at the things children make . . . shows how children's play is shaped by and expresses its social context."[18] While language is admittedly different from material culture like dolls or handmade playthings or journals, I build upon Bernstein and Sánchez-Eppler to argue that children's rhymes gathered by FWP fieldworkers can also serve as an underexplored entry point, as they catalog scripts bound contextually to place and time as dutifully recorded by adults in the presence of children enacting these scripts on playgrounds and around sidewalks. Ellison's ethnographic FWP work, then, offers additional insights as his accompanying field notes offer rich context that was not often logged in the reports of other fieldworkers.

In Ellison's field notes, we see how agential and knowing children engage in a long-standing practice of dialect signifying meaning specific to the speaker's culture and context. A useful parallel is Katherine Capshaw's close readings of the dialect poetry Paul Laurence Dunbar wrote for children during the Harlem Renaissance of the 1920s. Building on John Edgar Wideman and Lois Kuznets's work on play and the study of Black dialect specifically, she writes that "play with language can comment on, and often imaginatively change, the nature of social structures and relations. Within the African American community, such play advances a series subtext, for the structures of racism and inequity and likely targets of verbal inversion and subversions."[19] I argue that this same powerful linguistic play is present in the language of children recorded in Ellison's notes.

Ellison cataloged this language of play within children's rhymes during 1939–1940, years spent working for the New York Writers' Project and, in part, interviewing children and visiting playgrounds around Harlem. Sara Rutkowski's

Literary Legacies of the Federal Writers' Project reprints a handful of the jump rope rhymes Ellison cataloged, which she describes as "meaningful within a folk group, and even as they change over time, their form is familiar and culturally binding."[20] I argue that the language employed in this "binding" form can be read as anti-language, language that "convey[s] a certain tension," to pull forward Rutkowski's description of the rhymes.[21] This idea of anti-language was first developed by sociolinguist M. A. Halliday from real-life examples of languages formed by an "anti-society" (he draws primarily on examples from prisoners and criminals) that operate largely as "modes of resistance."[22] These languages create an alternate reality that becomes a "counter-reality, set up in opposition to some established norm" in which "it is not the distance between the two realities but the tension between them that is significant."[23] Therefore, anti-languages are created and sustained by a hyperawareness of power structures within society.[24] Notably, they are also the product of processes not of "construction but reconstruction" in which meaning is made not only in negotiation with semiotic systems but also in negotiation with other language users.[25]

My work with Ellison's archival material is informed by this idea of anti-language, a concept I use to study the process of the language formation of children within a rigidly classed society, I build on the work of Roger Fowler, for whom anti-language is not just verbal play but "facilitate[s] an alternative social and conceptual reality for [its] speakers."[26]

As anti-language defines its own parameters against discourses of power and privilege, what these rhymes offer is expressive talk that the child attunes to a subjectivity that is emerging from distorting social circumstances. For Fowler, "the element of verbal play links anti-language with the special rhymes and sayings of children's culture."[27] Anti-language, after all, "is constantly renewing itself—to sustain the vitality that it needs if it is to function at all," which we see in the variations of rhymes, variations often specific to the child's context.[28] It is important to note that the Opies demarked extreme variations like this as intentional, nonstandard choices that children make because of their lower class position, though this is not explicitly named and instead is implied in their analysis. In a section entitled "Secret Languages" within a chapter entitled "Some Curiosities," for example, they mark back slang as "slang, local dialect, a multiplicity of technical terms, word-twisting, codes, and sign language" as communication inaccessible to "outsiders," which "satisf[ies] an impulse common to all underdogs."[29] While a reader could assume that the Opies see children, broadly, as underdogs, there is not-so-subtle language embedded in the short section that clearly marks this as the language of "some classes of children" even as they acknowledge even some "respectable children" have been observed using it.[30]

While the Opies even go as far as to caution against such "curiosities" because of how "too much meaning can be (and very often is) read into the formulas of children's games and customs," Henricks's *Play and the Human Condition* brings together recent theories of play to reminds us powerfully of the role play takes in navigating what is normed within a culture and its opposite: what might be.[31] Two specific ideas bear note here. First, play helps make meaning that then moves one to action. As "a commentary on the lives of *communities*," he argues, play "emphasizes the way people fit their activity to society's broader terms" or, conversely, how they "[seek] alternatives to established cultural patterns."[32] This "develops, maintains, and assesses action strategies."[33] Second, play creates self-awareness, which requires cultural knowledge and incredible skill for navigating conflict.[34] "Creativity," Henricks writes, "is a disputatious process; so is the maintenance of what is created. And getting anyone to participate wholeheartedly in such a fragile, perhaps trivial affair is a challenge of its own sort."[35] I am interested in the ways the language Ellison recorded of Black children at play represents a kind of cultural production not often heard, looked for, and listened to in the 1930s: a way of making meaning that signifies an understanding of the limitations of *and* the joy within their cultural context as well as the agency embedded in their language choices.

"How does this child fit into his America?": Reading FWP Children's Rhymes in the Archive

The rhymes Ellison was collecting were intended for inclusion in a book about children's folklore by the New York Writers' Project. What remains of this unfinished and unpublished manuscript, *Children's Rhymes of New York City*, is housed in the Library of Congress. The folder in which this essay is housed is overflowing with scraps and paper-thin mimeographed pages of rhymes, a few with the cover sheet cataloging the location, date, and other identifying information of their collection and most others without any notes attached at all, cut into strips, and stapled in horizontal rows—six or so to a page—on typing paper. The folder also contains an opening essay celebrating the collecting of approximately one thousand rhymes from across New York City. Page five of the essay is a section entitled "Negro Folk Culture," purposefully separated from the rest of the essay in which the folk rhymes of white and immigrant children are described (though they are not raced as such and instead are presented as the unmarked default: "children").[36]

The language of this section is striking. Its overarching focus tends to be on the origins of the material, and the writer emphasizes that the "liveliest and most interesting of the rhymes are current among Negro children whose parents have moved to New York from the South" and admits that such rhymes show "innovation and invention" as they also demonstrate a "racial reaction to chauvinism and prejudice" present in the South and in New York. Yet, the focus of the remaining two paragraphs is that "old English rhymes" are more prevalent here "than in any other group." The author partially attributes this to the "earlier and more benevolent days of the pre-bellum South, [when] Negro and white children played together, sharing their games and rhymes." The essay blithely ends—"In any case"—with a short paragraph noting the pleasure of the writers to include "so many" of the "rhymes and games of Negro children from an intrinsic, lively and often lovely section of American folk culture." Among this discomfiting nostalgia for an antebellum South in which Black and white children are at play sharing language—white to Black, of course, is suggested—we find the focus of the celebration to be the Black child's ability to turn old English rhymes so generously "share[d]" into something "lively" and "most interesting." The folder does not suggest how the rhymes were going to be cataloged in this never-published book. The closest the contents of the folder get to suggesting an organizational structure is this introductory essay, and if it was the template, then the rhymes Ellison collected would have been cataloged by their difference and celebrated for their vitality. The rhymes described in the rest of the eleven-page essay are categorized by their function (e.g., "rhymes used for rope jumping") and their use in school curriculum.[37]

Filed one container away are most of what remains of the rhymes Ellison collected.[38] As I have read and cataloged the rhymes, I am struck by how children's anti-language in the rhymes (1) establishes a common discourse separating insiders and outsiders, (2) creates new narratives, and (3) reclaims (or relexicalizes) language.

The most common patterns in the rhymes record a discourse intent on marking insiders and outsiders. Many of these rhymes are taunts and some divide the child speakers from others in terms of racial or ethnic identity. The following rhyme is labeled as a taunt and recorded several times in Ellison's papers (although identifying markers suggest that there are multiple copies of the same rhyme):

> RED WHITE AND BLUE
> YOUR OLD MAN IS A JEW
> YOUR MOTHER IS AN IRISH POTATOE
> JUST LIKE YOU.
>
> (R.W.E.) Harlem Negro
> 130th and Lenox Ave.[39]

This is a variation of a common rhyme, noted by some folklorists as being popular during World War I and the 1920s with Jewish and non-Jewish children (the use of either the pronoun "my" or "your" signifies the users identity).[40] The first line of the rhyme, the colors of the American flag, establish the rhyme's starting point, a kind of stock patriotism that makes the slurs that follow sharper against this symbolic background.[41] What follows in other recorded versions of the rhyme include the same word used as an ethnic slur in the second phrase, "Jew," and then other ethnic slurs in the third phrase of the rhyme that are specific to the speaker's context (e.g., "Chinaman" or "Dago"[42]). With the rhyme Ellison recorded, we see the child speaker's use of "Jew" and "Irish Potatoe [*sic*]" as slurs that demonstrate the child's understanding of racism and prejudice specific to their context. Of note in this rhyme is the anti-language that carefully marks the outsider, allowing the unmarked insider to claim their power through the use of possessive pronouns.

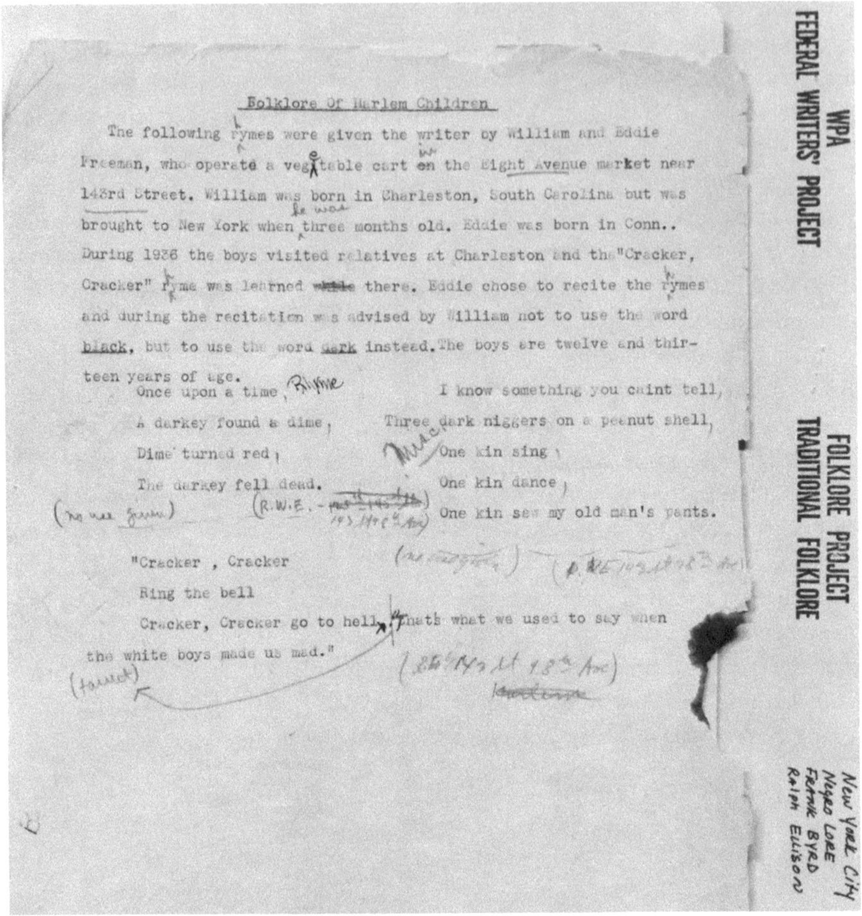

WPA
FEDERAL WRITERS' PROJECT

Folklore Of Harlem Children

The following rymes were given the writer by William and Eddie Freeman, who operate a vegtable cart on the Eight Avenue market near 143rd Street. William was born in Charleston, South Carolina but was brought to New York when three months old. Eddie was born in Conn.. During 1936 the boys visited relatives at Charleston and the "Cracker, Cracker" ryme was learned while there. Eddie chose to recite the rymes and during the recitation was advised by William not to use the word black, but to use the word dark instead. The boys are twelve and thirteen years of age.

Once upon a time,
A darkey found a dime,
Dime turned red,
The darkey fell dead.

I know something you caint tell,
Three dark niggers on a peanut shell,
One kin sing
One kin dance
One kin sew my old man's pants.

"Cracker , Cracker
Ring the bell
Cracker, Cracker go to hell, Thats what we used to say when the white boys made us mad."

FOLKLORE PROJECT
TRADITIONAL FOLKLORE

New York City
Negro Lore
Ralph Ellison

FIGURE 5.3 "Folklore of Harlem Children" annotated page from Ellison's interview with two brothers (A648).

Courtesy of the Library of Congress.

In the same folder is Ellison's record of three rhymes by brothers who "operate a vegetable cart," William, age thirteen, and Eddie, age twelve (see Figure 5.3). The last rhyme recorded on the page is as follows:

> Cracker, Cracker
> Ring the bell
> Cracker, Cracker go to hell

In this rhyme, Ellison's ethnographic notes mark not only the origin of the rhyme but also its intent. "That's what we used to say when the white boys made us mad," Eddie is recorded as saying. "Cracker" was slang for whites in lower-class positions.

The idiom "ring the bell," suggests the threat of an altercation, as to have one's bell rung is to be beaten in a fight or hit with such force that it ends the fight. Here, too, we see children of Harlem using anti-language to mark boundaries of who is inside and who must remain outside (and what might happen if those boundaries are crossed).[43]

Within the rhymes, we see a second pattern of using anti-language to create new narratives within specific contexts. In Ellison's 1939 report, "I won't go to Macy's" not only demarks the child's understanding of places that are off limits but also the consequences of seeking access to said places. "Macy's" seems to have been first published the year before in *New Masses* in an article entitled "Street Songs of Children" by Fred Rolland, who also worked for the FWP.[44] The iteration of the rhyme Rolland recorded is different, and Rolland's prefatory paragraphs are worth noting here at length:[45]

> American folklore of cities, villages, and farms find vivid and often delightful utterance in the rhymes of their children. Those rhymes, enriched by contributions of an endless line of immigrants, have been remodeled by succeeding generations of youngsters, and we find them today an entertaining and revealing mixture of tradition and modernization. Language to a child is synonymous with action. These are rhymes which require dramatic explanation through game, dance, or burlesque. The child's naïve representation of the conventions and actions of elders often produces a rollicking, if unconscious, satire.
>
> All poetry, to live, must be not only universal in content but also a repercussion of the age in which it was created. These rhymes of childhood have passed a stern test in being accepted by succeeding generations. They have been modified, of course, and therein lies much of their interest. We find innumerable versions of any one rhyme, and, in tracing its changes, we discover an authentic comment upon the changes in our society. The twentieth-century child who proclaims that he "won't go to Macy's any more, more, more" is already voicing his protest, superficial but indicative.
>
> These jingles are a product of group fraternization, amended, adapted, and accepted by collective approval. They come from sidewalks, back alleys, playgrounds, and playstreets, the folklore of the children of America.[46]

While parts of Rolland's approach engage in the typical deprecation of children's rhymes—"the child's naïve representation of the conventions and actions of elders"—he more powerfully lauds the "action" of a child's language and the collective construction of rhymes that provide "an authentic comment upon the changes in our society." Here the agential child chooses to repeat narratives that hold particular, agreed-upon meaning within their context, meaning that may only be conveyed in a particular moment in time and, therefore, is not represented in a permanent record.

Working with a 1954 recording of the "Macy's" rhyme from Hell's Kitchen, Molly Rosner argues that it demonstrates that children "could identify where they 'belonged' in consumer society—and where they didn't," and that through the process of play "they reify and challenge the norms they're encountering."[47] We see in Ellison's note that this was a ball-bouncing rhyme, which added emphasis to the key words in the rhyme. Most important, though, we see here the child's awareness and choice to repeat the rhyme and, in doing so, tell a story of what it means to be young and Black in Harlem. This abstract rhyme reifies a story these children knew to be true:

I WONT GO TO MACY'S ANY MORE, MORE, MORE!
THERE'S A BIG FAT POLICEMAN AT THE DOOR, DOOR, DOOR!
HE GRABBED ME BY THE COLLAR
AND HE MADE ME PAY A DOLLAR
AND I WONT GO TO MACY'S ANY MORE, MORE, MORE!

The rhymes Ellison recorded also show Harlem children's efforts to relexicalize language, a process "partial, not total" in which new words are used in ways "central to the activities of the subculture and that set it off most sharply from the established society."[48] While most FWP field workers recorded only the rhymes of children and, occasionally, the information requested on the agency's cover sheet, Ellison's field notes remain the exception and, therefore, offer this insight into the ways the anti-language of these rhymes was ever in motion and crafted in response to specific moments as well as broader contexts. For example, Ellison registers "one boy's attitude toward [Public School #89]," noting that "the first version [of the rhyme] was recorded before he knew his words were to be taken down, and the second, more respectable version, when he saw the pencil put to paper."

1. REMEMBER THE EIGHT
REMEMBER THE NINE
REMEMBER THAT 'CITY DUMP' 89.

2. REMEMBER THE EIGHT
REMEMBER THE NINE
REMEMBER THAT 'WHITE HOUSE' 89.

Here we have record of the child's language choices of the rhyme. The original—unstated—centers Public School #89 as the subject of the rhyme. The first recorded rhyme shows the child relexicalize (use different words for) the subject as the "CITY DUMP," an immediate shift that indicates the child's perception of the school. City dump, after all, not only signifies the child's distaste for school but also the child's framing of the school as being in possession of the city, as a product of the larger social structure which assigns value (or does not). Furthermore, the second recorded rhyme shows the child's awareness of an external audience, the expectation of how one is supposed to revere school, and the dexterity of the child's language to immediately relexicalize again—"WHITE HOUSE"—to adhere to what the child thinks an adult audience will see as—to borrow from Ellison—"respectable" language. The discursive power in the child's choice, however, is that the adjective "white" can also be read as denigrative, marking the school as a space of white control. The child's decision to make this more "respectable" revision can be read as his use of performative anti-language that to a listener might signify one thing and in the discourse community of Harlem children will later mean something entirely different.[49]

This example of improvisation and innovation of folk rhymes offers us the opportunity to see children in the process of defining their street, their neighborhood, their world. They speak in conversation with and against that which has come before, which is manifest in Ellison's attention to their language choices, both in word and use. For Ellison, it seems, the child's capacity for imagination, for invention, for that which continually resurfaces old questions, seeks new answers and brings forward possibilities to what he called in various essays "method[s] of reordering the world" that respond to the "moral and political problems which would not stay put underground."[50] Reading the language of these children in Harlem as anti-language suggests so.

Ellison's later essays and interviews often center folklore as preserving universal experiences brought forward by "courageous expression [that] announced the Negro's willingness to trust his own experience, his own sensibilities as to the definition of reality."[51] Furthermore, he continued to return to the language of children as a political force. In his essay "What These Children Are Like," a lecture given during a seminar considering the "Education for Culturally Different Youth" in 1963 in Massachusetts, for example, he questions the application of the label "culturally deprived" to Black youth and instead asserts that "[Black youth are] products of a different cultural complex." What unfolds within Ellison's essay is, I would argue, an introduction to the workings of anti-language within the language of Black youth. Contrary to the belief that "these kids have no capacity to manipulate the language," he asks, "How can we keep the discord flowing into the mainstream of the language without destroying it?" It must be forced to "sound and bend under the pressure of [Negro] need to express their sense of the real." Near the end of the essay, Ellison claims that Black slang "exists precisely because Negroes need words which will communicate, which will designate the objects, the processes, the manners and subtleties" of Black culture.[52]

Such discord is at the heart of anti-language, language which by definition exists "in an antagonistic relationship to the dominant culture."[53] Similarly, though focused more broadly on FWP texts written by Black authors, J. J. Butts's summative paragraphs in *Dark Mirror: African Americans and the Federal Writers' Project* dwell on the irony that if "heard correctly, these voices could have offered alternative understandings, local knowledge, a deep understanding of race, and, perhaps most importantly in the interplay of patterns and chaos, course corrections."[54] The rhymes Ellison collected require that we, as readers, first acknowledge children's capacity for and understanding of language and the ways in which it is used not only to reinscribe power within society but also to potentially reclaim it. And then, as modeled by his FWP methodology and lifelong insistence on the necessity of the idioms of Black youth, the work becomes ours: if "heard correctly," the discord we find insists we look around to see a society woefully out of balance and then return again to listen differently to the anti-language of the creative child.

NOTES

My research within Federal Writers' Project papers at the Library of Congress was made possible by my time as a Kluge Fellow, for which I am grateful. I would also like to thank the Department of English and the Office of Research and Graduate Studies at Illinois State University for its support in completing this work.

Chapter Heading Quotes: "The jungles and doggerels of childhood"—B. A. Botkin, *A Treasury of American Folklore* (New York; Crown Publishers, 1944), 768; "Simultaneously scripted and scripting"—Marah Gubar, "The Hermeneutics of Recuperation: What a Kinship-Model Approach to Children's Agency Could Do for Children's Literature and Childhood Studies," *Jeunesse: Young People, Texts, Cultures* 8, no. 1 (Summer 2016): 295; "How does this child fit into his America?"—This question comes from Ellison's unfinished novel, *Three Days Before the Shooting*... (89). The question is originally asked with sarcasm by the white reporter McIntyre. I would argue, however, that this question guides much of the novel's remaining pieces and parts. Put in the mouth of any of the main characters (and several of the memorable characters who dominate only a single scene, e.g., Miss Maud in Book II), the answer to this question becomes a map of sorts in which the reader can follow Ellison's oft-trod paths through the novel's different drafts. Strewn upon these paths are often children's rhymes.

1. Jerrold Hirsch, "Federal Writers' Project," in *American Literature in Transition, 1930–1940*, ed. Ichiro Takayoski (Cambridge: Cambridge University Press, 2018), 361.
2. Sara Rutkowski, *Literary Legacies of the Federal Writers' Project: Voices of the Depression in the American Postwar Era* (London: Palgrave Macmillan, 2017), 34. The largest emphasis of scholarly attention to the FWP in literary studies has been to trace the influence of the Project on major literary figures who were thus employed, such as Zora Neale Hurston, Richard Wright, Meridel Le Sueur, Nelson Algren, and Ralph Ellison.
3. B.A. Botkin, "WPA and Folklore Research: 'Bread and Song' (1939)," in *The Conservation of Culture: Folklorists and the Public Sector*, ed. Burt Feintuch (Lexington: University Press of Kentucky, 1988), 263. This shift—recording and studying folklore as performance—gained traction in folklore studies in the 1960s (Hirsch, "Federal Writers' Project," 372).
4. Botkin, *Treasury*, xxi; B. A. Botkin, "We Call it 'Living Lore,'" *New York Folklore Quarterly* 14 (Autumn 1958): 190; and Hirsh, "Federal Writers' Project," 366.
5. Elizabeth F. Boettiger, *Children's Play Indoors and Out* (New York: E. P. Dutton, 1938), 13.
6. Helen B. Schwartzman, *Transformations: The Anthropology of Children's Play* (New York: Plenum, 1978), 133. As Schwartzman notes in chapter 6, twentieth-century studies of children's play normed middle-class whiteness as the site of generative, functional play. Other groups of children, then, occupied deficit positions in research.
7. Thomas S. Henricks, "Play Studies: A Brief History," *American Journal of Play* 12, no. 2 (Winter 2020): 119.
8. Thomas S. Henricks, *Play and the Human Condition* (Urbana: University of Illinois Press, 2015), 209.
9. Henricks, *Play and the Human Condition*, 76.

10. While children's rhymes are now separated as a distinct category within the filing of the folklore collected and sorted within the Folklore Project files at the Library of Congress, the rhymes collected therein were recorded by a wide variety of field workers who also recorded other folklore filed across a host of categories. Each state's files are categorized primarily by the function of the folklore (e.g. "ghost stories," "dreams," and "local lore" are common across each state's slightly different files), though many states separated out the folklore of specific groups of people.
11. Peter and Iona Opie, *The Lore and Language of Schoolchildren*, rev. ed. (New York: New York Review Books, 2001), 4, 8.
12. Opie, *Lore and Language*, 2.
13. Opie, *Lore and Language*, 18.
14. Conrad, *Time for Childhoods* (Amherst: University of Massachusetts Press, 2020), 4, 9, 10.
15. Gubar "Hermeneutics of Recuperation," 293–295.
16. Gubar, "Hermeneutics of Recuperation," 304.
17. Bernstein, *Racial Innocence*, 29.
18. Karen Sánchez-Eppler, "Geographies of Play: Scales of Imagination in the Study of Child-Made Things," in *Reimagining Childhood Studies*, ed. Spyros Spyrou, Rachel Rosen, and Daniel Thomas Cook (London: Bloomsbury Academic, 2019), 41.
19. Katherine Capshaw Smith, *Children's Literature of the Harlem Renaissance.* (Bloomington: Indiana University Press, 2004), 124.
20. Rutkowski, *Literary Legacies*, 53.
21. Rutkowski, *Literary Legacies*, 50.
22. M.A.K. Halliday, "Anti-Languages," *American Anthropologist* 78 (1976): 570.
23. Halliday, "Anti-Languages," 576.
24. Halliday, "Anti-Languages," 583.
25. Halliday, "Anti-Languages," 575.
26. Roger Fowler, *Literature as Social Discourse* (London: Batsford, 1981), 147.
27. Fowler, *Literature*, 152.
28. Halliday, "Anti-Languages," 582.
29. Opie, *Lore and Language*, 320.
30. Opie, *Lore and Language*, 320.
31. Opie, *Lore and Language*, 306.
32. Henricks, *Play*, 2, 205.
33. Henricks, *Play*, 210.
34. Henricks, *Play*, 209.
35. Henricks, *Play*, 164.
36. Children's Lore, box A647, WPA, Federal Writers' Project, Folklore Project, New York City, Children's Lore, Miscellaneous, Library of Congress, Washington DC.
37. Ellison, A648.
38. One more folder also contains children's rhymes Ellison recorded, WPA A1086. "Copy 2" in the top left-hand corner labels this set of thirty-six pages, some of which appear to be final drafts of the rhymes largely unorganized in A648. A648 rhymes often have pen and pencil edits, which the copies at the beginning of A1086 typically do not. Lastly, some of the rhymes on pages filed in A1086 are numbered and labeled according to purpose (e.g. "taunt" or "ball bouncing"), suggesting a final draft Ellison might have submitted. Of

note is that in these supposed final drafts, Ellison's rich ethnographic notes are absent, suggesting that what was required of the assignment was only the text of the rhyme, the geographic location of its recitation, and its purpose.

The first drafts of Ellison's FWP field notes often included rhymes from his own childhood, labeled as "R.W.E. Oklahoma City, 1925." Carefully paired with rhymes from Harlem children, it is as though Ellison was reminded of the language of his own youth.

39. Ellison, A648
40. Nathan Hurvitz, "Jews and Jewishness in the Street Rhymes of American Children," *Jewish Social Studies* 16, no. 2 (April 1954): 142–143.
41. When used by Jewish children in 1925, the rhyme was shortened: "Red, white and blue / The color of the Jew." Here Hurvitz reads the evocation of the American flag by Jewish children as "an effort on their part to identify with a major symbol of American life" (142).
42. Emelyn E. Gardner, "Some Counting-Out Rhymes in Michigan," *Journal of American Folklore* 31, no. 122 (Oct.–Dec. 1918): 534.
43. Ellison, A648.
44. Jerre Mangione, *The Dream and the Deal: The Federal Writers' Project, 1935–1943* (Syracuse: Syracuse University Press, 1996), 252. It was hoped that FWP writers would find opportunities for publication of literary works influenced by their time on the Project. Only *American Stuff* (1937) was published by the Project; however, many other existing outlets, such as the magazine *Poetry*, published issues devoted to literature by FWP workers. The *New Masses* May 10, 1938 issue referenced here is another example.
45. In the rhyme Rolland records, the threat is that the policeman "will squeeze me like a lemon / Achalachke zol em nehmen." Roger D. Abrahams's *Jump Rope Rhymes: A Dictionary*, offers a history of the "Macy's" rhyme as recorded in popular and scholarly publications (97).
46. Fred Rolland, "Street Songs of Children," *New Masses*, May 10, 1938.
47. Molly Rosner, *Playing with History: American Identities and Children's Consumer Culture* (New Brunswick: Rutgers University Press, 2021), 4.
48. Halliday, "Anti-Languages," 571.
49. Ellison, A 648.
50. Ralph W. Ellison, "Hidden Name and Complex Fate: A Writer's Experience in the United States," in *Shadow and Act* (New York: Vintage International, 1995), 161, 164.
51. Ellison, "The Art of Fiction: An Interview," in *Shadow and Act*, 172.
52. Ralph W. Ellison, "What These Children Are Like," in *Going to the Territory* (New York: Random House, 1986), 68, 67, 69, 74.
53. Fowler, *Literature*, 146.
54. J. J. Butts, *Dark Mirror: African Americans and the Federal Writers' Project* (Columbus: Ohio State University Press, 2021), 165.

6

Creative Testimonio as Activism

A Case Study of Sophie Cruz and Sarai Gonzalez

CRISTINA RHODES

"Y no te preocupes si no te aprueban / Cuando te critiquen, tú solo di / Soy yo," sings the Colombian pop band Bomba Estéreo in their hit song "Soy Yo."[1] The band's urging to be oneself despite all critiques is accompanied in their viral music video by the amateurish hip gyrations and dorky adaptations of old dance moves, like the sprinkler, of then eleven-year-old Sarai Gonzalez. Gonzalez's visible resistance to societal norms alongside the song's message of selfhood creatively defies cultural coding of girls as unable to affect change. Gonzalez, like other young Latina activists, utilizes creative performance as a new mode of activism. As a whole, "girls' activism is an extremely underexplored scholarly topic, largely invisible in the academic literatures on girlhood and on social movements," and creative activism is even more overlooked.[2] Further, activism centering young Latinxs, let alone girls, is often centered around immigration, education, and other basic human rights. To extend to creative activism is a territory yet unexplored. But Sarai Gonzalez, and those like her, signal a paradigmatic shift in activism and Latina girlhood. Thus, this chapter provides a case study of two Latinx child activists—Sarai Gonzalez and Sophie Cruz—to demonstrate that action coupled with creative performance affects cultural shifts. In other words, I argue that figures like Gonzalez and Cruz, who use creative outlets like art and dance as their vehicles for change, do not just affect societal change via the normal patterns of activism, but also shift cultural paradigms that hold Latina girlhood as a space for forming domestic and familial identities and behaviors. Whereas cultural scripts of childhood within Latinx communities situate children as the inheritors of change, I also position them as the *instigators* of it.

I frame this creative resistance around the act of testimonio, a unique form of bearing witness within Latinx communities, which is often used "to change the hearts and minds of the reader, and impel them to social action."[3] This phrasing is important, that testimonio *impels* action means that it drives action, it forces action. Testimonio is reciprocal in nature, allowing the speaker to vent their experiences while simultaneously seeking change by those who listen to the testimony. Testimonio is most often spoken or written, using text or oral tradition to instigate change. As Lindsey Pérez Huber explains, "*testimonio*" is "*a verbal journey of a witness who speaks to reveal the racial, classed, gendered, and nativist injustices they have suffered as a means of healing, empowerment, and advocacy for a more humane present and future.*"[4] I extend testimonio to more creative and visual performances here, capitalizing on this volume's interests in creative works by children. Testimonio, within this context then, means a creative action that allows the bearer to give witness to their oppression and to morph that witnessing into an assertion of power within Latina girlhood. Whereas Latina girlhoods are often painted as lacking power and agency by strict adherence to gender norms, these acts of artistic testimonio creatively revise such restrictive cultural scripts.

While I look specifically at the way that Sarai Gonzalez uses dance and Sophie Cruz uses drawing as forms of testimonio and resistance, these are not the only avenues young Latinas can take to effect change. Rather, I center them because of the relative prominence of their actions; Gonzalez and Cruz's testimonios became viral moments on the internet, with their pictures or videos shared across social media platforms thousands of times. Gonzalez's dancing in the "Soy Yo" video is complemented by her larger-than-life personality. Likewise, Cruz's delivery of a drawing to the Pope demonstrates a very different kind of Latina girl than those typically portrayed in dominant media. In that moment, she was powerful, and her youth enabled that power. The visibility of their testimonios effects a cultural shift in the way that Latina children are viewed, positioning them to become activists more easily and readily than in prior generations. In this chapter, I will first explain the prior disconnect between activism and Latina girlhood, and then I will discuss Gonzalez and Cruz as case studies for how activism has shifted from being inaccessible to Latina girls to being a powerful tool of testimonio and change.

Activism and Latina Girlhoods

Understanding the unique positionality of Latina childhoods, and girlhoods in particular, is vital to understanding how activists like Gonzalez and Cruz defy cultural gender norms while simultaneously using traditional Latinx creative formations as activism. Western (and, importantly, white) cultural notions of children and childhood prize innocence, but taking on activist causes positions children as being aware of the bad in the world. Adults thus experience a level of discomfort and cognitive dissonance which pushes them to continue a metanarrative of disempowerment for young activists. Yet, in dispelling the romanticized notion of childhood innocence and need for protection, child activists confront adults' anxieties about their positions of power and control.

According to Jessica Taft, "Being an activist can help girls as they construct identities that are alternative to the dominant forms of girlhood."[5] In other words, girl activists like Gonzalez and Cruz reconstruct modes of girlhood through their action. Scholars like Emily Bent agree. In her analysis of the teenage activist X González, she asserts, "Girl-power stories present a straightforward process of empowerment for girls followed by large-scale sociocultural change in the world."[6] What is more, writing about their experiences with a youth arts and activism program, Sandra Spickard Prettyman and Elisa Gargarella explain that artists who are also activists "recognize their potential to take more active roles in transforming their own futures and the future of their communities."[7] Ultimately, the art activism I study here makes possible the kinds of societal change often forged through activism, and it also opens new pathways for Latina girlhood. Gonzalez and Cruz exhibit traits that are often at odds with the ideal for Latinas—they are powerful and in control in ways that bely culture's coding of them as weak or submissive.

Young Latinxs tend to engage in more prosocial behaviors; in other words, "a traditional Latino/a ethnic heritage is concordant with consideration for others, respecting others, and contributing to the group."[8] This is magnified for female-identifying children, because they are socialized to aid in family and community endeavors as part and parcel of subservience and secondary status. In her study of Latina girlhoods, Andrea Fernández-García explains that the patriarchy dictates girls' place in Latinx culture.[9] As patriarchal subjects, young Latinas are socialized to become curators of family peace and proliferation. Yet, Jill Denner and Bianca L. Guzmán contend, "young girls are influenced by their home environments, and they also influence their home environment in such a way that they are creating new cultural practices."[10] This shift signals that Latina girlhood is no longer a space of submissiveness; instead, young Latinas are creating new ways of being. Indeed, recent studies indicate that Latinx childhoods are in flux. Mario T. García's construction of the "Latino Generation" captures the fluid nature of Latinx childhoods more broadly, but also encompasses girlhoods.[11] This new generation has knowledge of past and present oppressions, and this particular epistemology allows Latinx youth to forge their own new identities and cultures.[12] The ideological and identity-based shift in cultural notions for Latina girlhoods, in particular, is significant and necessary. Empowered young Latinas are widely beneficial.[13] In other words, this shifting of Latina girlhood to be more proactive and empowered provides a model for a new generation of Latina girls, but also for a world that needs new modes of being—brought about through activism.

Creative Testimonios

For scholars of childhood, activism, and art, Gonzalez and Cruz stand as an example of change through their artistic endeavors. While both engage in creative testimonio, Cruz is less known for her artistic performance than Gonzalez. Cruz, the daughter of undocumented immigrants, became a prominent figure in the immigration activism community when she was only five years old. Cruz, afraid that her parents could be deported and her family separated, wanted to engage in activism and was ultimately chosen by an immigrant rights group to give a letter to the

Pope Francis during his visit to the United States in 2015. Cruz was able to catch the Pope's attention and, despite being warned off by security, delivered a letter and a drawing. It is the drawing that is of most interest here. The letter read, in part, "Nosotros los niños somos la esperanza, la Luz [*sic*], y el futuro. Oremos juntos por mi y por ellos, para tener la fuerza de seguir luchando por nuestros sueños. Tengo fe que pronto se ira el dolor y llegara la paz."[14] While it is arguable whether Cruz herself wrote this letter (and it certainly seems influenced by the adults around her, given Cruz's own tender age at the time), the drawing is that of a typical five-year-old.

Depicting the Pope holding the hands of a group of children, Cruz ostensibly among them, the drawing is done in bright colors. The figures themselves are relatively rudimentary, with two of the female-coded figures having triangles for dresses and only several of the figures having necks or other bodily features one would expect of more advanced artwork. As with the letter, it is debatable whether Cruz was coached on the drawing; regardless, the message attached to it is something that Cruz has spoken about without adult prompting, signaling that these are her own thoughts and desires. From left to right, the drawing depicts an African American boy, a Latina girl who is likely Cruz, the Pope, an Indigenous child with unclear gender coding, a white girl, and an East Asian girl—all of whom are holding hands and are standing on equal level. The drawing itself represents difference in skin color and in dress, as the Indigenous and East Asian children are both in what appear to be traditional cultural dress. The header at the top of the drawing affirms this somewhat salad-bowl multiculturalism. It reads: "Mis amiguitos y yo nos amamos sin importar el color de nuestra piel."[15] Cruz's assertion that her friends love each other and are not concerned with each other's skin color is a sort of color-blind (to use an ableist term) anti-racism, but it is also the kind of anti-racist sentiment that makes sense for a child to assert. Children, particularly non-white children and those who live in already diverse settings like Cruz, are more likely to form interracial friendships.[16] What is more, the focus on color also dovetails with Cruz's artistic endeavors, as she is meticulous about depicting each figure in the drawing as unique and bright. As an artist/activist, Cruz's testimonio is grounded in her desire for friendship, unity, and peace. Her drawing emblematizes this youthful desire for friendship and family without borders.

In the short documentary *Free Like Birds* (2016), released the year following Cruz's crashing of the papal parade and directed by Paola Mendoza, Cruz is depicted as "a luchadora, a fighter."[17] But, while the documentary does show images of Cruz at a karate dojo learning the art of self-defense as a parallel to her fight for immigrant rights, the scenes in which Cruz is interviewed depict her at a child's table, drawing. With a pencil or crayon in her hand and a shy smile on her face, Cruz answers the documentarian's questions, often focusing on her art while talking instead of looking at the documentarian or the camera. While *Free Like Birds* does little to frame Cruz as an artist, instead focusing on her as a fighter both literally and figuratively through scenes of her activism and practicing martial arts, its subtle emphasis on her art is nevertheless significant. It is in her most reflective moments, when speaking with the filmmakers, that Cruz as the artist is revealed. What is more, her interview in this short documentary extends her testimonio. Cruz's testimonio is neither static nor constrained to her performance to contact the Pope. Because I contend that such creative testimonios effect shifts in childhood power and agency, testimonio is necessarily a long process, and Cruz's interview demonstrates that the singular moment of her performance begins a shift in the cultural values attributed to her as a Latina and a child.

Cruz's now infamous drawing and letter given to the Pope envision a child's ideal of equity and friendship. Cruz's art, however mediated, is still an extension of the artist and her testimonio. It is telling that Cruz situates her avatar in the drawing as closest to the Pope; it is she who is holding his hand and, due to her colorful dress and braids, the eye is drawn to her rather than the taller figure to the right, the Pope decked out in his white robes. That Cruz is the visual pull of this image is telling of the ways that her art reframes Latina childhood agency and power. While Cruz's letter privileges the Pope, Congress, and then President Barack Obama as the changemakers of the world, her drawing tells a different story. In rendering herself in full color, the brightest object in the drawing, Cruz asserts her visibility and, with that visibility comes power. "The youth subject is a significant and highly visible component of testimonial networks and increasingly, a distinctive affective position within contemporary activist contexts."[18] So then, Cruz's artistic testimonio is the space within which she creates a new identity for herself and then, when this testimonio enters the public gaze, it extends the power of that identity to effect shifts in the cultural coding of Latina girlhood. Put simply, her drawing simultaneously imbues her with power and effects shifts in Latina girlhood agency and autonomy.

That Cruz is held as an example through the documentary and her subsequent invitation to speak at the 2017 Women's March on Washington exemplifies the impact of her activism. Gone is the image of a powerless girl worried that her family will be deported. In her place is a young Latina who took power over her situation through creative endeavors. Likewise, Sarai Gonzalez, the star of the aforementioned Bomba Estéreo music video, impacts concerns over childhood agency and autonomy through creative testimonio in her self-assured dancing throughout the video. Gonzalez's character in the video is a "spunky, just being-yourself-kind-of girl."[19] Although this is a character Gonzalez was hired to play, she explains that this character is so close to who she is as a person, "It was pretty easy to transform into that character."[20] Indeed, the character in the video and Sarai Gonzalez are deeply intertwined. In keeping with my assertion that we can and should value Cruz's contributions despite their potential mediation, I extend this to Gonzalez, who is very clearly playing a character outside of herself. Yet, while she does not necessarily play herself in the video, the real Gonzalez nevertheless shines through, thus when discussing the music video below I refer to this character simply as Gonzalez and underline how the generative space of the music video allows Gonzalez the freedom to blend her identity with that of the character she is portraying.

Indeed, Gonzalez explains her own activist stance on representational justice and the need for nontraditional role models when in an interview, she notes, "It doesn't matter what other people think about where you come from or how you look. It just matters what you think about yourself."[21] Gonzalez's testimonio is one of self-efficacy. In a world that does not always value difference, let alone difference embodied in a young Latina, Gonzalez's testimonio resistance through dance and style challenges dominant perceptions. And, importantly, always challenges Latinx cultural expectations. Drawing on her own experiences as a bicultural Latina (her mom is Peruvian and her father is Costa Rican), Gonzalez asserts, "Just be yourself."[22] Because I assert that Gonzalez utilizes this testimonio to challenge both dominant and intracultural paradigms, her identity as a mixed-heritage Latina who is self-assured and who defies gendered norms allows for such interventions.

Gonzalez embodies this ethos with her artistic resistance. Gonzalez who, in the videos is posed against waifish white girls with long, curling hair and rail-thin bodies, is their brown, chubby shadow. The video opens with Gonzalez seated at a bustling barber shop, her hair being coiffed into an eccentric style. When she is turned in the barber chair toward the mirror, she takes in her reflection and pauses for a moment. As she takes in her appearance, expression neutral, the audience may begin to cringe. Her hair is in pigtails and braids with thick, blunt bangs—certainly not a trendy hairstyle. The audience is invited to wait with bated breath for Gonzalez to reject the hairstyle, to curl into herself in embarrassment. But she does not. Instead, she gives a satisfied smile and Bomba Estéreo's "Soy Yo" opening notes begin. To the tune of the song's jaunty gaita flute (which Gonzalez mimes by playing a recorder in the video), Gonzalez dances her way down a city block, challenging those she comes across to dance battles or a pickup game of basketball. These background characters regard Gonzalez with varying levels of confusion and condescension, but Gonzalez does not care. She shines in these scenes, always taking the spotlight.

Cristina Herrera frames Gonzalez as "this adorable chiquita nerd."[23] She further elaborates that the video is "a powerful acceptance to be who she is, haters be damned. To put it plainly, this is one badass chiquita who relishes her nerdiness."[24] I take Herrera's analysis a step further, however. Gonzalez's visible presence defies norms. She wears overalls and a funky hairstyle and Coke-bottle glasses. She *looks* different and yet she asserts a powerful sense of self, not typically attributed to this brand of Latina or child. Unlike Cruz's resistance, which is to the oppressive governmental state, Gonzalez's resistance speaks directly to the sexualization and manipulation of the Latina body in the dominant imagination. Nevertheless, both use art to assert their new epistemologies and to re-create a better world order.

Gonzalez's creative impact on cultural scripts moves beyond the "Soy Yo" music video. Like Cruz, who was the subject of a documentary and invited to the Women's

March, Gonzalez's visibility in the music video catapulted her into public consciousness. In 2018, Gonzalez and award-winning Latinx children's author Monica Brown published the first in a series of early reader chapter books inspired by Gonzalez's life. While it is difficult to say the extent to which the books are Brown's words or Gonzalez's, as Kathy G. Short notes, activist children's "dependence on adults does not negate their ability to reason and for their voices to be considered."[25] Gonzalez's participation in the books' inception and creation still signals Gonzalez's power to make change. Further, the books make Gonzalez's brand of Latina childhood accessible for young people, thus concretizing her impact on childhood culture. In my review of the first book, *Sarai and the Meaning of Awesome*, for the website Latinxs in Kid Lit, I explain, "Gonzalez and Brown ultimately weave a tale that shares its abundance of hope with a readership who needs it. In a time when Latinx children are victimized by current political ideologies, seeing Sarai take charge and resist provides a necessary counterstory."[26] The book, which recounts a fictionalized Gonzalez trying to earn money so that her grandparents can keep their house, extends Gonzalez's resistance to dominant paradigms. Although the Gonzalez in the book is also a dancer, as she is in the music video, she uses another creative skill, baking, to earn money for her family and to advocate for her grandparents. The subsequent books in the series likewise situate Gonzalez in creative and change-making endeavors, such as music and poetry.

Impacts of Change

In the end, Sophie Cruz's and Sarai Gonzalez's artistic endeavors are not meant purely to be seen. Art is often housed in museums and archives or on display in a performance for a single night, but these creative testimonios have life beyond a singular moment, not just because they are shared via social media, but because they pushed observers to rethink the ways they regard art and childhood. Mendoza, the director of *Free Like Birds*, explains that Cruz "at the age of six . . . is our nation's conscience. She is our movement's inspiration. She is one of our leaders. She is why we fight."[27] This framing of Cruz as both a leader of the movement and the impetus for change captures the impact of testimonio. I began this chapter by asserting that Latina girls are the instigators *and* inheritors of sociocultural change. Cruz and Gonzalez, through creative testimonio, are making a better world for themselves, their families, and the Latina girls who will inherit their legacies and push those legacies forward into even greater equity.

Cruz's and Gonzalez's multifaceted creative endeavors demonstrate the dexterity and flexibility of creative activism by Latina girls. And their lingering impact signals the depth to which they made cultural changes. Gonzalez and Brown's book series recently saw the publication of its fourth volume, and Cruz was featured in the mural *Sophie Holding the World Together* at the San Jose Museum of Art.[28] Both girls have taken part in advocacy work such as Cruz's speech at the Women's March and Gonzalez's public service announcements on voting in the 2020 presidential election. In an increasingly digital age, Cruz's and Gonzalez's testimonios are more widely circulated and more easily accessible. Further, both Cruz and Gonzalez, who are now adolescents, have continued to make an impact. In 2021, Cruz was interviewed to promote her school, the Knowledge is Power Program Southern California (KIPP SoCal)—a public school system that "[believes] the purpose of education is liberation, in cultivating a place and space where diverse identities are affirmed, voices are heard, and our students can envision what a just world is and feels like."[29] Cruz's example stands as one for her younger classmates as they, too, are prepared to create a more just future. Additionally, Gonzalez recently gave a TEDxYouth talk about mental health.[30] The talk explains how vital it is for people to know how to access mental health resources and for everyone, especially young people, to destigmatize mental health and know the signs of when someone is in crisis and how to help. This continued activism shows that both girls are not one-hit wonders and that their activism has a continued impact.

Even as I give these multiple examples of the impact both girls have had, it is important to reinforce that their activism is extraordinary for Latina youth. Within dominant imagination and Latinx culture, Latina girls should not have the power and influence that I have argued Cruz and Gonzalez embody. Imagining children as activists is a task at odds with multiple cultural scripts of childhood. Writing about how images of children are deployed in propaganda, Karen Dubinsky notes, "Visual representations of children are rarely literal depictions of actual children."[31] But these *are* actual children, visible not just within their communities but within the hegemony and metanarrative. Understanding this visibility as creative testimonios sets in motion the reciprocal nature of this form of activism. Testimonio, by its very nature, means that once an audience has borne witness to the act, they must *do something* as a result of the interaction. While we cannot yet measure what audiences have done with their witnessing of these creative testimonios, we are in a position to anticipate the change set in motion.

NOTES

1. Bomba Estéreo, "Soy Yo," featuring Timbaland, track 4 on *Amanecer*, Sony Latin, 2015.
2. Jessica K. Taft, *Rebel Girls: Youth Activism and Social Change Across the Americas* (New York: New York University Press, 2010), 4.
3. Norma Elia Cantú, "Memoir, Autobiography, Testimonio," in *The Routledge Companion to Latino/a Literature*, ed. Suzanne Bost and Frances R. Aparicio (Abingdon: Routledge, 2012), 322.
4. Lindsey Pérez Huber, "Disrupting Apartheid of Knowledge: *Testimonio* as Methodology in Latina/o Critical Race Research in Education," *International Journal of Qualitative Studies in Education* 22, no. 6 (2009): 644.
5. Taft, *Rebel Girls*, 80.
6. Emily Bent, "This Is Not Another Girl-Power Story: Reading Emma González as a Public Feminist Intellectual," *Signs* 45, no. 4 (2020): 798.
7. Sandra Spickard Prettyman and Elisa Gargarella, "The Power of Art to Develop Artists and Activists," *International Journal of Education & the Arts* 14, no. 2.7 (2013): 13.

8. Cara Streit, Gustavo Carlo, and Sarah E. Killoren. "Ethnic Socialization, Identity, and Values Associated with U.S. Latino/a Young Adults' Prosocial Behaviors," *Cultural Diversity & Ethnic Minority Psychology* 26, no. 1 (2020): 103.
9. Andrea Fernández-García, *Geographies of Girlhood in US Latina Writing: Decolonizing Spaces and Identities* (Cham, Switzerland: Palgrave Macmillan, 2020), 14.
10. Jill Denner and Bianca L. Guzmán, *Latina Girls: Voices of Adolescent Strength in the United States* (New York: New York University Press, 2006), 231.
11. Mario T García, *The Chicano Generation: Testimonios of the Movement* (Oakland: University of California Press, 2015), 32.
12. García, *Chicano Generation*, 32.
13. Taft, *Rebel Girls*, 6.
14. Kenneth Moton, "Meet the Little Girl Blessed by Pope Francis," ABC News, last modified September 23, 2015, https://abcnews.go.com/US/meet-young-girl-blessed-pope-francis/story?id=33981305.
15. Moton, "Meet the Little Girl."
16. Marianne Modica, *Race Among Friends: Exploring Race at a Suburban School* (New Brunswick, NJ: Rutgers University Press, 2015), 11.
17. *Free Like Birds,* directed by Paola Mendoza (2016; Mountain Film), https://www.mountainfilm.org/media/free-like-the-birds.
18. Cardell, Kylie, and Kate Douglas. "Emma González, Silence and Youth Testimony." *Women: A Cultural Review* 31, no. 1 (2020): 2.
19. FUSION, "Life Advice from the Girl in Bomba Estéreo's "Soy Yo" Music Video," YouTube video, 2:10, October 11, 2016, https://www.youtube.com/watch?v=xoiiosTU7lo.
20. FUSION, "Life Advice."
21. FUSION, "Life Advice."
22. FUSION, "Life Advice."
23. Cristina Herrera, *ChicaNerds in Chicana Young Adult Literature: Brown and Nerdy* (New York: Routledge, 2021), 19.
24. Herrera, *ChicaNerds*, 19.
25. Kathy G. Short, "The Right to Participate: Children as Activists in Picturebooks," in *Critical Content Analysis of Children's and Young Adult Literature: Reframing Perspective*, ed. Holly Johnson, Janelle Mathis, and Kathy G. Short (New York: Routledge, 2016), 139.
26. Cristina Rhodes, "Book Review: *Sarai and the Meaning of Awesome* by Sarai Gonzalez & Monica Brown, illus. by Christine Almeda," Latinxs in Kid Lit, last modified November 8, 2018, https://latinxsinkidlit.com/2018/11/08/book-review-sarai-and-the-meaning-of-awesome-by-sarai-gonzalez-monica-brown-illus-by-christine-almeda/.
27. "Sophie Cruz and Migrants' Rights," Girl Museum, June 25, 2021, https://www.girlmuseum.org/sophie-cruz-and-migrants-rights.
28. "A Mural of Hope," San Jose Museum of Art, https://sjmusart.org/mural-hope.
29. "About KIPP SoCal," KIPP SoCal, last modified 2022, https://www.kippsocal.org/about/index.
30. TEDx Talks, "Mental Illness: Do You Understand? | Sarai Gonzalez | TEDxYouth@WHRHS," YouTube video, 13:48, July 13, 2021, https://youtu.be/d1zmJPtfOFk.
31. Karen Dubinsky, "Children, Ideology, and Iconography: How Babies Rule the World," *Journal of the History of Childhood & Youth* 5, no. 1 (2012): 12.

7

Acting Up

Child Actors as Authors and Collaborators in Contemporary World Cinema

PETER C. KUNZE

Nine years before he directed and wrote the Oscar-winning *Jojo Rabbit* (2019), Taika Waititi made another coming-of-age story, *Boy* (2010). Set in his Waititi's native New Zealand in 1984, *Boy* follows Alamein, a Māori child nicknamed "Boy" and played by eleven-year-old actor James Rolleston. Although Boy has been effectively abandoned by his father (Taika Waititi), he continues to worship him as a hero. In his father's absence, Boy attempts to carry himself with a more mature swagger, imitating the idealized masculine role model he imagines his father to be. When his father returns, Boy experiences hope, excitement, and finally the disappointment that his immature father will not be the father figure he so desperately desires. In this way, *Boy* alternates between comedy and melodrama in its inversion of the father-son relationship and its focus on fractured family relationships. As the title character, Rolleston bears the lion's share of the dramatic responsibility in the film, generating not only many of its laughs but ultimately demonstrating its heart.

In a climactic moment, a heartbroken Boy confronts his father, revealing that the buried money his father has been looking for has already been found—and eaten by one of the household goats (see Figure 7.1). Boy empties a bag of shredded money before his father as he coldly asserts, "There's your treasure." As his seated father goes to respond in anger, Boy, standing before him, slaps him across the face. Rolleston bites his lip and stares intently at Waititi. The father recovers, but as he shouts, "You little shit," Rolleston grimaces and slaps him again. Rolleston lunges forward, attempting to shake Waititi. The father does not fight back, instead attempting to restrain his son. Rolleston furrows his brow, muttering how he does not remember his father and demanding he explain where he was. Waititi makes his eyes bulge to convey the father's surprise at Boy's change in temperament and enactment of punishment, perhaps finally understanding and accepting the legitimacy of Boy's critiques and his own inadequacies as a father. This devastating scene is a sobering moment: the amiable, naive Boy has

FIGURE 7.1 Boy (James Rolleston) confronts his father (Taika Waititi).

romanticized his father to his friends and to himself, forgiving or ignoring his myriad shortcomings. But, in this scene, Rolleston sets aside the warm, goofy Boy he has portrayed until then, exploding with the anger he has been repressing. This cathartic moment is startling not only for its dramatic shift, but also for the skill with which the young actor delivers the scene.

Despite his clear talent, Rolleston's moving performance is inevitably crafted through the combination of his efforts and Waititi's screenplay and direction, as well as through the technical contributions of the cinematographer and editor, among others. Filmmaking is an inherently collaborative process, and as such, it does not lend itself to the models of authorship initially developed, frequently employed, and heavily debated by literature scholars. (Of course, that does not mean some film critics and scholars have not deployed them via auteur theory, an approach to film analysis that has been roundly criticized yet profoundly influential.) My point here is that studying child performance on-screen provides an avenue for examining child-produced culture which is not wholly distinguishable from the influence, intervention, and contribution of adults. In what follows, I frame screen performances by child actors as what Victoria Ford Smith calls "intergenerational collaborations"; whereas Smith turns to Victorian culture, especially literature, I would argue that a focus on recent world cinema provides at least one avenue for applying her thinking about the "larger investigation of the limits and possibilities of child agency taking place in a range of discourses and cultural venues" to a twenty-first-century global context.[1] While these collaborations are neither equal nor equitable, they nevertheless depend on directed and self-directed individual contributions. It also helps us to rethink agency and authorship in ways that may enrich not only film studies, but also other disciplines' investigations into similar concerns.

Studying Child Performance

The initial challenge in a critical study of child performances like Rolleston's is defining the object of study itself. Indeed, child performances are often performances of childhood by children themselves, extending how we may think through the concept of children's performativity because childhood itself has been read as a performance embodied by young people. As Robin Bernstein has observed, "Performance does not make children or childhood alone; rather, it is through performance that children and childhood coemerge and co-constitute each other."[2] My purposes here are fairly traditional in the application of "performance," strictly focusing on screen acting by children, but I share Bernstein's interest in its implications for our critical understanding of childhood. In what follows, I define "child" in its traditional Western understanding as under the age of thirteen, and my examples will include toddlers, young children, and preteens. My goal here is not to distinguish child performers as inherently different from their adolescent or adult counterparts; rather, it is the exact opposite. I hope to show that efforts to distinguish child and nonchild actors on the basis of craft or effectiveness are subjective and arbitrary. As such, I am more interested in the similarities between child performers and their elder counterparts at the level of artistry and storytelling than the alleged differences.

Earlier film studies scholarship on child performers has focused on child stars, especially white, presumably middle- or upper-class children in mainstream Hollywood fare. Unsurprisingly, Shirley Temple remains the most studied, not only for her popularity and commercial success, but also for her enduring cultural influence.[3] Sociologist Jane O'Connor historicizes and examines child stardom as a sociocultural phenomenon, while film studies scholars have produced individual case studies on the likes of Jackie Coogan, Freddie Bartholomew, and Hibari Misora.[4] More recent efforts consider the Disney tween stars as well as the rise of child performers in social media entertainment.[5] Much of this work tends to take an ideological approach that situates the performer within discourses of childhood or a historical perspective that connects industry logics and trends with the actor's career. What is less often studied in this important work is the actual screen performance that the child delivers, though this is changing with important contributions specifically out of film studies in the United Kingdom, including Karen Lury's *The Child in Film: Tears, Fears, and Fairy Tales* (2010); a 2012 dossier in *Screen*, coedited by Michael Lawrence and Susan Smith; and, more recently, Catherine O'Rawe's *The Non-Professional Actor: Italian Neorealist Cinema and Beyond* (2023). The shift from the meanings of the child image to a close analysis of the child performance on-screen not only expands critical attention to acting (by adults) further to include children and enriches scholarly interest in historical and contemporary discourses of childhood but offers a generative opportunity to examine and retheorize young people's agency in cultural production.

The limited attention to child performance prior to Lury, Lawrence, and Smith echoes a larger neglect within film and media studies of acting as a vital contribution to film production. This claim is not to suggest acting has gone completely ignored; after all, James Naremore's foundational study, *Acting in the Cinema*, was published in 1988.[6] Star studies, inspired in large part by Richard Dyer's seminal 1979 work, *Stars*, tends to focus on the star image, which includes and extends beyond the screen performance to include the range of discourses that help construct and maintain the star's public persona.[7] As a result, Pamela Robertson Wojcik notes, "close descriptions of individual performances" are forsaken in favor of broader issues that can be traced and examined across a body of texts, including films, interviews, publicity, and promotional materials.[8] Focused analyses of screen performances have improved in recent years, as seen in edited collections such as Murray Pomerance and Kyle Stevens's two-volume *Close-Up: Great Cinema Performances*, but even there we see no chapter on a child actor's performance, despite the crucial role of child actors in numerous cinematic masterpieces.[9] This point is less a criticism of Pomerance, Stevens, and their volumes than an attempt to underscore an implicit presumption noticeable across a great deal of film studies scholarship on acting. Indeed, the idea of a child actor delivering a crafted performance that demonstrates deliberate, revelatory decisions to convey emotion and meaning seems beyond most critics and scholars. When a child actor develops a superb screen performance, it is almost treated as fortuitous, even preternatural. In his review of *The Florida Project* (Sean Baker, 2017), for example, Justin Chang of the *Los Angeles Times* marvels how six-year-old Brooklynn Prince "goes so far beyond the precocious mugging that often passes for child acting that it all but defies that classification."[10] More often, child actors are seemingly understood as functionaries facilitating their more skilled adult counterparts or being deployed by the "true" author: the director.

The primary critical focus on the director, inspired by the auteur theory, displaces and erases the artistic contributions of directors' many collaborators. Although it was roundly critiqued from the time of its arrival in the United States in the 1960s, most famously by Pauline Kael, the auteur theory remains pervasive in popular film criticism as well as academic film studies.[11] In both arenas, critics and scholars alike have resisted the romanticization of film authorship with attention to screenwriters, producers, editors, actors, and even the studio system itself.[12] The auteur remains alluring in part because of its roots in literary approaches, wherein the director, like the poet, is an inspired artist working both within and against the constraints of their time to express themselves authentically. Marketing, advertising, and film criticism today continue to demonstrate what Timothy Corrigan calls "the commerce of auteurism"—that is, promoting a film on the basis of the supposed "auteur" responsible for it.[13] Despite this discursive persistence, notions of the author (or auteur) as singular, uncompromised, and authentic have been thoroughly scrutinized, especially in film, where a range of competencies are required to successfully complete a project.

The child performer is a productive focus for a study of authorship because, on the one hand, it is understood that the child is not performing according to their own devices alone. The director and the scene partner(s) are clearly making a creative contribution, as are the cinematographer, editor, and a range of other filmmaking craftspeople. And yet, to some unclear and indeterminate degree, the child performer is working to deliver a combination of talent, craft, responsiveness to direction, and fortunate accidents that ultimately comprise so-called movie magic. Therefore, the child performer on screen—and, by extension, on stage—exercises a degree of agency that is both hard to determine and yet impossible to refute.[14] As Linda Ruth Williams astutely notes in her analysis of Henry Thomas's performance in *E. T. the Extra-terrestrial* (Steven Spielberg, 1982), "The child actor is often framed as exploited, but (particularly in tearjerkers) he also exploits."[15] We can hopefully agree that the child performer does not act (in both senses of the term) alone while also acknowledging that their contribution is quite often a crucial element of a film's emotional resonance. An adult actor saying the same lines, making the same gestures, and mimicking the same expressions seems unlikely to produce the same affective response from the same audiences. A child actor's voice, face, and body are their instruments, and their ability to skillfully employ their physicality for storytelling purposes is crucial to a film's success as an artistic effort and, quite often, a commercial endeavor.

And yet, as Karen Lury observes, we do not imagine that children do not have access to the same language used by their adult counterparts to articulate the craft behind their appearance.[16] If a child actor were to sincerely tell an interviewer of their training, technique, and decision-making process, they would be seen as humorous or pretentious, perhaps just *strange*. Lury notes that they must be child-like without being childish, yet their performance is often imagined as either the result of being themselves or being oddly precocious.[17] There is a critical hesitation or even refusal to understand child actors as artists who craft performances in their own right, perhaps because we cannot imagine them as capable of such deliberation and intentionality. Yet how much intentionality must be behind an actor's performance to make it effective or "good"? Considering child performers as actors reminds us of the blend of intention and accident as well as the expression and manipulation within any actor's performance.

Studying child performers as actors, therefore, requires us to accept the disconnect between intention and result that is true of any actor's performance. It reminds us that agency can be expressed both purposefully and accidentally, and that the expression of that agency also may bear the mark of other collaborators, also contributing in a range of ways between intention and accident. As Marah Gubar notes in her discussion of child actors on the Victorian stage, "They modeled a form of nonautonomous agency in which being scripted by adults did not necessarily preclude them from functioning as intelligent, creative individuals."[18] To this end, we might say that the differences between the child performer and their adult collaborator are largely artificial, leading Gubar to argue that children and adults sharing the stage together as equals "undercut[s] the notion that children were a race apart."[19] Similarly, Victoria Ford Smith argues that analyzing such intergenerational collaborations reveals how the long-held, highly politicized distinctions between both groups cannot be maintained.[20] Close analysis of child actors' performances, therefore, complicates not only our notions of performance but of child authorship and of childhood itself.

While performance offers us rich possibilities for reexamining how we discuss children's agency, it also poses significant challenges for scholars in terms of how to do so. Child performances can be studied in a range of ways, including ethnographic approaches and interviews, but for my purposes here, I am interested in close textual analysis, specifically of performance. I turn to Cynthia Baron and Sharon Marie Carnicke, whose 2008 book *Reframing Screen Performance* calls upon scholars to study "the aesthetic choices actually seen on screen" because "what the actor does within the frame with body and voice, rhythm and movement, matters more than the presumed creative process."[21] Baron and Carnicke's charge reminds us that attention to intentionality, as literature scholars have long known, is often misdirected and futile. What we see clearly evident on screen, however, is ripe for analysis and interpretation. I adapt Baron and Carnicke's emphasis on "expressions, gestures, intonations, and inflections" to pay particular attention to what child actors do with their faces, limbs (especially hands), voices, and bodies.[22] Building upon the important work on earlier child stars, I extend the conversation by focusing on the crafted performances of actors of color in films produced outside of Hollywood that operate across different genres. Each respective performer—Zain Al Rafeea in *Capernaum* (Nadine Labaki, 2019), Maggie Mulubwa in *I Am Not a Witch* (Rungano Nyoni, 2017), and Myra Vishwakarma in *Pihu* (Vinod Kapri, 2019)—provides me with the opportunity to consider various theoretical concerns in studying, analyzing, and interpreting child performance. Doing so allows scholars to see not so much intention but action as an expression of child agency within screen media and within child-produced culture specifically. It also encourages us to see the child actor not as a symbol or sieve for ideological meanings but as an artist working within the entertainment industries.

Performing Childhood and Adulthood in *Capernaum*

In several ways, *Capernaum*, the 2019 Nadine Labaki film about a young Lebanese boy seeking independence from his abusive parents, directly extends from the Italian neorealist tradition. Much attention has been paid in the press to twelve-year-old lead actor Zain Al Rafeea being a nonprofessional actor as well as a Syrian refugee, and the loose, realistic storytelling nevertheless unfolds in a melodramatic mode, emphasizing personal struggle, morally conflicted situations, and emotionally gut-wrenching moments similar to those in *Roma città aperta* (*Rome, Open City*, Roberto Rossellini, 1945) and *Ladri di biciclette* (*Bicycle Thieves*, Vittorio De Sica, 1948).[23] Yet it also engages several social issues confronting contemporary

Lebanon, including immigration, poverty, sex trafficking, child exploitation, and human rights more broadly.

Since the lead character and the actor portraying him share a first name, I will refer to the character as "Zain" and the actor portraying him as "Al Rafeea" to avoid confusion in the analysis that follows. The film opens with Al Rafeea in a long shot, wearing only his underwear. His right leg is forward, turned out. His hands fall slack. His head is turned slightly to the left, eyes looking toward the camera. He glances around the room, scratches his leg. He is bored, perhaps unclear on why he is there. (The audience, too, is unclear on the nature of this scene.) He looks up. The next shot jumps ahead, where a doctor is examining his mouth. Al Rafeea looks forward passively, perhaps with defeat. The doctor turns off camera, reporting that Zain has lost his baby teeth and is perhaps twelve or thirteen years old. We then cut to a shot showing Rahil (Yordanos Shiferaw), a young Ethiopian migrant worker, in a line being interrogated by an off-screen voice. She answers with resignation, staring at her unseen interrogator. Both her and Zain's fates will soon intersect.

The film then transitions to the past, where we see Zain as a precocious child afflicted by poverty and the neglect of his downtrodden parents. His beloved sister Sahar (Cedra Izam) is forced to marry the shopkeeper (Nour el Husseini), an adult at least a decade older than the frightened young girl. Upset, Zain runs away and meets Rahil, who allows him to stay with her in exchange for babysitting her son, Yonas (Boluwatife Treasure Bankole). But Rahil's subsequent arrest for expired papers deputizes Zain as Yonas' full-time caregiver. While he initially manages the task, he soon becomes irritable and frustrated by the exhausting responsibility. A merchant (Alaa Chouchnieh), who Zain naively does not realize is a human trafficker, compels Zain to surrender Yonas to him. He also promises to assist Zain in leaving Lebanon, assuming he can provide the proper ID paperwork. This charge requires Zain to return to the home he has abandoned.

Al Rafeea must display a broad range of emotion from confidence to vulnerability to anger in this tense scene. He walks up the stairs slowly, almost meditatively. Tears are in his eyes as he slowly enters the room. He puts out his father's (Fadi Kamel Youssef) cigarette as he watches him sleep on the couch. Despite all the pain his family has caused, Zain still desires to protect his parents, evidence of the forced maturation he has experienced. He goes through drawers, examining the papers. He checks in on the crying siblings. He rejects his mother's (Kawthar Al Haddad) questions. He merely stares at her as she hits him. He insists he is not here to see her or his father; he only wants his papers. He says so assertively, as any parental authority they may have had is now void. His mother sarcastically responds, waking up the father. Irritated, his father tells him no one cares about us. Zain throws down a toy, but the father reminds him, "Don't play the big man with me, you little shit!" He grabs him by the shirt, and Zain acquiesces. He looks down, head tilted as his father goes through eviction notices and a hospital bill. He attempts to restrain his emotion as his eyes alternate between his father and the hospital bill. "We're insects, my friend. Don't you get it? We're parasites." His father's anger attempts to mask the embarrassing reality that there are no official documents to give him. He remains stoic, and his father impatiently throws him through the door and curses him. His mother now tries to protect him.

Al Rafeea shifts here from the adultlike confidence he has exuded to a more childlike ignorance, steeped in the fear of what might have happened. Zain innocently asks who went to the hospital. His mother says no more. He asks again, standing firm. He says it directly, but Al Rafeea expresses a slight hesitation in his voice to convey that Zain fears the possible answer. His persistence indicates an awareness that he is being protected from information, but any notion of his innocence was robbed of him long ago by his circumstances and misfortunes. Backing off, he instead affectionately asks his siblings who is in the hospital. His father threatens him further, insisting he leave. Al Rafeea's grimaces in pain as tears well in his eyes. His voice is strained as he insists on knowing who is in the hospital. He uses his left arm to gently shake his mother, demanding an answer he already seems to know. He ignores his father's protests as empty threats, attempts at self-preservation, but he remains persistent. His mother seems alternately embarrassed and defeated. His father begins to cry, and Zain steps back and cries. He gasps, using a hand to wipe his left eye. His pain turns to anger as he demands to know what this "motherfucker"—the shopkeeper who married his sister against her will—did to her. Al Rafeea pivots from ignorant child to weary but assertive adult. He walks over and pushes his father. His face is tear stained, his eyes, heavy. Realizing his sister is now gone, Zain takes action; Al Rafeea staggers to the kitchen and retrieves a butcher's knife. "I'll show you who's who, who's gone," he threatens as he runs out and down the stairs. He takes on the role he thinks his father should—the role his father failed to play when Saher was handed over. Al Rafeea indicates that the son has become the father, as Zain's desperate escape underscores a manic assertiveness. We learn soon after that the opening examination was part of his imprisonment for the attempted murder of the shopkeeper.

Despite its melodramatic storytelling, somewhat defused by its shaky camerawork to suggest some attempt at documentary-like authenticity, the film actively inverts its generic claims. Whereas the family melodrama traditionally exploits these emotional moments for dramatic effect and audience pleasure, ultimately leading toward the repair of the damaged relationship(s) and reunification of the family, the opening and final scenes of *Capernaum* underscore the active, necessary dissolution of the family unit as Zain pursues emancipation and, finally, documentation. Yes, Rahil ultimately is reunited with her son—a moment played for maximum emotional effect—but Zain's resolution offers no such reaffirmation of familial bonds. Instead, he finds us again in a government office, being instructed by an off-screen voice to stand on the line. He acquiesces with mild irritation. Al Rafeea's eyes remain heavy, while his face is fallen in resignation to his situation. The camera is now in a close-up, focused exclusively on Al Rafeea's face, which betrays a bittersweet combination of promising youth and world-weariness. His

FIGURE 7.2 Zain's (Zain Al Rafeea) smile expresses relief and hope.

eyes are heavy, his lips together and pushed slightly forward. The off-screen voice, until then a disembodied representation of state authority, flatly muses, "Smile, Zain. This is for your ID card, not your death certificate!" Al Rafeea tries and fails to stifle a smile, and his eyes brighten. With a flash of the camera, the shot becomes a freeze frame, and a melancholic violin solo plays nondiegetically as the camera very slowly tracks in before fading to black (see Figure 7.2). This final image—a long-awaited smile, frozen in time—hearkens back to *Les quatre cents coups* (*The 400 Blows*, 1959), where François Truffaut ends his classic study of juvenile delinquency with a freeze-frame of Antoine (Jean-Pierre Léaud) staring into the camera. But whereas Léaud's face is an ambivalent combination of freedom and fear, Al Rafeea's smirk conveys hope.

Capernaum demands a lot of its young actor. Whereas children in Italian neorealism are often supporting characters, left to motivate the adult protagonists and evince discourses of futurity for the audience, Al Rafeea carries the film, appearing in almost every scene. And his performance consequently has him ebbing and flowing, from exhaustion to anger and finally to relief, even joy. As such, it is perhaps easier to analyze and assess his performance in its ability to demonstrate the kind of range expected of adult actors, especially by Western standards of "good" acting. But as Al Rafeea plays various roles here—son, brother, roommate, surrogate parent—he also must waver between being a child and an adult by virtue of his varying circumstances. As discussed above, when Zain returns to retrieve his papers, Al Rafeea's performance accordingly must alternate between the vulnerability and passivity of a child, seeking the knowledge of the circumstances being denied to him by adults who feel he does not need to know and perhaps cannot handle it. Of course, when he does learn, his sorrow becomes anger, and he acts decisively in a way that recalls the kinds of assertive actions he has been taking as Yonas's reluctant protector.

In moving between childhood and adulthood, Al Rafeea's performance brings to mind Bernstein's observation above, which reminds us of the performative aspects of both "stages" of life. His ability to do so not only effectively but affectively conveys both a skill and an agency, perhaps cultivated and compromised by his collaborators—most obviously, Labaki, who also appears on-screen as Zain's legal representative. If both childhood and adulthood can be performed, then they are both "scripted" and constructed. As such, performance analysis not only provides an opportunity to better understand the agency of the creative child, but it also helps us to extend and enhance the ongoing critical examination of the child image in screen media and culture.

Consistency and Variability in *I Am Not A Witch*

In Rungano Nyoni's *I Am Not A Witch* (2017), a young girl named Shula (Maggie Mulubwa) unexplainedly appears in a village, inspiring a range of reactions in the individuals she meets. From the panicked cries of "witch!" by the villagers to the opportunistic machinations of a local bureaucrat, Mr. Banda (Henry B. J. Phiri), these varied responses paint a rich, conflicted, satirical tableau of the Zambian community in a manner not unlike Gabriel García Márquez's fable, *Un señor muy viejo con unas alas enormes* "A Very Old Man with Enormous Wings"). Indeed, the girl becomes a tablet of sorts unto which the community inscribes its fears, desires, interests, and shortcomings. Consequently, Mulubwa's performance is often fairly serious and unaffected. Her solemnity and stoicism prompt the question, "How much *performing* must one do to deliver a 'performance' as it is used in evaluations and analyses of acting?" In this section, I argue that Mulubwa's flat affect reveals quite more than we might imagine. The question of how much acting is necessary for "good acting" is subjective and ultimately pointless. Instead, we might focus on how what Mulubwa does not do still constitutes what she is doing, thereby providing us an opportunity to think more reflectively about acting, performance, and agency in the process. Furthermore, as the silent child figure, she also reminds us of the expectations, fears, and agenda inscribed onto young people's bodies by the adults charged with nurturing and protecting them.

The film opens with a group of primarily white tourists being taken to see a camp of women, who are later revealed to be witches. As the tourists wander in front of the barricade, the witches shake their hands and chat. The camera tracks left to right, capturing this performance for the white Western eyes, in many ways proxies for the Western viewers that may consume this film, a coproduction between Zambia, France, Germany, and the United Kingdom. The film sets up an opposition between these tourists (and the Black tour guide who brings them to the site) and the women who are being put on display for the amusement of these visiting Westerners. The subsequent scene, however, cuts to a villager (Eunice Mapala) filling a water bucket. On her walk back home, she stumbles, falls, and spills the water. The scene immediately cuts to a medium close-up of a young girl observing the fall. Mulubwa's face betrays no emotion, aside from a possible resigned sadness in her eyes. Her arms are slack at her side, and her mouth closed.

The next shot is an over-the-shoulder shot behind the girl, revealing the woman on the ground looking at her, surprised at the inaction of the girl toward her fall. The woman runs off, leaving the girl with the bucket. The following scene features a long shot that shows the girl returning the bucket, full of water, to the woman's home. The girl struggles to place it on the front steps, and when her knocks are not answered, she sits on the stairs, taps her foot, and looks off into the distance. Unbeknownst to the girl, the woman has appeared at the window, looking down at this mysterious helper. A voiceover from the next scene—a J cut, in film editing terms—of the woman accusing the girl of being a witch provides a sound bridge into the next scene where Shula stands before the local magistrate, while the panicked village observes. One man accuses the girl of having cut off his arm with an axe. The gruesome story is immediately defused when he admits it was a dream, prompting his dismissal by the magistrate. Men leaning in the window continue to harangue the girl, accusing her of being a witch, but Mulubwa still does not react. In the next scene, a back shot reveals a bureaucrat being bathed in a Western-style house that sharply contrasts to the village setting. He receives a call informing him about the unknown visitor. Corrupt and opportunistic, his scheming exploits the girl while furthering his lofty ambitions. Across these four scenes, Nyoni lays out the varying power dynamics of her film: West versus East, young versus old, men versus women, individual versus society. And with a seemingly passive Mulubwa at the center, the girl's passivity captures the cruelty inherent to each of those tensions.

Throughout *I Am Not a Witch*, the girl, soon renamed Shula by a witch, faces a range of reactions from the people she encounters that vary from care to exploitation. When she embarrasses Mr. Banda, for instance, he verbally accosts her, but she resists his aggression. Mulubwa merely leans back and blinks, obscuring her mouth with her garment. She only occasionally speaks, yet the camera is consistently centered on her reactions, focalizing the narrative through her experience of this often hostile environment. The film consequently alternates between a gentle social satire and a devastating critique of the mistreatment of children, especially young girls.

This oscillation is perhaps most evident in the end of the film. The camera tracks across the faces of schoolchildren, including Shula, playing telephone. Shula seems content: while the sadness remains in her eyes, she willfully engages in the game with her classmates. The camera cuts to a back shot, revealing the tether that witches are required to wear. Suddenly, Shula is pulled away by the tether. She reaches above her to grasp the tether, but her face remains relaxed, even stoic, as if resigned once more to the violence against her. A cut reveals her point of view, as we see a low-angle tracking shot of the trees she sees as she is pulled. We next see her in a cart. She has been kidnapped because it is believed she can help conjure rain. A long shot shows Shula sitting. She stands up and shuffles, moving her arms and hands in a rapidly increasing manner. The shot cuts to a low-angle close-up. Mulubwa's face is solemn, but her hands flap energetically, as if she is desperately trying to fulfill her charge despite her lack of understanding of witchcraft. The nondiegetic music underscores the urgency and panic Shula feels. Finally, a cut to the sun as the music fades away. The camera tilts down to show Shula continuing to dance, though much slower now, from left to right, as she picks up the dry crops and places them on her head. She stumbles, yet recovers, continuing to dance. She hums, but her labored breaths betray her exhaustion. The witches look on. Finally, a low-angle close-up shot of her legs reveals her urinating. She is finally carried off, completely exhausted; Mulubwa slackens her body and breathes laboriously. The cut this time takes us to her sleeping in a tentlike structure. The off-screen voice of an older woman asks her to explain why she is upset. Others join the inquiry, and Shula reveals she should have been a goat, since they can move and act freely. The women protest, telling her she would be eaten if that were the case. The scene jumps ahead to sometime later that night, where Shula arises, looks around, and exits the tent. She follows her tether through the dark. The camera fades to black. We learn soon after she has died, a victim of the enduring cruelty she has faced at the hands of the villagers and the bureaucrat.

Mulubwa's performance throughout the film is remarkably consistent. Unlike Rolleston and Al Rafeea, whose performances are marked by an ability to modulate and alternate, it is the consistency of Mulubwa's performance that makes it so effective—and ultimately haunting. Whereas many acting performances are celebrated in terms of their ability to move effortlessly between tones and emotions, the debut performance here by Mulubwa, a nonprofessional much like her counterparts in the Italian neorealist films, challenges us to develop alternate ways of assessing performance beyond seemingly effortless alternation and credible realism. Indeed, Shula persists, and Mulubwa captures that with a stoicism that conveys both acceptance and perseverance (see Figure 7.3). Mulubwa's slow movement of her eyes, her measured blinks, and a certain surrender in her face seem to suggest that the character's passivity is chosen rather than imposed. Since we do not get a climactic dramatic moment in the Hollywood sense in which Mulubwa gets

FIGURE 7.3 Shula's (Maggie Mulubwa) flat affect becomes a canvas for others' anxieties.

to act out or demonstrate that Shula has matured or resisted, one's understanding of her performance may be perhaps biased toward confusion or indifference. Her work here, though, is to conceal the work. In turn, much like the townspeople, the audience projects its own meanings onto Shula. I would argue the agency here is both an act of collaboration with Nyoni and others as well as a reminder to reconsider the criteria of evaluating acting performance, particularly its Western-influenced, Hollywood-shaped biases.

Pihu and the Question of Intention

What makes the Indian thriller *Pihu* particularly interesting for the scholar of child performance is its singular focus on the two-year-old child actor, Myra Vishwakarma. The film's premise is simple: a young mother has committed suicide, leaving her toddler to fend for herself in their apartment. As the title character Pihu, Vishwakarma's only visible costar is her mother's corpse (Prerna Sharma, Myra's real-life mother), leaving the young actress to carry the film. Filmmaker Vinod Kapri revealed that Vishwakarma's age meant they could only film for two hours a day, often following her around in the process.[24] Furthermore, her young age raises the question about how well she could take direction, let alone memorize a scripted part. Consequently, it appears that a great deal of the film was cobbled together from Vishwakarma moving about the space and being put into various scenarios. Therefore, as an acting performance, this reality may, in fact, give Vishwakarma more creative agency in the process. It fundamentally renegotiates traditional understandings of the actor and director relationship, placing more emphasis, too, on the cinematographer's, camera operators', and editor's roles in the process. Admittedly, *Pihu* is not the familiar collaborative cinematic effort we often imagine, but its exceptionality invites reconsideration of performance and agency in original and productive ways.

The film opens with giggling children and the patter of the attending parents. Chalk animations create a celebratory atmosphere, and it soon becomes clear that this is a child's birthday party. Pihu and her mother are introduced as a loving relationship. At the outset, it seems the film will be a lighthearted family film. But as the film cuts to live-action, the shot mimics the eyes of Pihu waking up. The story is focalized through Pihu, and the slow music creates a distinct contrast from the liveliness of the day before. This is the morning after: the house is now quiet, left in disarray from the previous day's celebration. Pihu is unable to wake her mother. What begins as a cute romp as Pihu explores the house on her own quickly becomes much darker as new dangers emerge—climbing stairs, popping balloons, running water, standing on an unsteady stepstool—and place her in peril. These varying risks, in turn, underscore her vulnerability without her mother's supervision. It also becomes clear that her mother is not sleeping, but instead has died: Pihu cannot awaken her after pained attempts and a suicide note scrawled on a mirror becomes visible. The film consequently varies from whimsy to suspense as

Pihu engages in consistently unsafe behavior and the possibility of adult intervention meets ongoing obstacles. *Pihu* claustrophobically keeps its viewers in the apartment with its title character, powerless to help her themselves. It never cuts to show us the trash man or guards or maintenance workers knocking on the other side of the door. Through phone calls, we hear—but do not see—Pihu's father, who is in Kolkata on business, as he excoriates his wife, checks in on Pihu, and (later) frantically tries to get home as he realizes something is awry. The child in peril has long been a convention within world cinema, but while those films frequently employ a melodramatic mode, *Pihu* more often uses suspense, curiously alternating between its generic claims to the commercial thriller and the socially conscious family drama.

In a series of increasingly more dangerous incidents, Pihu goes outside and looks out over the town as a series of high-angle and low-angle shots emphasize the precarity of her situation (see Figure 7.4). A low-angle shot through the grates in medium close-up would presumably place the camera on the other side of the rails, high above the city. While this shot lets us know the danger she is in, it also does the opposite, since such a shot if really done high above the city would be costly, challenging, and dangerous (save the use of some kind of drone technologies). Ironically, it reminds us of the staged nature of this study of child endangerment. Vishwakarma grips the rail and looks off frame, her voice modulating to capture the realistic way a child might call for someone she wants but cannot see. Vishwakarma's face is largely expressionless: Pihu still does not grasp that her mother is dead nor the severity of the dangerous state she is in. Her right hand rocks back and forth on the rails as her eyes seem to survey around her. Her mouth is ajar. Pihu calls out to her mother again. Vishwakarma pats the rail, calls loudly for the unseen Ishika below, and purses her lips. She pours water over the edge in amusement, much to the consternation of the people below. She pats back her hair with swift brushes of her palms. Her doll falls over the railing and lands on a pair

FIGURE 7.4 A shot from behind Myra Vishwakarma conveys Pihu's increasing peril.

of wires. She looks over to get it, trying to use her feet to assist her. The doll finally falls, a warning of what could happen to Pihu if she is not saved. Although her father is now rushing to get home, it seems unlikely he will be her savior.

Vishwakarma's actions unfold naturally in large part because they are completed at the toddler's discretion. She rocks back and forth, she tries to climb, and she remains unaware of the danger as seen by her smile and strain. This moment seems the most extreme form of the possible dangers. Its suspense is heightened by the naivete of the child and the awareness of the camera and, eventually, the off-screen voice of a concerned woman ("aunty"). But Pihu is nevertheless OK: killing off the protagonist—and singular character—is narratively impossible, and since Pihu is both so young and so defenseless, it is also inexcusable. In a way, one might understand *Pihu* as an ironic inversion of *Home Alone* (Chris Columbus, 1990); unlike the parental neglect that allows Kevin (Macaulay Culkin) to take control of the house and assert his dominance in protection of his home, here parental neglect leaves Pihu vulnerable to the myriad everyday dangers of the house. It therefore prompts a bit of an ethical dilemma: Are we watching this endangered child out of a sense of social concern or for the pleasure derived from a sadistic series of what-ifs? It also remains unclear to what extent Vishwakarma's actions are scripted or improvisational. The young star ultimately raises questions about the role of intention in the study of child-produced culture. The nature of the film, reaffirmed by the director, follows an almost documentary-like aesthetic in its use of tracking shots, its focus on the quotidian, its real-time pacing. While intention may be implicitly presumed within studies of acting, it seems unlikely that the actress has carefully planned a performance through rehearsal and preparation. But since she is the sole star, it is hard to deny she is not paramount to the production of the film. In fact, as mentioned earlier, the director has suggested that he spent a great deal of time with her and the film was made in short periods of filming over several weeks. So, while she is the youngest actress I examine here, the least likely to have formal training, and the least likely to carefully craft her performance, the quasi-improvisational nature of the film and the difficulty of carefully manipulating the performance of a two-year-old may in fact make her the most agential of the performers discussed in this study.

But since intention is arguably eroded or nonexistent, we must ask ourselves about the role of intentionality in theorizing child agency. One solution may be to think of agency not as steadfast and singular, but as a range of modes of action and expression. While Myra Vishwakarma's performance may not be a clear act of intentioned (and unintentioned) craft, it is an act of creation rooted in play, itself an important and often underestimated demonstration of childhood agency. One may understand her performance as mere play, but since the play is being limited and shaped, then recorded, edited, and released as a commercial film, it nevertheless becomes work. Consequently, a close analysis of Vishwakarma's performance in *Pihu* encourages us to think of the diverse ways in which children express agency, intentionally and unintentionally, and the broad scope that studying creativity and cultural production entails.

Conclusion

When we study art forms other than literature, we are quickly reminded that collaboration is fundamental and singular authorship is largely illusory, self-serving, and impractical. Agency is often used interchangeably with intentionality, but to what extent might fortuitous accidents constitute agency without intention? The emphasis on play as a form of intentional not-seriousness reminds us that one can act without a desired effect and yet still produce something interesting of value. The films discussed herein were produced as commercial endeavors; therefore, these young actors' "play" is work performed within an entertainment industry. We must consider modes of authorship as forms of labor as well as the possibility that child-produced culture is not, in fact, a subset of children's culture alone, at least to the extent that children's culture is understood as culture for children. Children create for their peers, but often for adults as well—perhaps even primarily for adults, as *Capernaum*, for example, received an R rating prior to its North American release. Therefore, a study of child performance is a reminder that child-produced culture is not only child-coproduced culture, but rather expands beyond culture for children to include culture for society at-large. In this way, it encourages us to more meaningfully center child agency and child-produced culture in humanistic studies of culture while at the same time reconsidering and retheorizing the very terms by which we attempt to do so.

NOTES

1. Victoria Ford Smith, *Between Generations: Collaborative Authorship in the Golden Age of Children's Literature* (Jackson: University Press of Mississippi, 2017), 261.
2. Robin Bernstein, "Childhood as Performance," in *The Children's Table: Childhood Studies and the Humanities*, ed. Anna Mae Duane (Athens: University of Georgia Press, 2013), 211.
3. See, for example, Kristen Hatch, *Shirley Temple and the Performance of Girlhood* (New Brunswick, NJ: Rutgers University Press, 2015).
4. Jane O'Connor, *The Cultural Significance of the Child Star* (New York: Routledge, 2008); Rob King, "The Kid from *The Kid*: Jackie Coogan and the Consolidation of Child Consumerism," *Velvet Light Trap*, 48 (Fall 2001): 4–19; Scott Balcerzak, "Dickensian Orphan as Child Star: Freddie Bartholomew and the Commodity of Cute in MGM's *David Copperfield* (1935)," *Literature/Film Quarterly* 33, no. 1 (2005): 51–61; and Deborah Shamoon, "Misora Hibari and the Girl Star in Postwar Japanese Cinema," *Signs* 35, no. 1 (Autumn 2009): 131–155.
5. See, for example, Morgan Genevieve Blue, *Girlhood on Disney Channel: Branding, Celebrity, and Femininity* (New York: Routledge, 2017), and Kyra Hunting, "Unwrapping Toy TV: *Ryan's World* and the Toy Review Genre's Impact on Children's Culture," in *The Marketing of Children's Toys: Critical Perspectives on Children's Consumer Culture*, ed. Rebecca C. Hains and Nancy A. Jennings (Cham, CH: Palgrave Macmillan, 2021), 105–124.

6. James Naremore, *Acting in the Cinema* (Berkeley: University of California Press, 1988).
7. Richard Dyer, *Stars* (London: British Film Institute, 1979).
8. Pamela Robertson Wojcik, "General Introduction," in *Movie Acting, The Film Reader* (New York: Routledge, 2004), 2.
9. Murray Pomerance and Kyle Stevens, eds., *Close-Up: Great Cinematic Performances Volume 1: America* (Edinburgh: Edinburgh University Press, 2018) and Murray Pomerance and Kyle Stevens, eds., *Close-Up: Great Cinematic Performances Volume 2: International* (Edinburgh: Edinburgh University Press, 2018).
10. Justin Chang, "Sean Baker's *The Florida Project* is a Magnificent Portrait of a Joyous, Troubled Childhood," *Los Angeles Times*, October 5, 2017, https://www.latimes.com/entertainment/movies/la-et-mn-the-florida-project-review-20171005-story.html.
11. For a representative selection of readings employing and critiquing auteur theory, consult John Caughie, ed., *Theories of Authorship: A Reader* (London: British Film Institute, 1981); Virginia Wright Wexman, ed., *Film and Authorship* (New Brunswick, NJ: Rutgers University Press, 2003); and Barry Keith Grant, ed., *Auteurs and Authorship: A Film Reader* (Malden, MA: Wiley-Blackwell, 2008).
12. See, for example, Richard Corliss, *Talking Pictures: Screenwriters in the American Cinema, 1927–1973* (Woodstock, NY: Overlook Press, 1974) and Andrew Spicer, A. T. McKenna, and Christopher Meir, eds., *Beyond the Bottom Line: The Producer in Film and Television Studies* (London: Bloomsbury Academic, 2014).
13. Timothy Corrigan, *A Cinema Without Walls: Movies and Culture After Vietnam* (New Brunswick, NJ: Rutgers University Press, 1991), 101–136.
14. For more on child performers on stage, consult Carolyn Steedman, *Strange Dislocations: Childhood and the Idea of Human Interiority, 1780–1930* (Cambridge, MA: Harvard University Press, 1995); Marah Gubar, *Artful Dodgers: Reconceiving the Golden Age of Children's Literature* (New York: Oxford University Press, 2009); and Dyan Colclough, "British Child Performers 1920–40: New Issues, Old Legacies," in *Entertaining Children: The Participation of Youth in the Entertainment Industry* (New York: Palgrave Macmillan, 2014), 73–90.
15. Linda Ruth Williams, "The Tears of Henry Thomas," *Screen* 53, no. 4 (Winter 2012): 464.
16. Karen Lury, *The Child in Film: Tears, Fears, and Fairy Tales* (New Brunswick, NJ: Rutgers University Press, 2010), 6, 156.
17. Lury, *Child in Film*, 152.
18. Gubar, *Artful Dodgers*, 159.
19. Gubar, *Artful Dodgers*, 174.
20. Ford Smith, *Between Generations*, 261.
21. Cynthia Baron and Sharon Marie Carnicke, *Reframing Screen Performance* (Ann Arbor: University of Michigan Press, 2008), 46.
22. Baron and Carnicke, *Reframing Screen Performance*, 60.
23. A. O. Scott, "*Capernaum* Review: A Heartbreaking and Defiant Look at a Boy's Life in Beirut," *New York Times*, December 13, 2018, accessed May 23, 2022, https://www.nytimes.com/2018/12/13/movies/capernaum-review.html.
24. "*Pihu* Movie Trailer: Trapped with a 2-Year-Old but Much Scarier," *Indian Express*, October 25, 2018, accessed June 23, 2022, https://indianexpress.com/article/entertainment/bollywood/pihu-trailer-vinod-kapri-5415983/.

PART THREE

Collaboration and Cocreation

8

"Mostly Written By"

A Cookbook Model for Reading Children's Art

IVY LINTON STABELL

Often, one of the few surviving artifacts of pre-1900 middle-class households is the family cookbook, a handwritten repository of generations of acquired domestic knowledge. These texts are charmingly eclectic and deeply informative works that reflect the idiosyncrasies and historical conditions of a cooking family—their traditions and tastes, their access to ingredients and kitchen technology, and who performed domestic labor and how they went about it. Recipes, medical remedies, cleaning techniques, gardening tips, economic advice, etiquette standards, anecdotes, financial records, and gossip all fall within these books' ambit. Manuscript cookbooks are often remarkably well preserved because they were so well cherished by the families that owned them. Next to the family Bible, these books often served as the family chronicle, recording births, marriages, and deaths. And significantly, it was not adults alone who had the right to inscribe this important record. For this reason, these distinctive texts do more than help us resurrect biographic detail or explore historical food culture; they allow us to draw inferences about families and children's places within them, and they offer an important site for theorizing young people's early authorship.

The Savery family's "Receipt Book" (1844–1853) typifies the manuscript cookbook genre in content and structure, and its perplexing front and back covers offer an illustrative example of what these collections can offer to scholars of children's creative output.[1] On the inside cover of this dignified leather-spined, marble-covered volume, the hand-lettered title page reads: "E. H. Savery's Receipt Book." Elizabeth Savery, mother of four by the time the book was begun in 1844, lived in Westchester County, New York, and in many ways it is logical to see her as the author of this work: the possessive grammar of the title page labels the book as her own, and adult experience is implied by a book that contains information about how to cure everything from ham to bilious cholic. Yet underneath this declaration, in the same hand, the title further declares the book to be "mostly written by her son Thomas Savery Jr."[2] What does the term "written" mean in this context?

Did he contribute the recipes? Is Thomas her scribe? Further complicating the matter, the inside back cover assigns authorship to a different brother, declaring "this was written by W.P.S., he being sick at the time with severe indisposition, which however as will be seen did not prevent him from being a good writer."[3] There's some cheeky response to this declaration; underneath this praise, the phrase "vain young man" is penciled in, and the same note about W.P.S. refers to a sister, R, who "gave it as her opinion that it was done 'miserably.'" Additionally, a dedication midway through the work states it is "To Elizabeth H. Savery from her sons Thomas Savery, John C. Savery, William Savery."[4] At first glance, these contradictory claims of authorship (and sister R's un-erased snarky review of their work) are baffling. Whose cookbook is it? Who is the author of this work?

The answers to these questions may seem specific to the ambiguously authored nature of manuscript cookbooks, yet studying this form provides a flexible and instructive model that can help children's literature scholars reframe our disciplinary understanding of authorship in ways that better reflect how children demonstrate their agency within the creative spaces they can best access. Within the domestic sphere, where children first find avenues of creative articulation, artistic expression is often collaborative, frequently derivative of established modes and makers, and typically incomplete by the traditional standards of authorship that privilege autonomous works, polished and delivered to a public audience. The Savery cookbook and the three other manuscript cookbooks this chapter will examine are representative of this informal artistic expression more common in domestic spaces, where authorship aspires neither to public consumption nor authorial distinction. The children involved in these four cookbooks never acted as sole untethered masters of their texts, but their creative actions still help us understand how children reacted to the lineage of ideas, authorities, and conditions they found themselves in, and how they participated in the formation of what was to come.

A Cookbook Methodology for Children's Authorship

Until very recently, children's literature scholarship has had little capacity to recognize children's creative output. The field has long centered around theories of childhood that figure adult agendas as the dominant force in imbalanced relationships between adults and children: adults, especially parents, teachers, and authors, impose their ideology and their will upon a passive child, who has little ability to resist or deviate from their agenda. In a foundational article, Perry Nodelman describes this adult authority as both seductive and absolute: "We woo them to our values. We tell them that their true happiness consists in pleasing us, bending to our will, doing what we want. We plant the seeds of our wisdom in them."[5] Children's impotence in the face of adult control has not left much room for scholars to imagine (or seek) ways children can and do respond to the world that preexisted their arrival. Yet even authors like Nodelman who helped consecrate these theories seem to recognize a gap in an inflexible understanding of adult-child dynamics. His very next sentence in the "woo them to our values" passage reads: "And we get very angry indeed when they dare to gaze back."[6] His acknowledgment that children can and do "gaze back" becomes an essential premise for scholars like Marah Gubar, Karen Sánchez-Eppler, Victoria Ford Smith, and others. Their curiosity about how children interact with both specific adult authorities and the ambient adult ideologies of their world—practices and beliefs about power, identity, childhood itself, and more—has led to a more flexible understanding of this power relationship. Under what Gubar refers to as "the kinship model," which emphasizes "relatedness, connection, and similarity without implying homogeneity, uniformity, and equality" among and between adults and children, there is greater capacity to recognize children's agency while continuing to acknowledge the many ways children's voices are mediated, shaped, and limited by social structures.[7] Using tools like Gubar's "kinship model" and corresponding scholarship that considers children as more vocal partners in the construction of culture, our field has begun to examine children's creative expressions, both as texts worthy of study and as a means of better understanding the (historically and culturally shaped) nature of conversation between generations.

Such work, however, requires a shift in our understandings of authorship itself. The notion of power as a force that flows in only one direction allows the terms of expression to be dictated by those at the top; in the case of literature, this means an overemphasis on the single-authored works of a mastermind, often imagined to be produced somehow independent of context. Victoria Ford Smith observes that "common definitions of professional authorship often exclude children or elide their participation, not only because children, who are often not paid for their contributions to texts, are considered (likely sometimes wrongfully) willing amateurs but also because accepted norms of authorship tend to reinforce existing biases about who is entitled such creative authority and therefore ignore purportedly 'passive subjects' such as children."[8] To restrict our ideas of authorship to only commercial, professional publications is to overlook work produced not only by children but by women and people of color as well, long denied the same access to or terms of publication. Such ideas of authorship also constrain what kinds of texts are granted legitimacy. Addressing the way accepted ideas of authorship tend to exclude women's writing, manuscript cookbook scholar Kristine Kowalchuk argues that we should not simply seek those female writers who were able to infiltrate a publishing world designed to exclude them but should instead adjust our notions of authorship to recognize the ways most women could and did meaningfully write. She asserts, "The reason why Virginia Woolf and others searched in vain for a record of women's lives and writing is that they looked in the wrong places; it is true that Judith Shakespeare did not become a playwright because her world did not cultivate, or even largely conceive of, such a possibility. But she likely did become, as Woolf suggests, a 'wise woman selling herbs' . . . and was most certainly a housewife, using the herbs herself and sharing written recipes with other women."[9] Turning our attention to literary forms like the manuscript cookbook that defy a standard of authorship focused on solitary composition, commercial distribution, and even our idea of a stable, finished product, can helpfully realign children's literature's ideas of how young people participate in the creation of texts and share them with other readers of all ages.

The Savery children's writing and the "Receipt Book" they created with their mother require such a revised concept of authorship. Though the title pages' conflicting attribution claims are unusual, the fact that (at least) four Saverys wrote together was not. Cookbook historians remind us that recipe authorship is hardly ever a single person's creation.[10] In most nineteenth-century households, cooking was a family affair, and though kitchens were typically governed by adult women, younger children were also involved in culinary labor; recipes are an intergenerational craft. Moreover, recipes are handed down from generations past, shared by relatives, friends, and neighbors, or copied from printed material. Often later users insert revision notes that shape recipes to their own taste; and every time a recipe is used, the current reader shapes meaning by interpreting the instructions and varying the results. To understand these many layers of authorship, culinary historian Henry Notaker offers medieval scribal culture as a corollary for cookbook writing. Prior to Gutenberg, he claims, authorship was understood as a range of activities from physically copying text, to locating passages to quote and comment upon, to composing new claims: "None of these roles involved exclusively writing one's own text. Originality was not an aim in itself; it was more important to imitate and transmit the work of one's predecessors."[11] Originality and individuality, similarly, are not the goals of the manuscript cookbook.

Scholars have further encouraged us to see even the simplest recipes as narratives themselves, dialogic works that connect many creators and users, rather than as mere technical writing or rote repetition. Cookbook theorists identify an implied narrative in a recipe that moves from disorder and craving to order and satisfaction. At the beginning of the recipe, the cake is an imaginary object of the reader's desire; by the end, the cake has been baked and the appetite fulfilled. Andrea Newlyn describes this narrative trajectory as the movement "from an unhealthy, inefficient and disorderly house to an organized, productive, and healthy home."[12] Cookbook scholars flexibly acknowledge multiple possibilities for identifying the work's protagonist; it could be the creator of the recipe, the scribe copying it into the book, or the reader acting upon these instructions in real life. Yet the form's engagement with an extended community of cocreators and readers is also significant because it can extend, reject, or edit the seemingly tidy narrative order the recipe offers. Attribution notes that describe the way a recipe has been handed off from one user to another (as in "Mrs. Smith's Chocolate Fudge") acknowledge the network of creators who built the text, disturbing expectations of single ownership of the work. Susan Leonardi contends that recipes with evaluative commentary invite readers into this community by prompting a response; when a recipe is labeled "A Very Good Cake Without Butter," "the reader not only *can* agree or argue but is encouraged to agree or argue."[13] In manuscript cookbooks, the dialogue between the community that shares advice and resources is frequently on display; and because the reader might simply pick up their pen to contribute a note in the margin, the dialogue between creators and readers is similarly perceptible.

Kowalchuk's point about the need to correctly calibrate what we recognize as literature is equally instructive for reading children's writing as it is women's. If we seek young people's authorial and artistic endeavors only in traditional spaces—the published work, the publicly lauded creation, the singly produced text—we will overlook the ways young people, too, could and did meaningfully create. As Smith's *Between Generations* depicts, even collaborations between adults and children that become public and published typically began in private, domestic contexts, infused with the codes and conventions of the family and the home. Works like manuscript cookbooks offered sanctioned spaces where young people could take early conscious steps as authors and as people with opinions and behaviors in agreement or not with the existing ideas of their first environments. Moreover, there are many similar kinds of texts worthy of study—letters, school assignments, visual art, songs, and more that children readily participate in.

Thinking of these cookbooks as a model for considering other kinds of works allows us to register three key features of much of child-produced culture. First, domestic writings may be private, but they frequently allow the author to grapple with potential future audiences. A young person's immediate family, with whom they were in daily conversation about the recipes at hand, might be their primary audience. But secondarily, they might have understood that the knowledge of the family cookbook was meant to be passed on, and so the manuscript cookbook provides a way of viewing how children confront the notion of legacy and posterity, even in their earliest utterances. Second, the cookbook is by definition a collaborative effort, and in order to understand how it works, we must concede the traceable and untraceable layers of authorship behind it rather than seek an urtext or originating hand that would elide the nuances of its production. Finally, manuscript cookbooks teach us to value works in progress and unfinished products. Much like children (and, really, all authors) themselves, manuscript cookbooks were dynamic works, changing as time passed and conditions changed. There is no "complete" version of a cookbook—it is forever in dialogue with both past and future. Recognizing and valuing works that are similarly constructed will enable a greater understanding of the way kinship manifested between adults and children before the twentieth century.

The Bones Family Account and Recipe Book, 1661–1788

The earliest children's cookbook writing we will examine here is the account book of the Bones family of Essex, England.[14] The book documents more than a century and a quarter of usage, and its eclectic content demonstrates the range of practical and creative uses a manuscript cookbook might have—and how children's contributions seamlessly blend with adults'. Unlike the Savery "Receipt Book," which was clearly created (and so titled) specifically for recipes, the Bones family book contains a little bit of everything. There are recipes for oyster loaves, orange pudding, seed cake, gingerbread, and more, which exhibit the access a middle-class family would have had to imported ingredients like sugar, citrus, and spices available in nearby London. In total, there are thirteen detailed recipes, inscribed in several different hands, with the rest of the 150-page volume primarily dedicated to the financial records of this merchant family. Generations of careful accounting reflects rents paid, annual agricultural product tallies, bills for laundry services, and even records of money owed to the family, seemingly copied into the book in the debtor's hand: "In All May the 28th 1747 I promise to pay to Mr. W. Bones . . . the Sume of Fifty Pounds."[15] There are pages and pages of math, adding and subtracting what the family paid and owed.

The Bones family account book presents as much more practical than the playful Savery book, yet even within the well-used pages of sober financials, children's hands are present, even prominent. Generations of Boneses signed their name to this book—there are signatures all over it. Most of them appear in neat, lineal script, suggestive of a practiced adult hand, yet periodically entire two-page spreads are dedicated to the wobbly and decadently large handwriting of someone still rusty at the task. It is of course possible that this was an adult first learning to write their name, but that seems unlikely, given the importance of literacy to this family's livelihood. Moreover, the childlike signatures are male names, and male members of the Bones family would likely have been initiated into the family trade early on. We can therefore infer that the Bones family account and recipe book, in addition to containing the household finances and favorite recipes, was also a tool of early literacy. Cookbook historian Janet Theophano's survey of manuscript cookbooks from this period suggests this is typical usage: "[Mothers] allowed, even encouraged their children to practice their letters in these books. Cookbooks from as early as the seventeenth century provide ample evidence of children's doodling, practicing letters, and copying recipes."[16] This is likely the best way to interpret a signature like "Christo-pher Bones, 1788": his first name, broken midway through and continued on the next line, evidences a writer still learning how to measure the space required for longer words.[17] On a nearby page, we see a youthful hand practicing a salutation typical of an eighteenth-century letter, another essential form for the middle-class learner.[18]

That the Bones children practiced their writing somewhere is not remarkable, but the fact that their practice appears within this indispensable family document suggests that their development was a valued family activity. We cannot explain the use of the account book as a copybook as a scarcity of resources: writing materials, especially for a family of the financial standing documented in the Bones accounts, would have been fairly accessible. Instead, the juxtaposition of the meticulous recipes and accounting with the children's practicing hands shows that generations of the Bones family did not see the precision needed for baking and keeping the accounts as demanding separate or sacred space away from the evolving work of early literacy. Instead, the written evidence of family labor—both financial and culinary—provides a context and a direction for the work of learning, demonstrating the future applications for the skill they were busy acquiring. That many authorial purposes combine in one space (and remain there—no one has excised Christopher Bones's scribbles) is important because it means this family prized unfinishedness and saw it as an important part of their labor. Rather than existing in separate, less lauded spaces, children and their developing compositions were an important part of generational survival: adults practice their trade and children are trained up into it, in turn instructing their own children. The Bones family account and cookbook reflects and respects this entire cycle.

Elizabeth Leggatt's Commonplace Book, 1759–1807

"Mother's Receipt Book" reads the faded script on the exterior leather cover of an eighteenth-century commonplace book belonging to Elizabeth Leggatt.[19] There can be no doubt whatsoever over the original owner of the volume, though it is unclear if Leggatt is the mother in question. On both the front and back inside covers, Elizabeth Leggatt is inscribed in full-page decorative script, though in two different hands. The front cover includes an earlier and more formal decoration, written out by someone whose flourish-laden penmanship rivals John Hancock's ("Miss Elizabeth Leggatt, her Book, February 6th, 1759, Steyning, Sussex"), while the back cover, inscribed a few years later ("Elizabeth Leggatt Her Book, Jan the 31 1762"), is more playfully decorated and is likely Leggatt's own handwriting.[20] Here, Leggatt embellishes her script with the care of a focused doodler, drawing tiny dots evenly around the perimeter of each letter. The look of this back cover seems to indicate a young person's hand—it bears close resemblance to many a modern teenage notebook—but the stronger evidence that this is the work of a young person is the fact that it seems to have been used first as a mathematics copybook. It is a workbook of sorts, with information and problems written out by the Hancockesque writer and answered by the hand that whimsically signed the back of the book. There are pages and pages of arithmetic lessons and tables of measurement in the first half of the book before the recipes begin, indicating the rigor of Leggatt's education. Halfway through the book, the recipes begin, first for a range of medical remedies for diseases like dropsy and piles, and then for foodstuffs like raisin wine, cheesecakes, and oyster ketchup. The use of this book as a cookbook is prompted by a poetic inscription on the first internal page of the book titled "To a Young Lady with a Present."[21] The inscription is not fully legible, but it is clearly a food-oriented gift, as it makes references to the "Birds you will roast" and declares an intention for the book: "The present is trifling yet still you will find / fine food for the Body as well as the mind."[22]

Despite her conspicuous signatures, Leggatt's presence in this manuscript cookbook is perhaps felt more in her authorial absence than in its presence.

Leggatt's handwriting can be seen throughout the arithmetic section; she carefully answered every prompt she was given. Yet her handwriting is almost entirely missing in the recipe section. Instead, several other hands seem to have penned most of it: someone named Elizabeth Irish also signs the book, and there is a chronicle of Irish family births within the volume, so perhaps these relatives or friends of Leggatt's may have done most of the recipe writing. Leggatt signs one recipe, and a few other similarly scripted ones nearby are likely hers as well, but we cannot know why she wrote so few recipes. What is plain is that if that front inscription directing her to roast birds and use her book for "the body as well as the mind" was intended for her, she mostly ignored it. Leggatt does use the gift—there are over fifty pages of arithmetic lessons diligently scripted into the pages. But she does not build a receipt book.

Maybe she was not a very good cook, or maybe her recipes were written into another notebook, long lost. But it is also possible that Leggatt rejected the prompt to write a cookbook. The kind of arithmetic she was studying gives us clues about the life Leggatt was being reared to. Though there are some standard tables and exercises, most of her recorded math problems are related to food. There are word problems and calculations about the cost of ham by weight, measurements of beer, and whether a cut of mutton or herring is more expensive. Leggatt was clearly being trained to run a household, and her life would center on the production and consumption of food. It is possible that she was wealthy enough to have servants who would have done most of the cooking. But whoever gave her this book intended her to be in the kitchen, roasting birds and scribbling away at content focused on both "the body as well as the mind." Others in her circle did so; this is a substantial cookbook with many recipes. But by limiting her participation in the coauthorship that governs the genre of the family cookbook, Leggatt pushed back against what was expected of her, at least in one small way. Her conspicuous absence in this cookbook that bears her name so prominently must be read as significant and agential.

Le livre de Matilda Livingston Rogers, 1850

Ninety years later, New Yorker Matilda Livingston Rogers's academic copybook also became a cookbook.[23] A young person is the mostly likely candidate for a book of schoolwork, but in this case we can confirm Rogers's age: the New York Public Library, where her book can be found, notes in the catalog listing that Rogers was born in 1836, making her fourteen years old when she began. Her green-marbled, hardcovered book is divided into two sections and functions: sixty-eight pages of French exercises precede the portion where the recipes begin. The title page, though, makes plain that the cookbook was a later conversion. The work is titled "Livre de Rhetorique fait a New York Ecrit par Matilda Livingston Rogers," and on the final page of lessons, the word "Fini" is embellished as though it were the sun on a horizon line, and in bolder, crosshatched script, she writes again, "Fin de la

Rhetorique."[24] The second half of the book presents a methodically arranged collection of around 170 recipes, separated into four sections: cakes, puddings, eatables, and bread.

This cookbook's purposeful design distinguishes it from the other manuscript cookbooks discussed here. As instruments of the kitchen, manuscript cookbook's recipes are typically added as needed, resulting in a hodgepodge reflective of trials and errors, needs and aspirations. Rogers, though, systematizes her collection. The order and cohesion of her text (cakes, puddings, eatables, bread) is indicative of how she imagined the purpose of her book. Sections are features of a preconceived work in which you strategically arrange material to help other readers navigate it. It is likely, therefore, that Rogers had other readers in mind, and arguably she contemplated publication, perhaps not in the sense that she hoped to put out her book, but certainly she was influenced by contemporary printed cookbooks and may have imagined herself creating something more in line with these works than a handwritten private volume. Though the practice of owning a collection of published cookbooks did not become commonplace until the late nineteenth century,[25] a few, like Hannah Glasse's *The Art of Cookery made Plain and Easy* (1747), which retained bestseller status for more than a century, and Eliza Acton's *Modern Cookery for Private Families* (1845), may have inspired the organization of Rogers's recipes. Rogers's recipe selection also reflects a sophisticated and on-trend palate. Her book includes local desserts like Washington Cake and Philadelphia Cake, the kinds of fare that appeared in the first decades of the young nation as Americans began to develop a distinct cultural identity. But Rogers also reflects the sophistication Americans sought, by including popular (and high-class) continental desserts like Floating Islands and Italian Cream that reflect the influence of European haute cuisine on Anglo-American menus.

Despite her clear vision for this work, Rogers is also not the only author of her cookbook. She has left ample room in each section, showing that even if echoing the structure of printed cookbooks, she intended hers to operate like other manuscript cookbooks by leaving room to add recipes, and indeed, at least three other hands add to the collection. The result is a book with a lot of stylistic variety: the handwriting differs substantially from page to page, the writers noticeably cross out mistakes in different ways, and other hands are more likely to record the recipe's origin than Rogers. But we can also see that these later writers *did* defer to Rogers's structure and vision for the cookbook. In one instance, a writer even seems to have moved some recipes from one section to another upon realization that they had not fit into Rogers's original sections; identical recipes for rolls, waffles, and water muffins are crossed out in the Pudding section, only to be rewritten under Bread. The added recipes also fit the general palate Rogers establishes, echoing her interest in sophisticated, likely somewhat expensive cuisine. These later contributors also added to the architecture of the book by adding two indexes that help an external reader navigate, again imitating published works.

The text is another product of collaboration; yet, significantly, of at least four scribes and countless recipe sources, Rogers is the clear governor the text, shaping the architecture of the work that later contributors follow. In the other cookbooks examined in this essay, we see books named after adults, bearing family names, and formed by adult agendas. In these examples, though children operate thoughtfully and creatively within spaces ordered by adults, they are not in command of how a book is arranged or used. But in Rogers's cookbook, the subsequent (possibly adult) contributors work within the textual world she has created. Moreover, they do so with the same sincerity we see in other texts: the recipes are just as detailed and the annotations just as earnest about how to improve a recipe or source its ingredients. Though such productions are rare, Matilda Livingston Rogers's cookbook shows us that it is possible for children to hold creative authority within collaboration.

The Savery Family Cookbook, 1844–1851

Let's close with the cookbook with which we began—the demonstrably, if confusingly, coauthored cookbook by E. H. Savery and her children. Though it is likely impossible to determine who crafted each part of the book, it is clear that the Savery children were more than mere scriveners. In several key spots, the multiple hands that composed this text color the way the reader is prompted to interact with the recipes. They add whimsical illustrations: a cat sitting on a mushroom next to "Mushroom (Kat)sup," one tomato chasing another next to "Tomato Catchup."[26] They write in jokes: next to a recipe for Mangoes [*sic*], "and so does Woman."[27] They instruct readers to cross-reference one recipe with another or even to look beyond the text: "see page 36 . . . or Mrs. Matlock's."[28] They cross out errors or mistakes in the text. And they challenge recipe claims, as in the case of the "cure for the cholera" recipe, which declares "thousands have been served by this simple remedy."[29] The same hand that writes the recipe also remarks, "I don't believe it" in the blank space below.[30] In these frisky additions, Thomas, W. P., perhaps snarky sister R, or even other unknown commentators who may have subsequently marked the text, approach this manuscript cookbook as playful, contestable terrain rather than as a sacred text to obey or memorize. Even if these child writers are simply copying down their mother's kitchen knowledge, it is important to see that they do not take a deferential attitude; instead, as fellow contributors to the text, they view that content as fair game for their interpretation and response.

The manuscript cookbook provides such a fascinating example because it is both authoritative and informal in its aims: it is the treasury of information in the kitchen, and yet its precious and preserved pages become places where one understands that any contribution can generate response. In this way, these cookbooks position the participating (or nonparticipating) child as an important voice, mingling among their elders and corresponding with their descendants. As the Savery cookbook reveals, it may be next to impossible to tease out every individual young contributor's mark on a text, but doing so is not the point. When children inscribe in the family cookbook, when they share one they have initiated with others, when they refuse to do much with this common and expected family document, they are interacting with the world as it stands before them. To write in such a text is to make your mark but also to understand that it will be subsumed into the whole. Commenting on anxieties that the manuscript cookbook form elides individual women's authorship, Kowalchuk reframes how to measure the writing within these books not as individual efforts but as connected pieces of a whole: "The imperative form receipt books use, for example, might not represent the assertion of an individual woman's instructions, but rather a disembodied authority of tradition, implying the way something simply *is done*."[31] A child's role within these collective works is not much about establishing their individual talent—it is instead to register themselves as the latest voice in a lineage of thinkers. The fact that their contributions have survived unredacted demonstrates how much that participation was valued in their day, and how much we should credit it now.

NOTES

1. Manuscript held in the Fales Library & Special Collections of New York University.
2. E. H. Savery's Receipt Book, 1851, New York University, Fales Library.
3. Savery.
4. Savery.
5. Perry Nodelman, "The Other: Orientalism, Colonialism, and Children's Literature," *Children's Literature Association Quarterly* 17, no. 1 (1992): 30.
6. Nodelman, "Other," 30.
7. Marah Gubar, "Risky Business: Talking about Children in Children's Literature Criticism," *Children's Literature Association Quarterly* 38, no. 4 (2013): 453.
8. Victoria Ford Smith, *Between Generations: Collaborative Authorship in the Golden Age of Children's Literature* (Jackson: University of Mississippi Press, 2017), 21.
9. Kristine Kowalchuk, introduction to *Preserving on Paper: Seventeenth-Century Englishwomen's Receipt Books* (Toronto: University of Toronto Press, 2017), 50–51.
10. U.S. patent law is also instructive: you cannot copyright a recipe itself, only explanatory material surrounding the ingredients and method (such as a narrative preceding a recipe or photographs of the finished dish). United States Copyright Office, *Works Not Protected by Copyright*, March 2021, https://www.copyright.gov/circs/circ33.pdf.
11. Henry Notaker, *A History of Cookbooks: From Kitchen to Page over Seven Centuries* (Oakland: University of California Press, 2017), 30.
12. Andrea K. Newlyn, "Redefining 'Rudimentary' Narrative: Women's Nineteenth-Century Manuscript Cookbooks," in *The Recipe Reader: Narratives, Contexts, Traditions*, ed. Janet Floyd and Laurel Foster (Lincoln: University of Nebraska Press, 2003).
13. Susan J. Leonardi, "Recipes for Reading: Summer Pasta, Lobster a la Riseholme, and Key Lime Pie," *PMLA* 104, no. 3 (1989): 342.
14. Manuscript held in the James Marshall and Marie-Louise Osborn Collection, Beinecke Rare Book and Manuscript Library, Yale University.

15. This IOU was presumably fulfilled, as the signatory's name has been crossed out. The Bones Family Account and Receipt Book, 1661–1788, Yale Beinecke Rare Book and Manuscript Library.
16. Janet Theophano, *Eat My Words: Reading Women's Lives through the Cookbooks They Wrote* (New York: Palgrave, 2002), 156–157.
17. Bones Family.
18. "Honored Mother Hoping these lines will find you in helth [*sic*] as [illegible] yours."
19. Elizabeth Leggatt Commonplace Book, 1759–1807, Yale Beinecke Rare Book and Manuscript Library. Commonplace books were informal journals that served as a repository for intellectual and cultural curiosities collected by the author, such as quotations, poems, prayers, etc.; the works might even serve as a scrapbook. It is not uncommon for recipes to appear in such texts.
20. Leggatt.
21. It should be noted that this inscription is not written by the same person who writes out Leggatt's lessons. Yet despite the different handwriting, I do think the note is meant for Leggatt, given its placement at the very start of the volume (rather than later in the volume where other parties' hands appear). But it is worth noting this as a mystery of the text; it is possible that it was added later and meant for another user of the book.
22. Leggatt.
23. Manuscript held in the Manuscript and Archives Division of the New York Public Library.
24. Recipe Book of Matilda Livingston Rogers, 1850, New York Public Library Manuscript and Archives Division.
25. Notaker, *History of Cookbooks*, 192.
26. Savery.
27. Savery.
28. Savery.
29. Savery.
30. Savery.
31. Kowalchuk, introduction, 42.

9

Negotiating Nightmares

Improvising with Children in Arthur Tress's *The Dream Collector*

VICTORIA FORD SMITH

Halfway through *The Dream Collector* (1972), Arthur Tress's published collection of photographs featuring children acting out their dreams and nightmares, the viewer encounters an image of a boy halfway up a cement staircase (Figure 9.1). The photograph is unsettling—a quality often associated with the work of Tress, who has become known for his interest in the surreal. The boy, small and shadowy, holds out his arms in exasperation. A group of children cluster behind him and, beyond them, a city skyline rises above a river. In the foreground, the staircase stretches toward the viewer, its cement broken and the way blocked by ropes. "He was trying desperately to get somewhere (he couldn't recall exactly where)," reads the caption by John Minahan, "but he was continually frustrated by a seemingly endless series of obstructions: stalled buses, flooded streets, locked gates, long fences, and—several times—broken staircases."[1] The distance between viewer and child, and between photographer and child subject, is untraversable. Staircases are designed to bridge distances, but this one is cluttered with obstacles, offering the possibility of connection only to deny it.

Several images in *The Dream Collector* depict children in poses of frustrated or arrested movement: a child buried in sand, another lodged in a large metal cone, a third peering out from the inside of an enormous fishbowl. Photography historian Moa Goysdotter observes that children in Tress's photographs often seem "unable to get away, trapped both in the image and the situation it depicts."[2] Tress's photographs imply that children, in their dreams (and ours), are immobile, frozen, stuck—and they are subject to something beyond physical paralysis. They appear totemic: forever acting out scenes of dreaming, abstracted to symbol.

However, in his introduction to the book, Minahan posits a different relationship between photographer and subject that is more dynamic and collaborative. Minahan writes that "a number of critics have suggested that the obvious success of Tress's dream photographs must be due in large measure to an extraordinary rapport with children, and this is quite true. Watching him work, you're aware of

FIGURE 9.1 Arthur Tress, *Boys on a Broken Staircase, Weehawken, New Jersey*, 1970. Reprinted in *The Dream Collector* (Richmond, VA: Westover Press, 1972). Copyright Arthur Tress Archive LLC.

an elusive 'chemistry' going on, extremely difficult to define."[3] Certainly some of the photographs in the collection required trust and dialogue between the photographer and his subjects, who are often arranged in unusual, uncomfortable, or potentially dangerous positions. The rapport Minahan assumes contradicts Goysdotter's reading of children trapped in photographs. *The Dream Collector*, then, presents at least two possibilities of intergenerational relationships at the same time: alienation and connection, subjugation and collaboration. Are the children in Tress's photographs props, partners, or somehow both?

That confusion makes *The Dream Collector* a useful case study. It foregrounds some of the questions most vexing to scholars interested in young people's creative agency—about the relationship between children's creativity and adult authority, and how preconceived notions of childhood inform and transform the stories we tell, and accept, about child creators. Tress's work thwarts our efforts to answer those questions in any definitive way. As I tried to piece together what I call the text's composition narrative—or the collective story of the book's creation, informed by multiple and sometimes contradictory accounts—my uncertainties about the photographs were not resolved.[4] Instead, they multiplied. I found contradictory stories, oppositional investments in childhood, and a range of understandings of adult-child power dynamics throughout the rich archive of material about *The Dream Collector*: the text itself, including Minahan's introduction and captions; reviews of the collection and related exhibits; my correspondence with Tress, published interviews with him, and his own writings on photography; and recent scholarship on the series' legacy. I was initially frustrated by the slipperiness of these photographs, but gradually my inquiry shifted. I was no longer interested in determining the precise process through which the images were created. Instead, I was invested in what we, as childhood studies scholars, might make of the conundrum itself. How can we understand an adult-child collaboration that is so crafty and undefined, so shape-shifting and uncertain? Below, in the sections titled "Ambivalence" and "Improvisation," I provide a record of my research process, unfolding information about *The Dream Collector* as I found it, including errors in my thinking and moments of confusion. In the final section, titled "Negotiation," I consider how childhood studies scholars might use what I learned to continue theorizing the messiness that arises when we try to fully understand children's creative agency.

Ambivalence

Tress began working professionally as a photographer in the 1960s and 1970s, traveling the world and working primarily in a documentary style, and he attracted significant critical attention in 1971 with an exhibit titled *Open Space in the Inner City: Ecology and the Urban Environment.* Hung in the Sierra Club's gallery in New York City and later released as a portfolio book, the series includes black-and-white photographs of people in industrial landscapes, including children without designated play spaces. Tress has noted that "the desolate piers, warehouses, and trash dumps were often used by kids as impromptu recreation areas and had already in themselves a feeling of surreal dislocation and melancholy peculiar to a dreamlike atmosphere."[5] As James A. Ganz notes, *Open Space* is "intertwined geographically, chronologically, and thematically" with *The Dream Collector*, "with a significant number of *Open Space* images resurfacing in the *Dream Collector* book."[6]

Before the publication of *The Dream Collector* as a book, Tress exhibited twenty of its photographs, mounted on black board, in an exhibit titled *Daymares: Photographs of Children's Dreams*, hung in the gallery attached to the Raffi Photo Lab in New York City in 1972. Peter Shults, founder and head of the agency Photo Researchers, saw the show and proposed a book of the photographs to Westover Press. The resulting hardcover book was released in 1972, featuring sixty plates with captions and an introductory essay by Minahan, a novelist and magazine writer. Later, it was reprinted in paperback by Avon Books. "You could pick it up for $4.95 at Greyhound Stations," Tress explains in an interview.[7] The images in *The Dream Collector* signaled a significant shift in his aesthetics, from the documentary to the surreal, and he was working in a similar vein to other groundbreaking 1970s photographers such as Duane Michals and Les Krims who, according to Goysdotter, drew upon "the inner life . . . as a source of images. The mind was the place for concepts and ideas to take form that were then realized by being staged and photographed."[8]

I first encountered Tress's photographs of children's dreams in the Westover edition of the series, and so I initially interpreted them through Minahan's introductory essay and captions. Minahan describes Tress's interactions with the young people featured within the book as close collaborations. He reports that Tress "went to grade schools and tape-recorded a wide variety of dream recollections by children of various ages. Then he began to photograph children in specific dream-like environments. . . . After studying elaborate, detailed maps of the city, he usually chose small isolated areas which he hadn't explored, areas that had a certain amount of open landscape, which is a frequent common denominator in children's dreams. He would then go to the area, become familiar with it, and attempt to tape-record and photograph the children there."[9] Minahan assumes a focused back-and-forth between Tress and individual children as the origin and method behind each photograph, and the captions he designed for each plate often reinforce this narrative. One photograph, for example, centers a young boy kneeling in an asphalt courtyard in Hell's Kitchen, eyes closed, hockey gloves poised confidently before his chest. The caption begins with a general description of dreaming, then pivots to the particular dream of the boy in the image: "Wish-fulfillment is a familiar identity-related dream. This boy told of recurring dreams in which he was a star player scoring goals in front of enormous crowds."[10] Describing a photograph of a boy hanging upside down out of a junkyard car—mouth agape, eyes wide, arms overhead—Minahan writes that "this boy remembered being chased by a huge tractor-trailer at very high speeds along a highway at night. As the truck gained on him, he suddenly realized that he didn't know how to drive, and therefore had to sit helpless as the truck somehow ran over his car, flattened it, and continued down the highway. The last image he recalled was seeing himself dead."[11] The clash between the viewer's probable idea of "appropriate" images of childhood and the photograph, in which the child's arched back and slack face suggest death, lends credence to Minahan's narrative of child participation. This unsettling image is far afield from what we expect to encounter. It *must* originate in the child's nightmare.

However, I found that the collaboration Minahan describes could not account for many of the book's photographs and even for several of Minahan's captions, which sometimes suggest a different method altogether. The second photograph in the book, for instance, features a naked, crying baby sitting at the base of towering trees, backlit by sunshine. This infant certainly could not relate and act out a dream for Tress as an older child could. That photograph's caption focuses not on the child's dream but on Tress's background: "Living in a sequoia forest near Santa Cruz, California, Tress studied, painted and photographed the huge, ancient redwoods, becoming fascinated by the dream-like qualities of his surroundings, particularly the shafts of translucent, almost vestigial light available during certain times of day."[12] Another photograph, perhaps in the same location, reveals a blond boy with his head back, eyes closed, mouth ajar, standing underneath a towering, gnarled tree trunk; there, Minahan writes that "as a child's mind moves through the environment, it projects its own imaginative wishes and fears," including "darker images" that "are more likely to be retained in the subconscious."[13] This child is presented not as an individual but as a universal, his dreams following the predictable patterns of the "child mind."

The uncertainties around the method Minahan describes are amplified in accounts of *The Dream Collector*'s photos circulated in the press in the 1970s. For example, the press release for Tress's 1972 *Daymares* exhibit, the show that featured many of the images that would be included in Tress's book, recounts a collaborative process similar to what Minahan describes: the photographer collected children's dreams through conversation, and Tress worked with those children to find ways to make their fantasies "visual actualities." However, the release also acknowledges that Tress's recreations are "a combination of actual dream, mythical archetypes, fairy tale, horror movie, comic book, and imaginative play."[14] New voices were piping up in Tress's "extraordinary rapport with children," voices that spoke not to children's individual experiences but to larger ideas of both childhood and nightmare. A few years later, this ambiguity resurfaces in a review of *The Dream Collector* in the *Boston Globe*. Writer C. R. Wasserman expresses the muddiness of the process behind Tress's photos, writing that "Tress serves somewhat as a medium in this collection, drawing not only on his personal dreams but also on dreams and fantasies told to him by children." Dubbing Tress a "medium" implies he was a conduit enabling children to communicate and stage their dreams, but Wasserman's comments also acknowledge the inevitable filter of Tress's experiences, assumptions, and motives. She ends by wishing for a representation of children's dreams untainted by adult interference: "One hopes a subsequent development will be for encouragement to be provided [to] children to record, and learn to transform, their own dreams and fantasies."[15]

Both the *Daymares* press release and Wasserman's review foreground a tension between, on the one hand, the insistence that Tress's photographs directly represented children's understanding and interpretation of their dreams and, on the other, the reality that those interpretations were filtered through the photographer and other influences, such as pop culture or psychology. (Tress is particularly interested in Jungian ideas of dreaming.) This tension frequently reappeared as I continued examining the book. In other words, as I read *The Dream Collector* alongside reviews, interviews, and other documents that offer parallel but slightly different stories of the book's origins, I began to suspect that the project was simultaneously deploying childhood in at least two contradictory ways. Accounts of *The Dream Collector* value the project as a documentation of individual children's dreams, even if that documentation was surreal and abstract. However, the images betray the influence of universal ideas of childhood and of Tress's own dreams, memories, and understandings of childhood.

Yet the specificity of Minahan's description of Tress's method, the occasional purported quotation from a child, and the details of the children's dreams included throughout the book all suggested that, despite my doubts, it was still likely that the images in *The Dream Collector* did account for the pictured children's experiences in some way. The photographs, I concluded, were interesting precisely *because* of their ambivalence, the way they pulled in two directions at once. I wondered if the book's unresolved quality might be a consequence, in part, of Tress's changing understanding of his own work at the time. My research into his career had already revealed a shift in his aesthetics around the time he began exhibiting images that would become part of *The Dream Collector*, and I would later read a 2010 interview with Tress in which he noted that he shot many of the photographs during a transitionary time. "It was a moment in my own artistic trajectory where I needed to move away from the prevalent documentary realism and street shooting of the late 60's [*sic*] into new areas of internal self-exploration," Tress explained. "The 'Dream Collector' images have one foot in each approach, and that is what gives them their compelling strength and intriguing [qualities]."[16] Both aesthetic impulses might be present in these photographs: the desire to record, visually, the children he encountered on playgrounds and in schoolrooms, in concrete courtyards and abandoned city spaces—a holdover from his early years as a documentary photographer—and a growing desire to move inward, to represent something of himself as much as, perhaps more than, depicting the child in front of the lens.

I drafted this chapter with these conclusions in mind. I took as my starting point Minahan's description of Tress's process and used the images, their captions, and the multiple origin stories that surrounded the book to undo that description, demonstrating its gaps and weaknesses and uncritical assumptions. In other words, I concluded that these images were marked by an unacknowledged ambivalence, and this conclusion felt persuasive to me. I had often encountered representations of childhood that were not as transparent as they purported to be, that were understandably pulled askew by the powerful gravity of our *ideas* about childhood.

Important to my analysis was one of the most famous images in *The Dream Collector: Flood Dream, Ocean City, New Jersey*, 1970. It captures a semi-flooded plain, interrupted by a ferry boat run aground on the horizon. (See cover image. Note that the boat is cropped out of the image on our cover.) A boy at the center of the image gazes out at the viewer, his arm and torso emerging from a hole in a damaged roof that has become dislodged from its building. The boy's blond hair is in disarray, and his face is smudged with dirt. This photograph is accompanied by one of the briefest captions in the collection: "Resignation and peace in the midst of a disaster."[17] I had located a 2012 *New York Times* article in which journalist Ted Loos describes the image's origins. He explains that it "was staged, but not planned in advance. [Tress] was driving along the Jersey Shore and saw a roof on the beach, with no house attached, and behind it an abandoned ferryboat. 'This boy came along on his bicycle out of nowhere, and I asked him to put his head through the roof,' Mr. Tress said. . . . 'He had this wonderful ambiguous expression.'"[18] This photograph was, to me, a compelling example of the tensions embedded in *The Dream Collector*. The child in the image did not narrate a flood dream to Tress, as Minahan's introduction implies. He is less cocreator than passerby, persuaded into the service of Tress's vision of childhood and nightmare, and his "ambiguous expression" helpfully resists interpretation. "He was glad to do it and just looked peacefully at the camera," Tress remembers. "And it was one of those strange moments that move the ordinary into a special archetypal place."[19] The child was an eager actor, but his participation was abstracted into a symbol.

Improvisation

As I put the finishing touches on my work, I reached out to museums that archive Tress's photographs to secure permissions to reprint *Flood Dream* and a handful of other images. When I did not receive a response, I reached out to Tress through his website, and he replied swiftly and generously. Amid our discussion of permissions, he sent me an important caveat: "Please be aware . . . that many of the images and the texts accompanying them in [*The Dream Collector*] were fabrications by the writer John Minahan. I was inspired by the imaginative world of children and did much dream research and wrote down 100s of dream themes on notecards that I used as reference but did not go out and actually record specific children's dreams and get them to act them out on the spot as the DC book implies. It is more of a work of fiction then [*sic*] a documentary."[20] During this email exchange, he sent me the exhibition catalog from his then running exhibit at the Getty Museum in Los Angeles—*Arthur Tress: Rambles, Dreams, and Shadows*—edited by James A. Ganz, who also contributed an essay on *The Dream Collector*. That essay made quick work of dismantling Minahan's narrative of the photos' origins. Peter Shults of Photo Researchers "was assuming the financial risk for *The Dream Collector* [and so] took certain decisions out of Tress's hands," Ganz writes. "In particular, believing that the images could not stand on their own, he hired John Minahan, a novelist who had worked as a staff writer for *Time* magazine and in television advertising, to produce an introductory essay as well as extended captions for the sixty plates."[21]

Ganz identifies several fabrications in Minahan's text, at times created "by Shults, with the collusion of the photographer himself." For example, "Minahan characterizes Tress as a kind of dream detective, scouring obscure corners of the city with a tape recorder and camera to document children's recollections of their dreams," but "Tress has confessed that he never owned a tape recorder and relied on his own sharp memory and notebook jottings to document his own dreams and those of friends, strangers, and children."[22] Ganz also states outright the conclusion I had come to after some hand-wringing: that while Minahan's introduction "would have the reader believe that Tress followed a uniform artistic program," the photos in fact were the product of several methods, many of them not the intergenerational collaborations they were purported to be. As an example, Ganz points out the final plate in the book, a photograph of a boy walking into the sea toward the ruins of a pier in San Francisco. Minahan's narrative caption explains that Tress asked the child to reenact his dream of a dead man walking into the ocean toward a distant gate. In fact, Tress took the photograph in 1965, years before he had conceived of *The Dream Collector*; "clearly," Ganz writes, Minahan "fabricated [the] narrative and retroactively assigned it to the earlier image."[23]

Admittedly, while I was excited to learn more about Tress's process, I found this new narrative baffling. After taking time to reflect on my earlier research and conclusions, I began to wonder why I had not found this information on my own—why I had not discovered, until I corresponded with the photographer himself, that the intergenerational collaborations at the center of *The Dream Collector* were, at best, *admittedly* complex or, at worst, pure fabrications by Minahan. I thanked Tress and admitted that the Minahan account is ubiquitous, that it had dominated what I found in my research. "Do you mind if I ask: are there other places/publications that discuss Minahan's fictionalizations?" I tentatively queried. His response: "Over the years I allowed the Minahan amplifications of my work to ride as it seemed to please people, with this image of the investigative photographer. I did feel that since Jim [Ganz] was doing a scholarly study it was a good time to adjust one's perceptions on the many complicated trails leading up to making the images."[24] That response provides at least one explanation for what I had found to be an uncritical reproduction, in reviews and descriptions of Tress's book, of Minahan's narrative. We *like* the idea that the children in Tress's book were transparent, that they are responsive to interpretation, and that our reading of them is correct (even if, as Tress notes, the images of children in *The Dream Collector* are often deeply unsettling).[25] Childhood is something we can see and understand. I too had found the story of the investigative photographer and his child subjects satisfying. It is what had drawn me to *The Dream Collector*, even if I had had my suspicions—a skepticism that led me to find that story's fractures and inconsistencies.

Armed with the information provided by Tress and several leads and sources he sent me, I began to find accounts of *The Dream Collector* that had escaped my initial research. These often were published in periodicals perhaps known to photographers but not readily accessible through my library's databases, and they reinforced Ganz's description of Minahan's fabulizing. Some are recent. For example, in a 2010 interview in *Shots* magazine, Tress describes asking children to enact dream scenarios but makes clear he had considered the scenarios beforehand. "Just by wandering around the city I would serendipitously find children playing in odd locations that would suggest possible reenactments," Tress explains. "I would ask the kids if they would climb into an overturned tractor or run away from a giant plastic roadside dinosaur."[26] The latter photograph, published in *The Dream Collector*, features a little girl trotting away from the dinosaur in question. Minahan's caption reads: "Tress accompanied her on [a tour of a park] and asked if she ever dreamed about monsters. 'Only once,' she said matter-of-factly. At which point she painted a vivid word picture of being chased by none other than *Tyrannosaurus rex* himself. 'It was kind of spooky,' she admitted."[27] Minahan's caption and its reference to the "vivid word picture" of the girl's dream stands in stark contrast to Tress's description of the photo, in which he names it as one of many images for which he recruited children to enact predetermined dream archetypes, "like being born, or being bitten or dying."[28] In 2017, seven years before Ganz wrote about Tress's methods for the Getty, he published an interview with Tress in *Esopus* magazine. Ganz jokingly characterizes Tress's directorial mode as "getting random people in the street to do bizarre things in front of the camera," and indeed Tress describes wandering the city with unusual props, such as a stuffed rat, to see if any dream scenarios arose from the dynamism among the object, the cityscape, and the people he encountered, including children. "More often I would find the object first . . . and I also came across these kids who were there, and so I would just incorporate these objects to create a more eerie, strange, science-fiction kind of feeling."[29] Object first, kids second, scene third.

However, I also discovered Tress had spoken about his multifaceted process in creating *The Dream Collector*, as well as the inaccuracies of Minahan's introduction, decades earlier, in 1982, in an interview for the *Photo Review*. "The way the book is written implies that this is the dream of the kid in the photograph. But that really wasn't the way it was," Tress explains. He attributes some of the dreams depicted in his series to conversations with young people but identifies a range of other sources—the childhood dreams of his friends, a study of Kafka's dreams, classic books on nightmares, his own experiences—all of which he recorded in notebooks, breaking them down into patterns before finding locations and children to enact them. In this interview, his interactions with children appear protean and shifting. At one moment the children are abstracted vehicles for Tress's self-exploration: "I think they were probably surrogates of my younger self."[30] Elsewhere, they are willing collaborators, poised to take direction to achieve his vision: "Children would ask, what are you taking those pictures for? And I would say, I'm doing a thing on dreams and then I would say, you don't mind hanging upside down (laughs) holding this dead cat in your hand? They would do it immediately. They had that sense of play and theater. But adults are very embarrassed because adults are concerned with what the photograph will look like afterwards."[31]

I was delighted by that anecdote—or as delighted as someone can be by a story involving a dead (and I hope taxidermied) cat—but that statement, and its underlying assumptions about the pliability of children's imaginations as compared to adults', also made my heart sink a bit. As someone interested in children as active cultural agents, and as a scholar drawn to young people's creative output, I understood my bias for detecting child agency, my inclination to look for ways their participation finds footholds, no matter how feeble, amid adult authority and assumptions. However, some of the ideas of childhood arising in my research seemed to diminish the role young people played in *The Dream Collector.* I was beginning to wonder if the childhood at the center of *The Dream Collector* had anything at all to do with the lived experiences of the young people in the book's photos. Could I disarticulate the child dreamer from the dream photographer? Was the child a participant at all or entirely a surrogate?

I found it useful at this point to turn to the rich range of metaphors Tress offers in his writings on photography. These metaphors capture an ambiguous understanding of the relationship between the agency of the photographer and that of the subject. Some suggest antagonism: the photographer maintains potentially malevolent control. For example, in 1974, while creating the photo-essay *Shadow,* Tress described the photographer as "the vampire of light" who "steals the souls of his subjects and changes them into eternal shades. He pushes them into the world of electronic illusion and negative transparency, making his model-victims submit to the cruel laws of media and instant transmission."[32] The photographer's almost supernatural ability to compel his subjects into attitudes that please him resurfaces in other writings; for example, in "The Photograph as Magical Image," Tress writes that the photographer "seems to be able to almost anticipate the activities of his subjects and sometimes actually appears to cause their occurrence by some mental willpower of his own that projects outward, making reality conform to his mentally conceived image of it that he records on film."[33] But typically Tress's faith in that power is more nuanced. In the same essay, he dubs the photographer not a vampire but a magician. "Often his best photographs are taken in a trance-like state where there is an almost unspoken mystical communication between his subject and himself," Tress writes, "and action is directed through nonverbal gesture and psychic transference."[34] A few years later, writing about another surrealist project, *Theater of the Mind* (1976–1977), Tress expressed a generative uncertainty about who precisely directs a photograph and its representation of a subject's inner world. "The photographic frame is no longer being used as a documentary window into undisturbed private lives," he writes, "but as a stage on which the subjects consciously direct themselves to bring forward hidden information that is not usually displayed on the surface."[35]

Tress is not referring directly to child subjects in those passages, but the power dynamic between photographer and subject, the representer and the represented, is relevant to *The Dream Collector* and beyond. The question "Who is in charge?" is familiar to those who research child-produced culture, and Tress's writings on photography reinforce the idea that this is often an unanswerable question—or the answer is adult and child, both and neither. Minahan encouraged me to read Tress's photographs in an either/or manner: *either* they aligned with the child-focused method described in the book's introduction *or* they revealed this story as fiction. A more nuanced composition narrative of *The Dream Collector* takes into account its contradictory origins to suggest that it is a not an ambivalent project, trying to be two things at once, but instead a work of collaborative *improvisation*, a term Tress and many who know his work frequently deploy to describe the playful back-and-forth of his process. Ganz, for example, introduces this term when interpreting *Flood Dream*, the image that, earlier in my research, had led me to question Minahan's child-centric narrative. Ganz calls the image "a miraculous product of creative improvisation. As is often the case in this series, his method followed a pattern of (1) random serendipitous amalgamation of setting, prop(s), and child 'actor,' (2) spontaneous playacting for the camera, with Tress directing the action, and (3) retroactive interpretation of the finished work."[36] This account begins to describe the intergenerational improvisation I intuited from engaging with *The Dream Collector*. However, Ganz minimizes children's roles in the photographs. He eliminates Tress's initial conversations with children, even though he later writes that *Flood Dream* had been inspired, in part, by "a specific dream that the photographer tape-recorded, 'in which a child explained that his house was washed into the sea by a flood and he watched it all from the roof.'"[37] And enclosing the word "actor" in quotes not only communicates that these young people were not actors (true) but also implies that their creative work was unserious, merely of childhood play—something Tress himself suggests and that I will discuss in more detail below—or that they were passive, *in*active.

Improvisation (for me at least) is associated with performance more than photography, although the line between the two is permeable in much of Tress's work. So it makes sense that one of the germs of *The Dream Collector*—one I discovered through my correspondence with Tress—was, in fact, a genre-bending, intergenerational performance. Tress highlighted in his correspondence with me that vital to his creation of *The Dream Collector* was his work in the years leading up to that project with Richard Lewis, an educator and fellow Bard College graduate. Lewis reached out to Tress in early 1971; he had recently founded the Touchstone Center for Children in New York and was working with children on various projects rooted in his belief that the imagination is central to child development. One of Lewis's workshops encouraged students to explore their daydreams through creative outlets, and he invited Tress to participate. Coverage in the *New York Times* of one of these workshops at PS 198 introduces Tress's collaboration and the participation of two children, Shaun and Nelson: "One week the teacher invited a friend, Arthur Tress, a professional photographer, who arrived with a duffle full of costumes—capes, crowns, horns, swords and monster masks. The children dressed themselves and took parts. Shaun became a unicorn, Nelson became a bearded king. [Nelson] also quickly asserted himself as the main author of an improvised story—about a king who wanted to capture a unicorn to present to the princess he was marrying. Then, functioning as a director, Nelson arranged the other children in a series of tableaux that Mr. Tress photographed. In the school's playground, in less than an hour, the children created an elaborate narrative in pictures."[38] According to Lewis, Tress filmed the children's playacting and created "still-picture dramas, which were developed and made into a series of 'dream books'—which could be read as a sequence of unfolding images and interpreted in endless ways."[39] Tress later described his work with Lewis as "a mind-expanding moment for me; a turning point—a kind of mental can opener."[40] The idiosyncrasies of my research had led me to the Touchstone Center, one of *The Dream Collector*'s *earliest* origin points, *last*. However, Tress's work at PS 198 was a "mental can opener" for me, too, and provides a compelling image of intergenerational improvisation: one that crystallizes the process I see at work in the composition narrative of Tress's book. The final product of these early collaborations, dream books capturing children's narratives in an adult's photographs under the direction of an educator, artifacts that resist linear and conclusive narration and so can be interpreted in "endless ways," felt like precisely the type of document I needed to find some closure to my research.

But they were not available for me to see. "I suspect that there was only one copy of the book, made by each child," Lewis told me, "and so they probably were taken home."[41] The books were, rightly, the property of their (partial) creators, and one more gap, for now, in my archive.

Negotiation

Most of the interpretations of *The Dream Collector* situate the series in Tress's ongoing career or in histories of photography. While all accounts of the photographs acknowledge and sometimes dwell on the fact that Tress's subjects are children, the book has not been part of conversations in childhood studies, and I believe our field can offer at least two useful perspectives to *The Dream Collector* and the improvisations behind its images. First, childhood studies scholars provide critical frameworks for thinking about children's creative agency, which in my reading is an open question in Tress's photographs. Sociologist Alison James charts how conceptualizations of child agency have shifted over time away from the assumption of independent action and toward a recognition of choices children make amid constraining social structures.[42] Literary and cultural studies scholars have amplified this perspective in recent years. Particularly useful are those theorizations that assume that children *exercise* rather than simply possess, or do not possess, agency, and that any practice of agency is a negotiation among individuals within systems of power. As Marah Gubar argues, "If we as scholars want to claim that children have agency, then, we must concede that the kind of agency they have is not synonymous with autonomy."[43] Disarticulating agency from autonomy is a vital critical move: it illuminates a spectrum of potential relationships between children and the adults who create alongside them. As Madeleine Leonard argues, "The meaning and experiences of childhood are constantly negotiated and renegotiated between adults and children."[44] That negotiation, as Rachel Conrad points out, can take many forms; adults can "recognize, acknowledge, facilitate, preserve, ignore, obscure, erode, or obstruct the agency that children claim, practice, or express."[45] These theorizations of child agency provide a useful framework for understanding the rich range of children's creative engagements with adults. Free from the expectation of autonomy and armed with the possibility that intergenerational collaboration, as Conrad's list indicates, can manifest in radically different ways, scholars can better understand examples of child-produced culture that certainly involved, and sometimes center, adults.

This elastic paradigm of children's creative agency accommodates *The Dream Collector*'s improvisations. In fact, Tress's series is useful in demonstrating that a *single cultural artifact*, when its composition narrative is understood in its full complexity, is a shape-shifting endeavor. Its improvisations, like understandings of child-produced culture originating in childhood studies, make clear that, in practice, the roles of adult and child are flexible; throughout the creative process, the two occupy ever-changing positions, at times directing, at times following direction. Sometimes, Tress and the other adults who participated in the images' creation and, later, circulation and interpretation are amicable collaborators who "recognize, acknowledge, facilitate" children's voices. This is certainly true at the project's early origins at PS 198. Tress and Lewis were invested in allowing children to direct their own dream scenarios, and often they actively resisted interpreting young people's words and images. When Nelson, one of the child participants, drew "a scene of violence involving four figures," it was unclear "whether they were animals or human or some combination of the two. . . . Nelson didn't say and Mr. Lewis purposefully never asked." Later, in recording children's daydreams, Tress limited his role to prop master, providing the duffle bag of costumes, and dutiful photographer. "The children dressed themselves and took parts," the *Times* reports, and Nelson "quickly asserted himself as the main author of an improvised story."[46] However, elsewhere in the long history of *The Dream Collector*'s creation, Tress and others obscure or obstruct children's practice of agency: when Tress uses children to stage a preconceived nightmare, for example, or when Minahan, perhaps at the publisher's bidding, fictionalizes a child's perspective to align with an appealing narrative.

The Dream Collector also crystallizes what childhood studies can offer to studies of photography—in particular, a sense of the history of visual and ideological constructions childhood. For much of photographic history, children have been subjects of, or subjected to, the camera's eye, framed through the stubborn tradition of Romantic childhood. Yet, as Anne Higonnet argues, buried in the proliferation of photographs of Romantic children is that conceit's undoing. Photographers' obsession with the Romantic child, and the "rather wild instability" of the supposedly objective photograph, inevitably reveal the tensions in that figure and its constructed nature.[47] Moreover, as researchers have sought out avenues to amplify children's voices and as photography has become an increasingly accessible medium, studies have, at times, turned to photographs taken *by* children.[48] Tress's *The Dream Collector* and, especially, his creative partnerships with children and the self-consciously improvised images those collaborations have produced, underscore both the instability of the concept of childhood Higonnet identifies (sometimes it is archetype and symbol, sometimes it is an individual, embodied child who challenges our assumptions) and the possibility of child participation that characterizes those recent studies.

This history of photography's investment in Romantic childhood destabilizes some of the rhetoric around childhood embedded in *The Dream Collector* and its composition narrative. While Ganz acknowledges how Tress's improvisational approach allowed him flexibility in negotiating the ideas, subjects, props, and settings of his photos, it does not account as fully for how Tress negotiated the ideas and expectations typically assigned to adults and children. Who leads and who follows? Who acts with intention and who does so without self-consciousness? Those expectations, cultural constructions of youth and adulthood that have been so widely accepted as to be practically invisible, are also elements of the environment Tress and his collaborators responded to. For example, both Lewis and Tress are invested in ideas of children as more imaginative and less inhibited than adults, and at times that inflects their reading to children's ideas and creations. Lewis, for example, was disappointed when one child, prompted to represent his daydreams, drew an image of Porky Pig rather than something more radical; the child was a little older, Lewis explained, and therefore "further away, in [his] ardently Wordsworthian view, from a young child's freshness of vision."[49] And Tress was attracted to children's dreams at the outset in part due to the work of Carl Jung, whose theories run parallel to Romantic ideas of childhood innocence. For Jung, children's dreams, unlike those of adults, are relatively unclouded by the interference of personal associations and, as Jolande Jacobi explains, the child's psyche is "still completely interwoven with its primal source"; therefore, "the dreams of children provide particularly suitable material for the investigation of the nature and operation of the [Jungian] archetypes."[50] The influence of Jungian childhood is evident when Tress reflects on *The Dream Collector*, even years later: "The child and I together sought out that participatory instant of magical thinking by an unsophisticated openness to playful possibilities inherent in all acts and objects. A crooked stick became a snake; a reflection of a face in water became a skull. . . . I learned that for children, as well as for myself, that there is a very thin veil between the world of the actual and the make-believe. The dream-life slides easily between the two, using the same metaphors and signs."[51]

Conclusion

It is noteworthy that Tress describes his own understanding of dream and reality as comparable to that of his child subjects. *Together*, they sought out playful possibilities. For both adult photographer and child subject, the line between the actual and the make-believe is porous. As someone who studies children's literature, this is a familiar refrain. I often encounter the assumption that those who most successfully document childhood are, essentially, children themselves. Celebrations of childlike adults might be framed as complimentary, but they are often deployed in infantilizing or even pathological ways. Consider Virginia Woolf's assessment of Lewis Carroll, another photographer of children: "His childhood was sharply severed. It lodged in him whole and entire. He could not disperse it. And therefore as he grew older this impediment in the centre of his being, this hard block of pure childhood, starved the mature man of nourishment."[52] Minahan describes Tress in a similar way, albeit with less morbidity and more Romanticism, when he claims that the key to the photographer's "unusual harmony with children is that he is 'childlike' himself, in the true sense of the word. That is, his imagination is still essentially *unsophisticated*—and therefore genuinely creative. Like children, he hasn't yet lost the capacity to wonder, to see the invisible, to dream in the daytime."[53] Such statements strive to dissolve the distance between adult and child, to make that gap traversable, but in fact they reify it. Only *certain* adults can reinhabit childhood, and they do so only by abandoning their "sophistication." The rest of us are inevitably separated from children, from childhood, by that broken staircase.

However, after my circuitous and sometimes frustrating exploration of *The Dream Collector*, I find that Tress's work suggests something more complicated. He does acknowledge the constructed boundary between adults and children, and the photographs that stage the potential antagonism between generations are some of the most striking in the series. They depict children snared, haunted, or trapped by adults. A blond boy stands on a suburban street, held back by a tall, black-cloaked and hooded figure behind him. A white-gowned girl gazes at the viewer from the end of a walkway leading to a lonely house, its doorway blocked by a tall, menacing adult.[54] But that adult-child stalemate is tempered by what I see as Tress's investment in affinities between adult and child.[55] Interspersed among the photographs of alienation and aggression are images that depict not the dreamer but the dream alone, from the dreamer's perspective. Looking at the photograph, the viewer, whether young or old, knows this scene, recognizes this nightmare: a smirking father figure standing among bullet-hole-riddled targets, a ripped window screen revealing a leering face.[56] While harrowing, these photographs represent shared experience, the continuities of the child's and the adult's inner worlds.

And not every shared dream is so ominous. Others hint at the promise of connection, a collective dreaming into joy. One of the most famous images from *The Dream Collector* features three children, arms outstretched, silhouetted against chain link (Figure 9.2).[57] Tress remembers taking the photograph in a Queens playground: "A boy had climbed a baseball backstop fence. He reached the top and was lying flat. I took a few snaps and then asked his friends if they would join him up there. They did, and it seemed to me that the three boys there resembled a flock of birds silhouetted against the dark sky. This had the potential for a dream photo

FIGURE 9.2 Arthur Tress, *Flying Dream, Queens, New York*, 1971. Reprinted in *The Dream Collector* (Richmond, VA: Westover Press, 1972). Copyright Arthur Tress Archive LLC.

to illustrate the idea of one of the most frequent of all dream motifs: Flying."[58] The boys might become other creatures altogether, birds against the sky, but their avian nature is typical in its strangeness. It is a dream adults, including Tress, share.

NOTES

1. Arthur Tress, *The Dream Collector*, text by John Minahan (Richmond, VA: Westover Press, 1972), 52. *The Dream Collector* is unpaginated. I've designated the first page of the introduction page 1 and numbered subsequent pages accordingly.
2. Moa Goysdotter, *Impure Vision: American Staged Photography of the 1970s* (Lund: Nordic Academic Press, 2013), 117.
3. Tress and Minahan, *Dream Collector*, 3.
4. For a sustained explanation of composition narratives, see the introduction to Victoria Ford Smith, *Between Generations: Collaborative Authorship in the Golden Age of Children's Literature* (Jackson: University Press of Mississippi, 2017).

5. Arthur Tress, quoted in James A. Ganz, "Collecting Dreams," in *Arthur Tress: Rambles, Dreams, and Shadows* (Los Angeles: Getty Museum, 2023), 56–57.
6. Ganz, "Collecting Dreams," 57.
7. Russell Joslin, "Arthur Tress: *The Dream Collector* Revisited," *Shots* 109 (Autumn 2010): 37.
8. Goysdotter, *Impure Vision*, 90.
9. Tress and Minahan, *Dream Collector*, 3.
10. Tress and Minahan, *Dream Collector*, 66.
11. Tress and Minahan, *Dream Collector*, 72.
12. Tress and Minahan, *Dream Collector*, 12.
13. Tress and Minahan, *Dream Collector*, 84.
14. Arthur Tress, "The Dream Collector," excerpt from a press release for *Daymares*, in Arthur Tress, *Arthur Tress: Talisman*, ed. Marco Livingstone (New York: Thames and Hudson, 1986), 150.
15. C. R. Wasserman, "Fears Seen through a Child's Eyes," *Boston Globe*, April 17, 1973.
16. Joslin, "Arthur Tress," 36.
17. Tress and Minahan, *Dream Collector*, 70.
18. Ted Loos, "Lost, Now Found: Visions of 1964," *New York Times*, April 8, 2012.
19. Joslin, "Arthur Tress," 38.
20. Arthur Tress, email message to the author, November 23, 2023.
21. Ganz, "Collecting Dreams," 61.
22. Ganz, "Collecting Dreams," 62. Later moments in this chapter will reveal contradictory accounts of whether or not Tress used a tape recorder, which is a small detail. However, a tape recorder does suggest an investment in the embodied voices of children. Tress generously sent me scans of his notebooks, in which he recorded information about children's dreams.
23. Ganz, "Collecting Dreams," 63–64.
24. Arthur Tress, email message to the author, November 28, 2023.
25. One of the more delightful anecdotes in Ganz's account of *The Dream Collector* centers how upsetting the photographs can be. Ganz recounts a meeting between Tress and Maurice Sendak. Tress recalls that Sendak "was a bit taken aback" by the dream photographs. "He thought they were a bit too direct and I think too dark in tone. From his point of view, where the illustrated dreams in his own work are more lyrical and not frightening, perhaps my more gothic and sinister interpretations were a bit over the top." Ganz, "Collecting Dreams," 59.
26. Joslin, "Arthur Tress," 43.
27. Tress and Minahan, *Dream Collector*, 82.
28. Joslin, "Arthur Tress," 43.
29. James A. Ganz, "Arthur Tress: Dreaming in Color," *Esopus* 24 (Spring 2017): 216.
30. Stephen Perloff, "Arthur Tress: The Dream Collector," *Photo Review* 15, no. 4 (Summer 1982): 13.
31. Perloff, "Arthur Tress," 14.
32. Arthur Tress, "Apropos 'the shadows,'" in Livingstone, *Talisman*, 151.
33. Arthur Tress, "The Photograph as Magical Image," in *Rambles*, 9.
34. Tress, *Rambles*, 9.

35. Arthur Tress, "Family Portraits: the Techniques of *Theater of the Mind*," in Livingstone, *Talisman*, 151.
36. Ganz, "Collecting Dreams," 66.
37. Ganz, "Collecting Dreams," 66. Note here the tape recorder reappears, despite other sources indicating that Tress did not own a tape recorder.
38. Joseph Lelyveld, "Class 4–4: Childish Fantasy Is More than Make-Believe," *New York Times*, May 3, 1971.
39. Richard Lewis, *Living by Wonder: Writings on the Imaginative Life of Childhood* (New York: Touchstone Center Publications, 2006), 60.
40. Joslin, "Arthur Tress," 36.
41. Richard Lewis, email message to the author, December 6, 2023.
42. Allison James, "Giving Voice to Children's Voices: Practices and Problems, Pitfalls and Potentials," *American Anthropologist* 109, no. 2 (2007): 269–270.
43. Marah Gubar, "The Hermeneutics of Recuperation: What a Kinship-Model Approach to Child Agency Could Do for Children's Literature and Childhood Studies," *Jeunesse* 8, no. 1 (Summer 2016): 293.
44. Madeleine Leonard, *The Sociology of Children, Childhood, and Generation* (Los Angeles: Sage, 2016), 149.
45. Rachel Conrad, *Time for Childhoods: Youth Poets and Questions of Agency* (Amherst: University of Massachusetts Press, 2019), 9.
46. Lelyveld, "Class," 39.
47. Anne Higonnet, *Pictures of Innocence: The History and Crisis of Ideal Childhood* (New York: Thames and Hudson, 1998), 109.
48. Several studies of photographs taken by children have been published in the social sciences, especially in anthropology and sociology, and theorize photography as a means for children to become participants in, rather than simply subjects of, research. See, for example, Vu Song Ha, "'Closer to My World': Children with Autism Spectrum Disorder Tell Their Stories through Photovoice," *Global Public* 11, no. 5–6 (2016): 546–563 and Wendy Luttrell, *Children Framing Childhoods: Working-Class Kids' Visions of Care* (Bristol: Bristol University Press, 2020).
49. Lelyveld, "Class," 39.
50. Jolande Jacobi, *Complex/Archetype/Symbol in the Psychology of C. G. Jung* (London: Routledge, 1999), 133.
51. Joslin, "Arthur Tress," 42.
52. Virginia Woolf, "Lewis Carroll," in *The Essays of Virginia Woolf*, vol. 6, ed. Stuart N. Clarke (London: Hogarth, 2011), 210.
53. Tress and Minahan, *The Dream Collector*, 3.
54. Tress and Minahan, *The Dream Collector*, 89, 31.
55. Tress would likely resonate with Gubar's kinship model of childhood and its insistence "first and foremost on how alike younger and older people are. Only after emphasizing this elemental similarity do they acknowledge—using obstinately tentative language—the possibility of age-related differences and deficiencies." Gubar, "Hermeneutics," 300.
56. Tress and Minahan, *The Dream Collector*, 27, 43.
57. Tress and Minahan, *The Dream Collector*, 91.
58. Joslin, "Arthur Tress," 38.

10

Choreographing Kinship

The Adult-Child Pas de Deux in *Day on Earth* and *Lineage*

MARAH GUBAR

As a childhood studies scholar who specializes in theater history, I have always depended on the expertise of archivists. But never until now have I had the experience of a librarian setting before me two artworks that spoke to one another so eloquently that I felt compelled to carry forward the work of creative juxtaposition that their curatorial pairing set into motion.

Tucked away in the wildly rural yet art-infused edge of western Massachusetts known as the Berkshires, the Jacob's Pillow Dance Festival is a magical place to visit at any time. But my July 2021 trip there felt even more precious than usual after a year spent hunkering at home under the shadow of a global pandemic. Before I arrived, I wrote to Norton Owen, the Pillow's director of preservation, to explain that I was working on a project that involved bringing childhood studies and dance studies together to analyze a phenomenon that I call the adult-child pas de deux: any choreographed sequence (i.e., not just ballet) in which an adult and a child dance together for an extended period of time. Having studied ballet and tap as a child and throughout my time earning a BFA in musical theater at the University of Michigan, I already knew about many adult-child dance duets on stage and screen, from the tap routines Bill "Bojangles" Robinson choreographed for himself and Shirley Temple in 1930s films to the poignant dream ballet that Peter Darling designed for *Billy Elliot: The Musical* (2005), in which the boy playing Billy as a child dances to the strains of *Swan Lake* with an older performer representing his adult self. Were there also intergenerational pairings in the modern dance tradition that I could learn about during my visit to the Pillow?

I was a little nervous about how my query would be received, not just because I worried that there might be a dearth of relevant materials at the Pillow, but also because of the snobbish response I got the first time I asked an archivist for assistance with a child-centered project. Some years ago, I was trying to figure out when and how children's theater emerged as a separate subcategory of drama, and the man then in charge of the Harvard Theater Collection discouraged me from visiting Cambridge by sternly informing me that not only did his library not house the particular material I sought, but also that "we have made a *point* of not collecting anything to do with children."

Temporarily cowed, I sought out other, more hospitable archives and eventually tried to counter such ageism by publishing an article demonstrating that child performers and playgoers were so omnipresent in nineteenth-century theaters that almost all forms of American popular drama from that era could be considered children's theater; only in the early twentieth century did artists and commentators begin drawing a sharp line of division between child- and adult-oriented productions and deeming the former less worthy of critical attention than the latter (meaning that Harvard had collected a good bit of material related to the rise of children's theater despite itself).[1] Dance, I discovered, had played an unexpectedly pivotal role in this process, since the nineteenth-century all-child pantomimes and operettas that paved the way for the emergence of children's plays were themselves inspired by the popularity of an internationally famous juvenile ballet company, Les Danseuses Viennoises, who enjoyed phenomenal success with mixed-age audiences across Europe and North America in the 1840s.[2]

If one way of refusing to take children seriously as artists involves a reluctance to archive and engage critically with their work, another is that on the rare occasions when such art does receive scholarly attention, particular pieces tend to get singled out and treated as exceptional anomalies rather than being contextualized as part of any kind of artistic tradition.[3] With regard to the adult-child pas de deux, for instance, several excellent essays concentrate on analyzing the famous Robinson and Temple staircase dance, while others focused on the whole of *Billy Elliot* contain some insightful commentary about its younger-and-older-self pas de deux.[4] But to my knowledge, no one has yet characterized the adult-child dance duet as an artistic trope or trend with a history worth tracing. While my decision to lump quite different kinds of dances together under this rubric might seem odd, I am motivated by the idea that viewing such intergenerational pairings as isolated anomalies has prevented us from seeing continuities in how dancing children function in different eras, not to mention appreciating the radical force of deviations from these long-standing norms. Plus, as dance scholars now acknowledge—and the history of the adult-child pas de deux confirms—the lines between ballet, musical theater, social, and modern dance are extremely permeable, with artists often working in and being influenced by multiple movement traditions.

Fortunately for me, Owen did not draw snobbish distinctions but instead performed his own act of inclusive coupling by encouraging me to view taped performances of two quite different modern dances featuring intergenerational pairings. When I arrived, he had already cued up for me the José Limón Dance Company's 1995 rendition of choreographer Doris Humphrey's *Day on Earth* (1947), which he explained was a classic work by a pioneering figure in the development of modern dance, featuring a central male protagonist who moves from solo laborer to romantic partner to loving father. I was grateful for this introduction, because at that point I had never heard of Humphrey, who—as I subsequently learned—contemporary dance critics sometimes describe as a "lost" or "worse than forgotten" choreographer, for reasons I will expand upon later in this essay.[5] That same day, Owen also alerted me to the existence of *Lineage* (2000), a much shorter piece that eleven-year-old dancer Lingji Hon choreographed and performed with her father as part of *Dances by Very Young Choreographers*, a program directed by award-winning dance educator Ellen Robbins and presented at Jacob's Pillow in 2001. Later, when I interviewed Hon and then Robbins, I would learn that Hon—who began taking classes with Robbins when she was around five years old—came up with the idea of designing an adult-child dance duet on this theme when she was nine and performed two earlier versions of it as part of programs that Robbins organized in New York City for her students to share their work with parents, friends, prospective students, and the general public.

To be honest, I had not even dared to hope that the archive would contain an adult-child pas de deux choreographed by a child, much less one that seemed to talk back to its more famous predecessor by making its youthful protagonist more centrally involved in the action of the dance. Whereas the *Day on Earth* child serves as a supporting player to her father, *Lineage* positions child and father as fellow participants in an interactive relationship involving affection and aggression, negotiation and compromise.[6] When I floated to Owen the idea of reading *Lineage*'s more fraught but also more egalitarian adult-child engagement as a riposte to *Day on Earth*—since the two dances also feature some striking similarities—he gifted me a piece of insider knowledge gleaned from his prior job working with the Limón Dance Company.[7] A few years before Robbins led the class for aspiring dancer-choreographers from which *Lineage* emerged, she helped train the two young performers who alternated in the role of the child for the 1995 production of *Day on Earth* that I had watched, meaning that she had brought an intimate knowledge of Humphrey's work into the room when she was assisting Hon in the creation of *Lineage*.

Indeed, Robbins later confirmed that she recommended and helped to prepare "many" child dancers for different productions of *Day on Earth*. She also shared with me that Humphrey's influential treatise *The Art of Making Dances* (1959)—which features lots of small creative assignments for novice choreographers—was "one of the few books" that influenced how she helps young people learn to choreograph their own dances, a scaffolded process that involves inviting less experienced pupils to engage in short, carefully structured forms of improvisation and more practiced ones to craft their own dances while getting feedback from Robbins and their fellow classmates (as Hon did while creating *Lineage*).[8] For this reason, as I will demonstrate, we can trace a line of influence from Humphrey to Robbins to Hon: even though Hon herself only got to know Humphrey's work as a college student, some of the eloquently expressed ideas about stage design and the stylization of everyday gestures that Robbins absorbed from *The Art of Making Dances* inform the structuring of *Lineage*, as they do the work of many adult choreographers of modern dance.

At the same time, though, the effect of having a child function not just as pupil and performer but also as choreographer sets into motion an exciting shift *away* from dance tradition, too. Whereas Humphrey's artistic choices in *Day on Earth* hearken back to a Romantic tradition of "othering" and objectifying children by portraying them as asocial, artless playthings, Hon's in *Lineage* portray parent and child as fellow acculturated and agential beings, neither of whom is completely autonomous since both are engaged in a fraught yet loving negotiation between honoring tradition and cherishing novelty. Being influenced by one's predecessors, *Lineage* suggests, is a point of kinship between younger and older people, not a sharply differentiating factor (even though adults often have the power to exert a higher degree of sway over children than vice versa). To second and support this point, I will trace how deeply the adult Humphrey was shaped by Romantic tropes she absorbed not just from Anglo-American poetry and dance, but also from her own Robbins figure: Mary Wood Hinman, a leading American researcher, teacher, and choreographer of folk dances in the early 1900s, whose classes Humphrey began attending when she was about eight years old.

All of these American artists and educators were working within and against the constraints of a culture that routinely denigrates dependency on others, conflates agency with autonomy, and fetishizes originality. In such societies, positive portrayals of interdependency, symbiosis, and collectivity are by no means thick on the ground, nor commonly celebrated as canonical texts. Recuperating the lost lineage of the adult-child pas de deux helps us to appreciate dance's special capacity to depict dependency not as a deficiency or difference that divides some human beings from others, but rather as a uniting factor and thing of beauty. In any pas de deux, but especially in ones that feature intergenerational pairings, significant asymmetries may exist in terms of who the partners are and what they do without canceling out the fundamental kinship they share by virtue of being fellow dancers. When that happens, such dances can help us to conceive what it might be like to inhabit a more flexibly equitable and mutually supportive society by serving as a moving metaphor for the adult-child relationship that is in line with the caringly egalitarian vision of what it means to be a child that I call the kinship model.[9] Surprisingly, this turns out to be true even of some dances that participate in a Romantic style of choreographing for children that I trace back to the Viennese Children and forward to *Day on Earth*. So, after pinpointing some problems with that choreographic mode, I then make use of that same choreography—and the reactions of socialists who unexpectedly loved it—to nuance overly reductive accounts of Romanticism that fail to register the egalitarian impulses that this movement included. Romantic discourse about childhood was more multifaceted than childhood studies scholars generally allow, encompassing not just reifying difference-model depictions of youth that objectify children as asocial "others" but also respectful kinship-model portrayals of younger and older people engaging in harmless and even joyous and mutually transformative acts of intergenerational communion.

Before diving back into the distant past, though, let me first elaborate on the sharp contrast between how the child dancer enters in *Day on Earth* versus how she first appears in *Lineage*, which positions Hon's child to play a more central role than Humphrey's. In both of these artworks, a young dancer of about ten years old portrays the child character. But in Humphrey's dance, the child does not appear until roughly halfway through the piece, when a cloth covering is drawn aside to reveal her prone body, which lies lifeless on the ground until her parents infuse vitality into her. Only when her mother makes a series of beckoning hand gestures that tacitly command the child to sit up, lie down, and roll over does Humphrey's child begin to move, obeying these physical commands like a well-trained pet or an adult-controlled puppet. Doubling down on the implication that children begin life in a wholly inert yet weirdly disciplined state of compliance, Humphrey then has the father pick the child up and swing her up and down in an *en face* lift reminiscent of a ballet "fish dive" (Figure 10.1 and 10.2).

The parents then pass the child back and forth between them before laying her down on the ground again while they dance together, thus exacerbating the impression that their offspring lacks even the smallest degree of self-propelling agency. In other words, Humphrey's child initially functions less like a fellow person than as an inanimate prop or plaything manipulated by adults.

The opening of *Lineage*, by contrast, immediately establishes adult and child as partners in an interpersonal relationship generated by the youth's arrival, which draws the elder into a new plane of existence. As the dance begins, a long rectangle of light falls across the dark stage, as if a door in the wings has fallen open. Through this illuminated passageway spins the child, who periodically pauses to mime the pulling of an invisible cord. Each time she does so, a man—whom the title *Lineage* invites us to read as a male ancestor or elder—takes a slow step after her, lunging forward on bended knee as if the other end of the cord were attached to his chest (Figure 10.3). A haunting and reiterative musical motif accompanies this movement. As the child whirls around, four distinct yet muted bell tones chime out, the last of which is much higher than the ones that precede it; when she pauses to pull the unseen cord, a low gong tolls which at first sounds like a single note, but eventually grows more complex and polyphonic, like a foghorn accompanied by a multilayered hum of ocean and city sounds.

We can read this invisible rope as a riff on the umbilical cord, one that doubles down on the intimate interchange enabled by that two-way conduit by positioning the child not as an inert, passive object of care, but rather as a full subject—an active partner and participant—in her own growth process. Throughout *Lineage*, the child character's subjectivity finds expression in solo spinning, which suggests both inward-facing introspection and the aspirational act of seeking out new experiences and forms of personal expression. This in-and-out dynamic, which intensifies later in the dance as the child whirls away from and then back toward the adult, gets established in the dance's opening moments through both movement and musical phrasing: as the child revolves internally

FIGURE 10.1 AND 10.2 Carla Maxwell (Woman), Paul Dennis (Man), and Chelica Kimerling (Child) perform Doris Humphrey's *Day on Earth* (1947), staged by Lucy Venable from the Labanotated score, Limón Dance Company, The Joyce Theater, New York City, NY, November 22, 1995.

FIGURE 10.3 Sat Chuen Hon and Lingji Hon perform Lingji Hon's *Lineage* (2000) in *Dances by Very Young Choreographers*, directed by Ellen Robbins at Jacob's Pillow, Doris Duke Studio Theatre, Becket, MA, June 28, 2001.

around her own axis, she is also traveling downstage left, even as the "dah-dah-dah, DUM" of the bell evokes someone marshaling their inner resources for a big move outward. Yet such self-propelled motion exists not apart from but rather inextricably interwoven with other-directed movement which reads as both constraining (child and adult are yoked together, as if by rope) and sustaining (the deepening aural complexity of the low-pitched gong suggests that interpersonal communion is both grounding and generative).

This ceaseless in-and-out dynamic ensures that even as the child in *Lineage* starts off manifesting a higher degree of agency than her counterpart in *Day on Earth*, such agency never feels synonymous with perfect autonomy. That, I think, is one of the great strengths of Hon's dance: it acknowledges that no one—not even the most self-reliant adult—is wholly uninfluenced by and independent of other living beings and the cultural environment they inhabit. A key way in which *Lineage* dramatizes this point is that the movements made by the adult dancer closely echo and build on the ancient Chinese tradition of Taiji Quan (also known as "tai chi"), thereby signaling how deeply his character, too, has been influenced by the cultural lineage transmitted to him by his predecessors.

As the adult dancer lunges chest-first toward the child, it is clear that this dance will explore the nature of a heartfelt intergenerational bond, which we can read as a parent-child relationship because Hon performed this dance with her father, Sat Chuen Hon. At the same time, though, costumes and music underscore that *Lineage* is not just about a one-on-one adult-child relationship, but also about the broader question of how the child will engage with her Asian ancestry. The father's white, full-length, and "very traditional" Chinese robe (as Hon described it to me) hints at Sat Hon's real-life status as a Taiji Quan master and anticipates how he will attempt to impose the slow, yielding rhythm of Taiji movements onto his daughter in the next section of the dance. In contrast, the daughter wears a much shorter, bright red tunic that is more reminiscent of an ordinary shirt than a ceremonial gown; and this vibrant splash of color on a mostly dark stage anticipates the heated resistance the daughter will express in the middle section of the dance, when she mimics but then decisively rejects some of the steps her father models in order to strike out on her own self-selected paths.

Part of the power of the opening sequence of *Lineage* lies in how it evokes not just any child-and-adult pairing, but rather the more particular situation of a family navigating a transition between two cultures: when the child enters first and tows her parent after her, we can interpret this moment as attesting both to how the birth of any new person pulls their caregiver(s) into a world of novel experiences, and to how children in an immigrant family often immerse themselves more quickly and fully than their elders in the new culture, so much so that they sometimes serve as translators, facilitators, or guides for their parents. For even as the light-induced doorway effect situates this action as unfolding at a threshold between two realms, the music that accompanies this dance represents a generative fusion of Eastern and Western traditions. The haunting bell-and-gong motif that opens (and later, closes) the dance was borrowed from a piece by Collin Walcott, a cofounder of the American jazz and world music band Oregon, while the more instrumentally complex and lushly lyrical middle section was composed by the Tibetan-born Nepalese Buddhist nun Ani Choying Drolma, whose "music combines Tibetan melodies with traditional and contemporary instruments, like singing bowls and synthesizers."[10]

Both Hon and Robbins recalled that Hon had come up with the idea of designing a dance about lineage using the Drolma song after hearing it played at home, while Robbins suggested the pointillist Walcott motif as an aural bookend later on in the creative process, with Hon agreeing because she liked how "mysterious" it sounded.[11] Their collective decision to intermix two separate musical scores feels especially appropriate because part of the power of this opening sequence of steps derives from how it melds together two movement traditions to create something that feels both familiar and new, reiterative and original. As Hon explained to me, she began learning the series of thirteen movements that form the basis of Taiji from her Chinese-born father at the same time as she began studying modern dance with Robbins, during her early childhood in New York City. No wonder, then, that *Lineage* repeatedly echoes both this carefully prescribed series of movements and the modern dance tradition forged by figures such as Isadora Duncan, Humphrey, and Martha Graham during the first half of the twentieth century.

Even as the father's glacially deliberate knee bends in the opening sequence evoke the slow and yielding spirit of Taiji, for example, he also follows directly in the footsteps of the male protagonist of Humphrey's *Day on Earth*, whose first entrance consists of a series of low, slow lunges from upstage left toward downstage right. When I asked Robbins to say more about the role she played in the evolution of *Lineage*, she recalled Hon coming up with the lion's share of the steps (including the child's whirling-and-rope-pulling moves) while she "probably" made suggestions about the larger structure of the dance, such as how it unfolds along a diagonal trajectory, with some of the most dramatically memorable steps happening upstage right (at the beginning) and downstage left (at the end).

This tentative recollection is supported by the fact that one thing Humphrey does in *The Art of Making Dances* is to diagram the relative strength and weakness of different locations on the stage before expressing her hope that, once equipped with this information, "Many fascinating experiments will occur to the student and the teacher. For example, deliberately try to build a diagonal sequence from an up corner to downstage, which will stress strong climactic movement in the two weak areas and be timid in the three strong places."[12] The opening and closing sections of *Lineage*, set in relatively weak parts of the stage, do indeed feature especially strong and memorable movements, including a powerfully resonant final tableau in which adult and child twist toward each other, with the child's right palm coming to press against the adult's (Figure 10.4)—a move that recalls another Humphrey exercise that prompts novice choreographers to experiment with creating their own variations on the stylized handshake.[13]

It feels especially appropriate that *Lineage* ends with parent and child coming together on common ground because this dance is infused from the start with a more deeply egalitarian spirit than *Day on Earth*. Although many of Humphrey's other dances—including *The Shakers* (1931) and *New Dance* (1935)—challenge patriarchal individualism by centering matriarchs or celebrating collectivist group activity, in *Day on Earth* she hews more closely to the norms of the sexist, ageist society she inhabited by situating her male character as the primary begetter and breadwinner of the family. Striding onto the scene alone, his solo pacing from upstage right to downstage left is accompanied by lifting, throwing, pushing, and pounding arm gestures that evoke the rigors of manual labor. Moreover, because he periodically returns to this lone exercise after various female figures in his life come and go—soon after she arrives, his flighty first lover disappears; then, the child he has with his more serious second partner leaves home; and finally, the second lover dies—Humphrey's father figure is clearly set up as the central character of a dance whose title invites us to regard him as an abstract "everyman" in whose experiences of labor, love, and loss "we must all of necessity read something of ourselves," to quote dance critic John Martin, who reviewed the earliest New York City performances of *Day on Earth*.[14]

Working half a century later, Hon shifts us away from this tradition of universalizing adult male experience as the norm from which all other forms of life deviate or descend, not least by having her two main characters enter in reverse generational order. As we have seen, if anyone gets set up as a string-pulling puppeteer in the opening sequence of *Lineage*, it is the female child: ingeniously

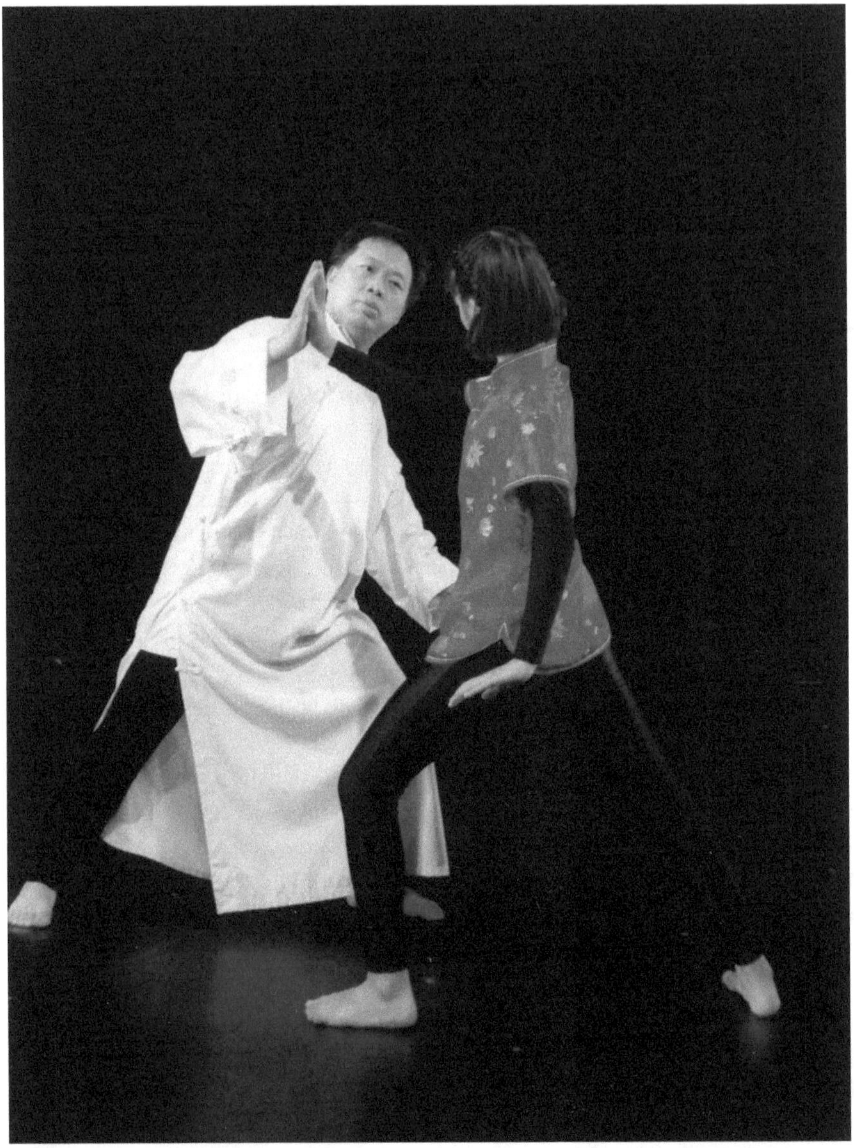

FIGURE 10.4 Ellen Robbins scrapbook photograph of Sat Chuen Hon and Lingji Hon in *Lineage*, taken by Faye Ellman, undated.

literalizing her title, Hon has the younger dancer conjure up the invisible yet powerful "line" that connects two people despite their difference in "age," thereby suggesting that caregiving is an inherently *reactive* process that involves responding to what the child is already being and doing. Yet as *Lineage* unfolds, it becomes increasingly clear that Hon does not simply flip the conventional script by stripping the patriarch of primacy and power and giving these qualities to the child. Rather, she portrays the elder-youth relationship as a simultaneously sustaining and constraining form of intimacy that is always already informed by a push-and-pull dynamic of affection and aggression, resistance and compliance.

Thus, after the child's arrival pulls her parent into a new phase of existence, the second section of this dance depicts them striving to get to know each other better while simultaneously engaging in a power struggle in which they take turns having the upper hand. First, the daughter lunges behind her father for a playfully evasive hide-and-seek movement in which he twists in one direction and then the other, fruitlessly trying to catch sight of her. Once they lock eyes in a way that suggests their familiarity with each other is deepening, he lays a gentle but heavy hand on her shoulder and they revolve around such that he is now standing behind her. Both facing forward, parent and child slowly raise and lower their arms in unison, but because he is so much taller than she is, *he* now seems to be exerting an invisible yet commandingly puppeteer-like power over *her*, especially since she drops her gaze downward at this moment in what looks like an expression of submission.

The effect of this moment is that of a wayward spirit being temporarily soothed—or smothered—into a state of stillness. Because this lowering-of-the-arms movement resembles an early step in the Taiji sequence, moreover, it is associated not just with the weight of paternal authority, but also with Chinese heritage more broadly, which the child seems to experience as a somewhat burdensome imposition, since she looks around in a panicky way while the arm raising is happening—as if to say, "What is happening here?"—and then quickly extricates herself from the imposed cone of calm that descends upon her. As a wistfully yearning classical guitar melody by Drolma begins playing, the child reaches one arm out and away from her father, then back, then out and away again, as if torn between the competing desires of seeking out novelty and finding shelter in familiarity and tradition.

As a drumbeat gradually infuses a more driving rhythm into Drolma's still-lyrical music, this in-and-out dynamic repeats and intensifies. When the child ducks out from under the loose embrace of her father's encircling arms and moves downstage left, she sets into motion a tumultuous third phase of the dance, during which the father continues doing Taiji-influenced moves at center stage while the daughter repeatedly breaks away and then darts back toward him in a series of quicker and more various exploratory movements. As she moves out and away from him, the child often performs spins that turn her inward, including one in which she wraps her arms around her own body as if absorbed in the contemplative work of gauging what her personal feelings and impulses are. At the same time, she alternates between emulating and rejecting her father's movements, as when she, too, strikes a familiar Taiji pose but then suddenly drops out of it while making an emphatic "No!" gesture that involves crisscrossing one splay-fingered hand over the other in front of her and then sharply separating them.

Similarly, after a moment of close connection when she and her father gaze intently at each other, the child suddenly knocks his hand away from her, causing him to lean back and close his eyes in a pained wince. Each partner, it seems, has the power to wound the other; and what happens next reveals that the felt obligation to care for the well-being of the other goes both ways, too. Realizing that her elder is upset, the child reengages him with a loving gesture that revives his spirits, a touching moment that paves the way for the more harmonious final section of the dance, in which adult and child do Taiji steps together before the child once again reaches yearningly out and away before twisting her upper body back in and toward her elder, such that they wind up pretzeled into the pressed-palm pose that concludes the dance (see Figure 10.4).

Because they lean their upper bodies toward each other in such a slow and solemn way, this prayerlike variation on the stylized handshake trope is infused with an air of caring connection. Yet to my eyes, it also has the feel of a slightly tense and somewhat contentious compromise, since the child's upstage twist obscures part of her face from the audience, as if she has had to sacrifice part of her psyche to make this moment of unity happen. Her palm against his thus evokes not just amity and unity but also the dynamic pressure exerted when two opposing forces meet. Or perhaps we should read this moment as achieving a "yin-yang" balance, in which contrary forces are not at odds with one another so much as interrelated, complementary, and mutually constitutive. For as Hon explained to me, "Taiji" is not just the short term for Taiji Quan, but also "the name of the 'yin-yang' symbol. So, 'Taiji Quan' means 'the practice of the yin-yang.'"[15] Rooted in Taoism, Taiji Quan is a physical and spiritual practice that seeks to find balance and harmony between the light (yin) and the dark (yang) aspects of existence, a tradition Hon alludes to in this final tableau by having adult and child approach one another using moves reminiscent of Taiji's Brush Knee Twist Step.

I believe that this moving moment in Hon's dance duet could help contemporary childhood studies scholars nuance how we conceive of adult influence over children. As cultural historian Robin Bernstein notes, such sway too often gets characterized as a one-way, "top-down" form of negative pressure, as if the only way to avoid idealizing it would be to equate it with authoritarian coercion or colonization: all dark and no light.[16] Yet it should be possible to register the discomfiting fact that asymmetries in ability, experience, and power often render younger people more vulnerable to outside pressures than older ones while still acknowledging that such susceptibility is a matter of degree, rather than a difference in kind. Registering and destigmatizing the fact that adults, like children, are to some degree also reliant on and shaped by others helps us to recall that such indebtedness can be sustaining as well as constraining: supportive nurturance and emancipatory pedagogy are just as real as hegemonic manipulation and coercion. Rather than comparing the adult-child relationship to colonization and debating whether we should be "for" or "against" the concept of agency,[17] we can instead engage in the more creatively challenging work of crafting more compelling accounts of how nonautonomous agency manifests itself in somewhat asymmetrical relationships.[18] What alternative analogies could we use for the adult-child relationship, we might ask ourselves, which could serve as a recurrent reminder that children and adults are akin to one another, not least in the sense that no one's agency emerges out of a cultural vacuum, but rather amid, through, and in conversation with preexisting structures and ways of being in the world?

The pas de deux, it seems to me, could function as one such metaphor, since this flexible artform is so well suited to dramatizing the fact that even somewhat asymmetrical relationships are not necessarily oppressive; sometimes, they are mutually enlivening, enjoyable, edifying, or transformative.[19] In *Lineage*, for example, there's no denying that the bigger, older partner seems to be wielding more sway over the smaller, younger one than vice versa: because the central drama of this piece is whether the child will or will not participate in the reanimation and perpetuation of the Taiji tradition that the parent embodies, she seems more influenced by her parent than her parent is by her. The ambivalence encoded into their final posture brilliantly captures how cultural inheritance can be both sustaining and constraining. For the simultaneously harmonious and fraught nature of this posture signals the child's status as a person who is both self-motivated and other-influenced: not a merely passive puppet but rather a nonautonomous agent enmeshed in the messy process of embodying a socially structured way of being in the world that does and does not feel like a good fit to her.

One of the first things Hon told me about *Lineage* was that "in retrospect, I realize it was truly a premonition of my life," since after venturing abroad to pursue a career as a multimedia artist in Berlin, she has doubled back to teaching Taiji Quan to other dancers, "so now I am continuing my father's lineage." Yet later on in our conversation, her description of an art film she had recently created made clear that Hon continues to interrogate as well as embrace this male-dominated tradition. The film, she explained, was about "how I found my way in Taiji being a woman, and being a pregnant woman." Her cameraman was taken aback, she added, when she chose to conclude it with "a scene that's completely red," which she did because this color—associated in Chinese culture with luck, vitality, and life—was not only her favorite as a girl but now reflects her growing desire as a woman and new mother to recuperate moments in the past when "Chinese culture was [more] matriarchal": "to celebrate women's power" by acknowledging and honoring the existence of "matriarchal cultures which celebrate blood, which celebrate women, which celebrate birth." Similarly, the contrasting costumes worn in *Lineage* attest to how the child Hon and her father embodied their Chinese identity in different ways: though both of the tunics donned in this dance were actual items of clothing that Hon and her father wore for family celebrations in Chinatown, her subtly patterned, richly red top—which was not actually a tunic, "just a favorite shirt of mine that was too big for me"—is less formal and more variegated than his long, plain, white gown.

When I asked Hon why the younger partner enters first, she replied that the child pulling the parent onstage dramatizes how "the younger generation" draws on the past to "summon something very ancient," and then parent and child participate together in a tradition—the "sacred dance" of Taiji Quan—that precedes both of them. I am struck by how this account underscores the kinship between adult and child as beings whose agency is not wholly untrammeled but rather emerges out of and expresses itself through existing structures, influences, and traditions. People of all ages are simultaneously dealing with the past and confronting novelty; the seemingly self-motivated child who leaps onto the scene solo turns out to be absorbing, rejecting, and reenacting her father's mode of moving through the world, even as the highly practiced parent is being pulled into a new world of experiences that are particular to his relationship with this unique and somewhat unruly, somewhat compliant child.

Hon's use of back-and-forth and in-and-out movements to register the pleasures and difficulties of acculturation represents a marked departure from what we might describe as an up-and-down aesthetic embraced by Humphrey and many other Western choreographers who hew more closely to a Romantic tradition of representing childhood as a time of untrammeled freedom and fun. In *The Art of Making Dances*, Humphrey explains that one of her guiding principles is that "youth is 'down' as little as possible; gravity holds him lightly to earth. Old age gradually takes over and the spring vanishes from the step until the final yielding, death," which she describes as a fully "horizontal" state of stillness in which the vital "speed and bounce" of youth has been altogether drained away.[20] No wonder, then, that Humphrey launches her child dancer in *Day on Earth* into a lift in which she reaches skyward and then gives her many playful skipping and hopping steps. Her alignment of youth with giddy heights recalls the strand of Romantic discourse that portrays children as natural or even supernatural beings—bounding roes, eddying leaves, woodland sprites, otherworldly angels—who float free of the "earthly freight [of] custom" until the deadening process of aging and acculturation pins them down "with a weight,/ Heavy as frost, and deep almost as life!"

Those lines are lifted from William Wordsworth's famous "Ode: Intimations of Immortality from Recollections of Early Childhood" (1807), which depicts aging as an inexorable downward slide in which the "Delight and liberty" of early childhood—associated with heavenly "clouds of glory"—gradually devolves into the earth-bound drudgery and prisonlike constraints of adulthood.[21] Elaborating on this theme in a poem addressed to six-year-old Hartley Coleridge, Wordsworth portrays this little boy as an otherworldly "faery voyager" who seems to "float . . . on air": wholly untouched by the "soiling" culture he inhabits, this "exquisitely wild" child is perceived as navigating through life on his own totally authentic terms, whether by dancing about with a "breeze-like motion" or singing a "self-born carol."[22]

As keen-eyed satirists such as Wordsworth's contemporary Thomas Hood recognized, such highly idealized depictions of purely natural and weirdly autonomous children ignore the messy reality of what it means to begin life in an extended state of dependency on others, as all human beings do.[23] Rather than conceiving of children as fellow people immersed from birth in a network of interactive and mutually influential social relationships, Wordsworth often depicts children as static, isolated figures who have more in common with natural objects than human beings. His Lucy Gray, for instance, dwells among "untrodden ways" and gets compared to a hard-to-spot flower, a solitary star, a floating cloud, and so on.[24] Indeed, her alterity is so extreme that the poet-narrator has an easier time imagining her dead and gone than engaged in the ceaseless back-and-forth negotiations that comprise communal life with other people; in poem after poem, he dwells on how death preserves Lucy's status as an inertly impervious "thing" among things, as when he envisions her "Roll'd round in earth's diurnal course/ With rocks and stones and trees!"[25]

Theatrical ballet-mistress Josephine Weiss, who designed the dances performed by the Viennese Children in the 1840s, successfully translated this strand of Romantic thinking about childhood into movement in ways that appealed strongly to audiences and influenced other choreographers. Reviewers on both sides of the Atlantic could not get over how rapidly these "little fairies" would "fly about the stage," bounding from combination to combination and then "trip[ping] away, as if it had been but a sport and they were skipping off to other gambols."[26] Like Wordsworth, Weiss often situated her playful children in pastoral scenes, as in her especially popular *Pas de Fleurs* (*Flower Dance*), in which approximately forty little girls were costumed as "idealized peasant damsels" and given semicircular arches and round hoops of flowers to hold, which they used to transform themselves into a large bouquet and smaller bunches of flowers.[27] Talk about Romantic objectification: Wordsworth's Lucy Gray gets metaphorically *compared* to blossoms, but the Viennese girls corporeally *became* them onstage, alternating between steps that suggested they were playing with flowers and ones that positioned them as being flowers.

Boston-based pit musician Thomas Ryan supplies us with the most detailed description of how this dance objectified children that I have been able to find. When the curtain rose on an 1847 performance of the *Pas de Fleurs* in Boston, he recalls in his memoir,

> the children were seen to be built up, about thirty of them, in the form of a huge bouquet, round which were two garlands or rings of flowers (children) that swung slowly around the middle mass. Then the latter disentangled themselves and spread out on the stage in bunches, and the animated movement began. Every kind of figure was made by groups of children,—swinging stars, chains, threading needles, and dancing round the May-pole, which with its long colored ribbons remained on the centre of the stage.[28]

Like many other admirers of the Viennese Children, Ryan pronounces himself at a loss for words as he tries to explain why such performances engendered floods of tears and wild applause from audiences, sending onlookers into a state of "ecstasy" so extreme that he describes it as "a kind of emotional insanity."[29] But it seems clear that their appeal stemmed in part from how successfully these children embodied the strand of Romantic discourse about childhood that paradoxically envisions the child as a naturally unconstrained will-o'-the-wisp and, at the same time, as an inanimate, reified, and controllable object. Over and over again, Anglo-American reviews praise the Viennese Children for combining the utmost "freedom and ease" with rigorously maintained "artificial discipline" and "military exactness," as when the London *Times* marveled at how "the precision of clock-work is attained, with the appearance of the most unrestrained freedom."[30]

This history can help us make sense of the odd duality built into the child's role in *Day on Earth*, such that the daughter figure seems at once passively compliant and wildly free. For while I have not yet found proof that Humphrey knew about the Viennese Children, she was certainly familiar with another international blockbuster that featured an even more airborne iteration of the Romantic child: J. M. Barrie's Peter Pan, a boy-bird hybrid who consorts with fairies and stars and who literally flew through the air (on a wire) in the stage version of Barrie's story. Barrie's phenomenally popular show—which debuted in London in 1904 and New York in 1905 and then dazzled Anglo-American audiences in countless touring productions and revivals—has exerted a long-lasting influence over the adult-child pas de deux. In the *Billy Elliot* dream ballet, for example, choreographer Peter Darling has adult Billy not merely lift child Billy up in his arms, but literally launch him into the air (on a wire) to circle higher and higher above the stage, a clear allusion to Barrie's hyper-canonical drama.

Like Wordsworth's Lucy Gray, Barrie's Peter Pan embodies the fantasy that children can instantly and effortlessly transcend their cultural origins to exist in a state of wild autonomy, as indicated by the eternal boy's triumphant boast that "I ran away the day I was born," fleeting up and away like "a little bird that has broken out of the egg."[31] That said, the brilliance of both *Peter Pan* and *Billy Elliot* is that they simultaneously indulge in this fantasy and underscore its status *as* a fantasy. Unlike Peter, "ordinary" children such as Wendy Darling and her brothers are thoroughly acculturated beings who cannot fly without supernatural assistance (lessons from Peter, plus fairy dust).[32] Similarly, when child Billy floats up, up, up into the air over a set that has suddenly been emptied of everything except stage fog, this magical moment at once dramatizes his unlimited potentiality to transcend the structural obstacles that stand in the way of him becoming a professional dancer *and* depicts the idea that grinding poverty, class prejudice, sexism, and homophobia will not hold a working-class child danseur down as a "dream" that is so fantastical that even the immutable law of gravity has been temporarily suspended.

Eleven-year-old Doris Humphrey, whose parents ran a boarding house that catered to theatrical troupers, was taken to see Barrie's drama in 1907 when the first American production starring Maude Adams as Peter traveled to Chicago. We know about this theatrical outing because Humphrey's mother mentions it in a letter to a friend, in which she describes how little Doris attended a costume party dressed up as "Tinker Bell the fairy in 'Peter Pan' which she saw a few weeks ago."[33]

Moreover, one of Humphrey's earliest dances—*Moment Musical*, composed while she was a teenager studying dance with Mary Wood Hinman—features a group of children skipping about with "hands held well forward as if playing the Pipes of Pan," just as Adams did both onstage and in a publicity photo for *Peter Pan*.[34] Humphrey had been studying dance with Hinman for several years by the time she went to see *Peter Pan*; at fourteen, she began working as Hinman's assistant teacher, and before she was twenty, she had choreographed four dances for children—including *Moment Musical*—that Hinman chose to include in *Gymnastic and Folk Dancing* (1914–1916), a multivolume work which included sheet music and detailed instructions for staging many dances for children.

Whereas Barrie produced an ambivalently ironic representation of the Romantic "Child of Nature," Hinman and young Humphrey exhibited more undiluted enthusiasm for the idea that children are asocial "others."[35] No reader of *Gymnastic and Folk Dancing* could fail to notice Hinman's celebratory embrace of Romantic writers whose idealization of rural life had helped to set into motion the newly intense interest in collecting folklore that began gathering steam in the nineteenth century, work that Hinman carries on and extends in this project. In volume 3, for example, she broadcasts her indebtedness to Wordsworth by opening with not one but two epigraphs drawn from his poems,[36] one from the "Immortality Ode" and the other from the equally famous verse known as "the daffodil poem,"[37] in which a roving poet-narrator admires a crowd of "Daffodils . . . / Tossing their heads in sprightly dance."[38] Moreover, Hinman includes two dances for children choreographed by Humphrey in this volume, the titles of which signal how deeply her star pupil was influenced by "[my] wonderful teacher" and, by extension, Wordsworth: Humphrey dubbed these dances *Will o' the Wisp* and *Daffodils*.[39]

Like the routines that Weiss crafted for the Viennese Children at the tail end of the Romantic era, these two early Humphrey dances feature a lot of skipping, bounding, and playing around. In *Will o' the Wisp*, for example, young children enact the role of elusive spirits who flit around and past one another with "quick running step[s]." "Waving their wings," half the company drop to their knees near the end of the dance, joining hands "very low" to form a kind of limbo stick that their peers can playfully jump over before all rise and exit "with flying step."[40] Similarly, *Daffodils* nods not just to Wordsworth (by having the child dancers repeatedly nod at one another, like his head-tossing blossoms), but also to dances such as the *Pas de Fleurs* (because Humphrey's children, like their Viennese counterparts, seem to flicker in and out of flower form).

In her opening instructions for *Daffodils*, for example, Humphrey calls for the children to form two concentric circles in which "all are flowers with arms for leaves. Those on the outside are visiting their playmates."[41] In line with the strand of Romantic discourse that stresses the asocial alterity of young people, these directions script young dancers to embody both vegetative, rooted inertness and restless, playful mobility. Perhaps because she recognized that such difference-model duality risks objectifying young people, contemporary dance educator Elsa

Posey decided to tweak this narrative when she restaged *Daffodils* in 2005 by encouraging the outside circle of child performers to think of themselves as gardeners rather than flowers.[42] Given the leading role that this group takes in the skipping section that follows, her directorial choice makes sense; and I appreciate how it invites girls to play a more active, agential role than that of decorative flower by inviting them to conceive of themselves as caregivers as well as receivers.

Meanwhile, in a sign of how artworks associated with children tend to go unstudied by scholars, the only researcher who has analyzed young Humphrey's four dances for young people is Barnard College student Gina Marie Borden—a former pupil of Posey's—who wrote an undergraduate thesis about the dances after performing in them when she was a member of Posey's Children's Dance Company. As Borden notes, many accounts of Humphrey's career fail to mention that she began her career as a choreographer by composing children's dances, an omission that impoverishes our understanding of her later work. Correcting this ageist oversight, Borden observes that *Will o' the Wisp* and *Daffodils* were designed for dancers of approximately the same age as the child featured in *Day on Earth* and include similar "Child of Nature"-style choreography. For example, *Day on Earth* features a "simple and playful" skipping step in which the child "steps with her right foot, and hops with her left leg in a parallel *passé*—almost exactly as it is done in *Will o' The Wisp*."[43]

Acknowledging Humphrey's indebtedness to Romanticism helps to explain an otherwise puzzling aspect of *Day on Earth*: namely, that although the child does dance one-on-one with her father for a sustained period of time, somehow this duet does not feel as much like an adult-child pas de deux as we might expect. The most obvious reason for this is that the child is introduced as part of a trio that includes both her mother and father. As a result, everything that follows feels like an extended pas de trois in which various parties come and go but the underlying structure remains triangular, especially since the remaining partners often seem to be reacting to—and often, mourning—the absence of the departed ones. But I think there's another less obvious factor that contributes to this effect, which is that the *Day on Earth* child, after initially seeming to have no self-propelling agency at all, suddenly starts to partake in the weird autonomy enjoyed by many Romantic "Child of Nature" figures, often skipping off to perform playful solo steps that—as dance critic Marcia B. Siegel observes—suggest she is "engrossed in her own private world of games and wonder."[44] Whether she is being tossed around like an insensate prop at the start of the dance or flitting hither and yon like "a delightful elf" who disappears altogether toward its end, Humphrey's child seems oddly inert, impermeable, and independent rather than deeply engaged with and influenced by her parents.[45]

In the closing moments of *Day on Earth*, to be sure, all the characters come together, and the child takes up the central position that her mother had occupied at the start. Yet even this moment of generational transfer stresses difference and distance rather than kinship and connection: the adults lie down on the ground and shroud their still bodies with a large cloth, as if dead, while the child sits up and stares out at the audience with her hands tightly clasped in her lap. Since the child at this moment represents the living present and future of her family, we might have expected her to assume a more active pose, perhaps one that signals how her way of being in the world has been shaped but not wholly constrained by her past relationships with the loved ones lying prone at her feet. Instead, she assumes a position so resolutely self-contained that she reads once again as an isolate, archetypical "Child" rather than a specific someone enmeshed in ties that bind a particular group of human beings together.[46] No wonder, then, that contemporary dance critic Jennifer Dunning faults *Day on Earth* for featuring a "cardboard Every Family"[47]: this final tableau depicts generational transfer not as a messy process of social transmission among individuals, but rather as an abstractly natural cycle of life and death, in which generic, passive specimens of humanity get "Roll'd round in earth's diurnal course/ With rocks and stones and trees!" Indeed, publicity photos for *Day on Earth* in 1948 depicted the dancers posed on a windswept, grassy beach, priming viewers to conceive of the human life cycle depicted in the dance as a timeless, universal, and wholly natural process.[48]

As its title signals, *Lineage* focuses much more intently on the issue of influence, introducing audiences to a more particularized child protagonist whose status as a socialized being is made evident not just in the more culturally specific choreography but in every detail of the stage design. The shaft of light that falls onto the stage before the child enters, for example, notably does *not* evoke natural light, such as a dappled sunbeam filtering softly through the leaves of a woodland setting. Instead, as I have noted, its smooth-edged rectangularity calls to mind what happens when a door opens and light spills over from one human-constructed realm to another. As a result, when the child enters and tows her father behind her through that liminal space, the multiple interpretations of this moment described above all rest on the assumption that aging is an interactive process in which it matters who we are with and what kind of sociocultural world we inhabit.

When I asked Hon and then Robbins how this evocative lighting design came to be, I was delighted to learn that it was not imposed onto the dance after its creation by an adult professional with no input from Hon. Rather, as Hon was choreographing this dance in New York City, she was in conversation with an award-winning lighting designer engaged by Robbins, Philip W. Sandström. Hon and Sandström met and had a conversation during which she shared with him her ideas about what the dance was about, and he suggested some options for what lighting choices might work best. An established artist in his own right, Sandström created the lighting design for *Lineage*. But they also came up with it together, engaging in an artistic pas de deux that any choreographer and designer will recognize, familiar as they are with how nonautonomous the act of creating a dance (or any theatrical performance) typically is.

Speaking of influence, one of my favorite moments in my interview with Hon came when I asked her what had prompted her to design a dance about grappling with one's lineage, and she cited a totally unexpected source of inspiration. "What really made me start to think about this [theme] and wanting to make a piece with my father," she told me,

> was that I'd seen *The Lion King* with my mom—not the movie, the Broadway show—[and] I really liked this one song called 'They Live in You.' That's the song [the father lion] Mufasa sings to [his son] Simba about his ancestors, and how they live in him. And I remember that the song really stuck with me, and I started thinking a lot about ancestry and how you carry your ancestors [within you and] carry on their lineage, so to speak.[49]

One thing that makes *Lineage* so richly worth analyzing, I think, is how interestingly indebted it is to other creative traditions, from the ancient art of Taiji to Humphrey-style modern dance to this contemporary Disney musical. Studying it has been a gift to me as a critic, not least because doing so has prompted me to recognize that I can treat indebtedness to others as something I positively value in the work of a child artist (as I often do when writing about adult artists). I needed that nudge because when I first began giving academic talks about children's creative efforts, skeptical colleagues barraged me with questions about whether such material was "really" generated by the child, as opposed to puppeteer-like adults exercising prescriptive power from behind the scenes. Attempting to combat such suspicion by seeking out archival proof that child creators were functioning as wholly independent agents, I now realize, was a mistake: first, because it turned out that even the strongest evidence of youth self-motivation was not enough to change the minds of committed skeptics; and second, because it limited my own thinking to commit myself to defending a fantasy about personal autonomy that I now realize I would rather interrogate than perpetuate.

In highly competitive cultures that are more apt to express anxiety about influence than celebrate it, dance has a special potential to destigmatize dependency. For this art form so often portrays people leaning on and being supported by one another that it widens our range of options for how to regard reliance on others, often depicting this tenuous state not as a despised deficiency or difference that divides us, but rather as something beautiful and challenging that unites us: a source of kinship that derives from our shared status as embodied, vulnerable, mortal beings.

Indeed, even *Day on Earth*, which I think adheres too closely to the reifying "Child of Nature" paradigm, still manages to represent reliance on others as something younger and older people have in common. As I turn back to Humphrey's dance one last time to track how she depicts dependency, I could choose to interpret this aspect of her work as a rejection of Romanticism, since Romantic writers indisputably played a key role in popularizing a still-pervasive habit of fetishizing originality and autonomy. But I read it, instead, as a sign that this artistic and philosophical movement offered a more variegated picture of childhood than its critics generally admit: while difference-model discourse that positions the innocent child as an otherworldly "other" is undeniably present (as in many—though not all—Wordsworth poems), so, too, is kinship-model discourse that portrays innocence as a joyful state of harmless playfulness and open-hearted vulnerability that both children and adults can embody (as in William Blake's *Songs of Innocence and Experience*).

Blake was the adult Humphrey's favorite Romantic poet, so it makes sense that when we take a closer look at how the adults move in *Day on Earth*, we can see that this dance cannot be dismissed as merely "othering" the child. For not only do the adults engage in the same sort of joyously playful movements as the child does (which I will describe in greater detail in a moment), dependency on others also emerges as a source of kinship between older and younger characters rather than a differentiating factor. The child's initial state of prone helplessness and extreme susceptibility to the wills and whims of other people differs in degree but not in kind from how the other, older characters behave: all three of the adult dancers at times collapse down to the floor, lean heavily on outside sources of support, and get bandied about when other people's actions send them into emotional tailspins.

After his first lover leaves him, for example, the *Day on Earth* man reaches desperately after her, and then—with his arm still outstretched forward—dramatically collapses backward onto the floor, so laid low by grief that all he can do is roll over and then stagger offstage altogether. He is drawn back onstage only after the second woman faces down the dark wings that swallowed him up and engages in a series of steps that anticipate the imaginary rope pulling in *Lineage*. Reaching her arms straight out in front of her, the female puller in this case starts moving backward while bending her elbows such that her forearms cycle in and around, in and around. This piston-like motion seems to tug the man—also walking backward and leaning back toward her—onto the stage to join her. Still unready to embark on a new relationship, the man again retreats offstage. Undaunted, the woman repeats this series of steps a second time, whereupon the man reappears face-first and stays with her, such that we feel she has successfully infused him with new life, willing him into being hopeful and brave enough to love again even though doing so exposes him to the risk (and eventually, the reality) of more heartbreak.

Similarly, even the man's first lover, who fleets across the stage with him during their joyfully expansive pas de deux, also throws herself onto the ground at one point and, at another, faces upstage and leans backward such that the back of her head rests into the curve of the forward-facing man's outstretched arm, after which they scuttle along sideways for a few steps with her fixed in this touchingly yielding yet also slightly awkward position. Because the woman's neck, chest, and torso are exposed to the sky, this precarious pose signals not just that she is depending on her partner for support, but also that such reliance is a risky move that requires self-revelation and makes her more vulnerable to pain. Apparently unwilling to tolerate such risk, the young woman—having been gently lifted to her feet by her partner after throwing herself to the ground—suddenly flees the scene, effectively dropping her lover before he can drop her.

We can connect the fact that everyone in *Day on Earth* spends some time on the ground to Humphrey's well-documented commitment to "fall and recovery" as "the very core of all movement." Indeed, she articulates this "theory of motion" at the very moment in *The Art of Making Dances* in which she associates youth with upward movement.[50] As if aware that this characterization risks portraying children as wholly different than adults, Humphrey quickly stresses the kinship between youth and age by observing that "*all* life fluctuates between the resistance to and the yielding to gravity. . . . This lifetime span is filled with thousands of falls and recoveries."[51] Nor does she wish to characterize aging as a terrible fall from grace, as indicated by her closing caveat: "This is not to suggest that youth is good and old age is bad, but is merely a clinical observation as to the way these impressions of young and old arise rhythmically" as bodies engage with one another in life and onstage.[52]

In keeping with this emphasis on cross-age kinship, it is not just the child who jumps for joy, skips, hops, and plays little games in *Day on Earth*; the adults do, too, and not only to humor the child, but also to entertain themselves before she is born. There are, for example, beautifully exuberant sequences in the pas de deux performed by the man and his first lover that remind me of nothing so much as "parallel play," the term developmental psychologists use to describe how young children who have not yet begun to engage interactively with peers play alongside (rather than with) one another. At these moments in *Day on Earth*, the lovers jaunt together across the stage to the buoyantly chirpy yet also profoundly dissonant strains of Aaron Copland's 1941 Piano Sonata, not touching each other but performing the same moves side by side, as when each scoops their curved arms skyward first one way and then another, as if lofting giant beach balls into the air. Given that these two adults also impishly engage with each other in ways that anticipate the hide-and-seek and limbo games that the child later plays with her parents, it is no wonder that Martin observed in his 1948 review that Humphrey's "composition for the child is of a piece with the work as a whole."[53] In other words, the child's steps—though not exactly the same as those performed by the adults—are closely akin to them; though less technically challenging, they are still (as Martin admiringly notes) quite "tricky."[54]

I have not said much about Copland's music, in part because it is hard to improve on Martin's brilliant description of it, which highlights the notably un-Romantic nature of its abstraction. "It is difficult music," he observes, "spare and sinewy, with phrases that use all kinds of rhythmic irregularities to get themselves shaped in their own design. Beneath its surface the choreographer has seen its hardy sweetness, its earth quality, its stalwart, unsentimental statement of beauty."[55] From the slow, stately, yet also jarringly discordant chords that accompany the man's solo lunges to the merrier fast sections whose rhythmic hairpin turns make the couple and trio dancing in *Day on Earth* seem exhilarating but also unpredictable and disorienting, Copland's score lends a usefully unsettling undertone of astringency to even the most jejune choreography.

As sentimental as it may sometimes seem, moreover, Humphrey's choreography often features unexpected tensions and depths that make it more similar to Copland's moodily complex music than it initially appears. Consider, for example, the child's entry into the dance, which on first viewing I dismissed as both sappy and objectifying. Yet if we start from the premise that none of the characters in *Day on Earth* are fully self-sufficient and self-supporting, then another, more appreciative interpretation of the child's initial helplessness comes into view: far from ignoring the messy reality of what it means to begin life in a state of heightened dependency on others, Humphrey dramatizes the embodied, lived experience of relying more heavily on physical support from others when we are a babe in arms than when we are an older child or adult. Moreover, just as Copland's often dissonant music has a sweet-and-sour quality to it, Humphrey's choreography likewise registers the difficulties as well as the delights of dependency. When the child's parents rock her back and forth, for instance, these transfers and lifts do not actually conjure up a saccharine scene of loving, protective care (see Figures 10.1 and 10.2). That is because they are performed so quickly—and the child is hoisted up so high—that they take on a distinct edge of danger and risk, much like the moments when passionate romantic attachments render the adults more vulnerable, open, and exposed to others, and thus more likely to be hurt or harmed by them.

Viewed in this light, *Day on Earth* bodies forth a relatively nonidealized vision of care. Even as it depicts the deep satisfaction and joy that lovers and parents and children derive from one another's company, it also dwells on the spirit-sapping grief that can descend upon them when their loved ones stop loving them, or leave home to live elsewhere, or die. Watching *Day on Earth* in 2021 and comparing it to contemporary dances such as *Lineage* makes salient how Humphrey centers the experience of an adult male and a heteronormative nuclear family. Yet it is also worth noting that for a modern dance choreographer in 1947 to make the everyday domestic activity of childcare a major theme—and to feature a child dancer in such a substantive role—was perceived by both Martin and Humphrey herself as a "bold and dangerous" choice.[56] Not only did this move introduce practical problems such as finding and training child performers (and hoping they would not grow out of the role too fast), it also constituted a radical departure from the common practice of centering modern dances around larger-than-life figures from Greek mythology or world history committing epic crimes and descending into irredeemable depths of "bitterness," "guilt," and despair.[57] Somehow, Martin marveled, Humphrey managed to make a dance focused on the quotidian pleasures and obligations of family life exciting, even though the narrative of *Day on Earth* "has no fireworks, no particular spectacular appeal."[58]

Given that Humphrey challenges traditional gender norms in so many of her other dances, why does she center a male character in *Day on Earth*? Once again, filling in a bit more of the cultural context that Humphrey was working within and against helps us to appreciate that this choice is edgier than it initially seems. Having embarked on a career as a dancer-choreographer at a time when American women still were not allowed to vote, Humphrey had by this point also mothered a son at a moment when female dancers "weren't taken seriously if you had a child."[59] As Siegel notes in her invaluable biography *Days on Earth: The Dance of Doris Humphrey* (1987), Humphrey's working-class, socialist husband, who absented himself from the domestic scene "much more of the time" than she did because of his chosen career as a sailor, nevertheless "made her feel that was she was abdicating her responsibilities as wife and mother every time she embarked" on a work-related trip, even though she carefully arranged for hired caregivers or friends to look after her young son when she could not.[60]

Reading this passage in Siegel's book—which Owen had pulled off the shelf for me during my visit to Jacob's Pillow—it struck me how critical it is to register not just male presence but also female absence in *Day on Earth*. What sets the father-daughter pas de deux into motion in this dance, after all, is the departure of the mother, whose sojourn to parts unknown is sustained long enough to suggest that she has other activities and relationships in her life that quite naturally take her beyond the bounds of the family circle. When she returns, a joyous reunion ensues that is notably unmarred by recriminations, guilt, or punishment. In other words, this is a dance in which a male partner cheerfully throws himself into the activity of caring for a child before, during, and after a period of maternal absence. What a dream come true for an ambitious working mother! Once we register this point, *Day on Earth* comes to seem more akin to other mid- and late-career Humphrey dances, which often body forth a hopeful vision of a more egalitarian world, as when she chooses to focus a dance around the Shakers because this female-founded religious sect lived communally, engaging in collective labor and allowing women as well as men to function as spiritual leaders.

The path Humphrey herself took to cofounding a dance company—and how she collaborated with others within that company—likewise attests to her commitment to building a better, more equitable world. Having left the famous Denishawn company after its founders proposed excluding Jewish dancers in order to keep their troupe 90 percent Anglo-Saxon, Humphrey teamed up with fellow dancer-choreographer Charles Weidman to cocreate a more inclusive company that nurtured the career of the Mexican-born Limón, who played the original man in *Day on Earth*.[61] Later, when Limón formed his own company, Humphrey agreed to serve as his artistic director, a precedent-breaking role reversal that Siegel notes was of a piece with her general commitment to rejecting "the autocratic role of the modern dance choreographer-director" and instead giving "dancers status as collaborators and managers of their artistic output."[62] The first dance Humphrey created for Limón's new company was *Day on Earth*, an instant success that became a key piece in their repertoire. Notably, the 1995 performance of *Day on Earth* by the Limón Company that I watched in the Pillow archive features two Black dancers in the roles of Man and Child, Paul Dennis and Chelica Kimerling. This casting choice at once pays homage to and doubles down on Humphrey's original decision to make her "Every Family" multiracial.

Within the field of childhood studies, the term "Romantic" often gets deployed as a negative label that we slap onto cultural artifacts in order to dismiss them as tritely sentimental, dangerously essentialist, and theoretically uninspiring. Yet the egalitarian inclusiveness that animated Humphrey's life and work does not so much depart from as partake in and expand on the youthful radicalism of Romantic poets who, inspired by the unfolding revolution against autocratic power, class stratification, and economic oppression in France, embraced the creed of "*liberté, égalité, fraternité*." Earlier eighteenth-century English poets such as Alexander Pope and William Cowper had focused their verse on high-status figures from myth, history, or contemporary culture or "assume[d] without question" that they could confidently generalize about "the poor" in ways that served to legitimate existing social hierarchies.[63] In contrast, Wordsworth and Samuel Taylor Coleridge centered many of their *Lyrical Ballads* (1798) around particular individuals existing at the margins of their culture whose life experiences trouble rather than justify the status quo, including a very old man disabled by—yet still engaging in—painfully hard labor and a "mad" mother cruelly abandoned by her baby's father.[64] Similarly, Blake's moral indignation at the exploitation of enslaved and impoverished people led him to fault both capitalist nation-states and organized religion for failing to live up to radically egalitarian example set by Jesus in the New Testament, a point he dramatizes by including poems such as "The Little Black Boy" and "The Chimney Sweeper" in his *Songs of Innocence and Experience* (1789/1794).

Loving Blake as she did, Humphrey corporealizes his kinship-model vision of innocence as a joyous, trusting, but also vulnerable mode of responsive engagement with others that is available to people of all ages, classes, and ethnicities. Indeed, another reason why the children's dances that she choreographed as a teenager are so worth recuperating is that the mutually supportive collectivism of these pieces prefigures the caringly egalitarian ethos of her unusually ensemble-centered works for adults. In *New Dance*, for example, a mixed-gender group of grown-ups enjoin one another in Blakean bursts of "cooperative energy," as jubilantly large-scale unison movement shares the stage with duo, solo, and small group effervescences that attest to how heterogeneity need not disband but rather can strengthen social unity.[65] Indeed, Humphrey remained so intent on celebrating "the healing, inspiring powers of group action"—as opposed to showcasing her own idiosyncratic star power—that Siegel cites this tendency toward "self-effacement" as a contributing factor to her fall into relative obscurity as compared to more self-promoting dancer-choreographers such as Graham.[66]

Whether Humphrey recognized it or not, by designing hopefully utopian dances in which "individual display . . . seems discountenanced" in favor of carefully coordinated group movement, she was also following in the footsteps of Madame Weiss and the Viennese Children.[67] For as Ryan recalls, that troupe's collective ability to merge into and out of highly intricate patterns involving multiple dancers was regarded as "so unlike anything before witnessed by a majority of the audience, that they felt as if they had had a dream or vision of Paradise."[68] But what, exactly, was the content of this utopian "dream," such that its realization onstage struck onlookers in the 1840s as so "unprecedented" as to "baffle[] all description"?[69] After all, idealizing representations of innocent, otherworldly children had been in circulation in multiple artforms for decades by this point in time, and the Romantic ballet in particular was such a well-established phenomenon that its popularity was already on the wane.[70] What, then, was so striking about these dancing children, and why were Anglo-American audiences so deeply moved by them?

Two interrelated factors—both related to corporeality and collectivity—seem relevant to any effort to account more fully for the intensity of the emotional responses that the Viennese Children engendered in onlookers. First, longtime theatergoers were stunned by the "unprecedented" standard of excellence the troupe set in ensemble dancing, repeatedly noting how extraordinarily well-synchronized the children were compared to other corps de ballet comprised of older dancers.[71] Although the Viennese Children differed in age and size, they were lauded by the *Montreal Transcript* for achieving an effect of unity and coordination so strong that "it seems as if one set of muscles animated all," such that "96 legs are, artistically speaking, but one pair of legs" and "the whole troop [seems] endowed with one dancing soul."[72] Their astonishingly rapid, intricately patterned, and perfectly coordinated movements, London's *Morning Post* observed, "prove . . . that the ballet corps of all theatres are woefully neglected and mismanaged, and that *maîtres de ballet* have to begin a new course of study to redeem the stage from the slow unsightly mechanism of their awkward squadrons."[73] Indeed, according to dance critic Joan Acocella, the ensemble work at the Paris Opera "improved noticeably" after a French review advised the "notoriously sloppy" corps of this famous institution to emulate the synchrony, precision, and energy of the younger troupe.[74]

Second, the sense of somatic fitness and all-around happy "healthfulness" these working-class children conveyed—despite having reportedly been born into the most "abject poverty"—was widely interpreted as bodying forth a vision not just of personal flourishing but of social transformation into a state of universal well-being and harmonious "unity" that viewers recognized was still more dream than reality.[75] At a time when scores of impoverished, underfed, and unwell children were highly visible on city streets, many contemporaries of the Viennese Children shared American author Lydia Maria Child's "mingled feeling of delight and sadness" at witnessing that the bodies of working-class children could instead attest to "the hidden power, and grace, and beauty, which lie infolded [*sic*] in the mechanism of the [human] frame. [The Viennese Children] show us the wonders which may be accomplished by exercise and training. They show us that not a tithe of our physical powers is developed, and how frequently they are misdeveloped," harmed or stunted by social circumstances.[76]

When suspicious contemporary critics focus solely on how the bodies of young people get eroticized in such accounts—which did sometimes happen—they disregard the fact that corporeal flourishing can be valued for nonsexual reasons, too.[77] Watching these working-class children embody a state of (apparent) physical well-being prompted a range of reactions. Some onlookers worried that the Viennese Children's labor might be much harder and more exploitative than it seemed.[78] Others fantasized about how different the world would be if all children could have the benefit of being offered the kind of careful instruction provided by Madame Weiss. "The process by which she has swayed at the same time mind and body—imparting to the former the most lively perception and intellectuality, and to the other ease, suppleness, and grace," one such commentator noted, "is truly marvellous, and is worthy of investigation for far higher purposes."[79] Whether they are worrying about the children's artistic labor or praising it, however, such accounts serve as a salutary reminder that the Viennese Children owed their success not merely to their physical attractiveness but also to the education, effort, and acuity that enabled them to become such skillful dancers.

No wonder, then, that "the happy, bright faces and the gleeful play" of these child performers "stirred up the deepest emotions of the spectators": they seem not just to have embodied a decades-old Romantic image of innocent alterity but also to have given some audience members a glimpse of a "simply ideal" future world in which children of all classes could flourish both physically and mentally, having received enough nurturance and support to actualize their positive potentialities.[80] Indeed, socialists writing for the *Harbinger*—a radical American periodical published by the utopian Brook Farm Community—were among the most enthusiastic spectators of the Viennese Children, lauding the group for manifesting "variety in unity" and "blissful harmonious coöperation, to a world all torn and rent by competition."[81] Inspired by French utopian socialist Charles Fourier, these radical thinkers regarded ensemble-produced art such as symphonies and group dances as attesting to "the innate passion of the soul" to experience the "correspondence between all the parts and moments of the great Whole of being," a way of thinking steeped in early Romantic "symphilosophizing" done in concert by the Jena Set, which envisioned nature as an interconnected whole and human creativity as communal and symbiotic.[82] Anticipating Humphrey, nineteenth-century socialists hoped that collaborative artistic endeavors would not merely serve as a useful metaphor for a more egalitarian and mutually supportive society, but would literally help to bring into being "the unity of ages, nations, [and] races" through the kinesthetic act of coming together to collectively create and live through a beautiful shared experience.[83]

As I was reading *Harbinger* articles that enthused about how such art helps us to envision alternatives to "an abominable order of society which establishes arbitrary distinctions of class, and attaches arbitrary honor or shame to various occupations," it occurred to me that I had not fully registered the significance of the man in *Day on Earth*'s status as a manual laborer, which is signaled not just by his physical gestures but also by the rough-textured work clothes that constituted Limón's original costume.[84] If it does not now read like a glaringly transgressive choice to make a working-class man the central figure of a concert dance, then that strikes me as a sign that some progress has been made toward creating a more egalitarian world. Nor do I think it naive to believe that artists and art educators, including Romantic ones, played a part in helping such shifts happen. Besides being a fan of Wordsworth, Humphrey's "wonderful teacher" Hinman also collaborated with social justice activist Jane Addams and progressive educator John Dewey to give immigrants and young children opportunities not just to perform her choreography but to engage themselves in collaborative "dance building" that she regarded as both a means and a model for civic engagement.[85]

We can thus trace the lineage of Humphrey's commitment to interactive pedagogy—in which students of dance not only learn other's people's principles of movement but also are "encouraged to expand or embroider on these in their own way"—back to Hinman.[86] And we can also trace it forward to Robbins, who began by teaching Hon basic steps and elementary improvisation and later made room for her student to choreograph her own dance, in conversation with her teacher, parent, peers, and professional artists such as Sandström. Following in Humphrey's footsteps, Robbins often makes use of a sewing metaphor to describe how she invites her youngest and least experienced pupils to cocreate dances in which she does the lion's share of the choreographing, but leaves some "seams . . . open so that there are parts that dancers . . . create" to help complete the work.[87] Yet when I asked Robbins whether her sewing metaphor was inspired by Humphrey's, she shook her head, smiled, and linked this locution back to a different kind of lineage. "My grandparents were needle workers," she said, "and my mother was a fine seamstress."[88]

NOTES

A series of supportive partners lifted me into the joyous work of writing this essay, beginning with Pete Kunze (who incited me to write about dance before I felt ready to take that leap) and Norton Owen (who showed me where to leap to). Lingji Hon and Ellen Robbins not only inspired me with their artistry but also enabled my research by sharing their memories, photographs, and recordings of *Lineage*. Carl Holt found me dance documentaries I didn't even know existed and contributed other above-and-beyond forms of research assistance. Eva Sanders Allen and Elena and Estelle Bovay shared their knowledge of dance history and terminology with me, while Robin Bernstein, Ben Mangrum, Emily Richmond Pollock, Kieran Setiya, Victoria Ford Smith, and Courtney Weikle-Mills supplied beautifully kind and canny editorial advice.

1. That essay ("Entertaining Children") came out several years after the one that initially prompted me to reach out to the (now retired) Harvard curator ("*Peter Pan* as Children's Theatre"). More recently, I have learned about the richness of Harvard's Theater Collection by working with Matthew Wittmann, who is a wonderfully open-minded, knowledgeable, and hospitable host to scholars and students who visit the Houghton. See "Entertaining Children of All Ages: Nineteenth-Century Popular Theater as Children's Theater," *American Quarterly* 66, no. 1 (March 2014): 1–34, and "*Peter*

Pan as Children's Theater: The Issue of Audience," in *The Oxford Handbook of Children's Literature*, ed. Julia L. Mickenberg and Lynne Vallone (New York: Oxford University Press, 2011), 475–495.

2. Freda Crisp, Ivor Guest (117–120), and Joan Ross Acocella document the international success of the Viennese Children. On the role this troupe played in the rise of children's theater, see my essays "Who Watched *The Children's Pinafore?*" (421–423) and "Entertaining Children of All Ages" (10–14). Consult Crisp, "'Scandalous' and 'Delightful' Viennese Children on Tour," *Dance Magazine* 43, no. 8 (August 1969): 29–31; Guest, *The Romantic Ballet in England* (Middletown, CT: Wesleyan University Press, 1972); Acocella, "Enchanting Children: Upstaging the Stars," *Dance Magazine* 54, no. 12 (December 1980): 54–56; and Gubar, "Who Watched *The Children's Pinafore?*" *Victorian Studies* 54, no. 3 (Spring 2012): 410–426.

3. Inspired by literary critic Maria Nikolajeva's concept of "aetonormativity" (8), I've dubbed this dubious move of forgetting the antecedents of works of art created by children "aetonormative amnesia" ("Seen and Heard," 43). See Nikolajeva, *Power, Voice and Subjectivity in Literature for Young Readers* (New York: Routledge, 2010), and Gubar, "Seen and Heard: Remembering Children's Art and Activism," *Los Angeles Review of Books* 20 (November 2018): 42–51.

4. On the Temple-Robinson staircase dance duet, see James Snead (47–66) and Ann Murphy; on the *Billy Elliot* older-and-younger-self pas de deux, see George Rodosthenos (287–288), Helen Freshwater (168–169), and Robert Gordon (436). See Snead, *White Screens, Black Images*, ed. Colin MacCabe and Cornel West (New York: Routledge, 1994); Murphy, "Bill Robinson and Shirley Temple Tap Past Jim Crow," in *The Oxford Handbook of Screendance Studies*, ed. Douglas Rosenberg (New York: Oxford University Press, 2016), 731–747; Rodosthenous, "*Billy Elliot the Musical*: Visual Representations of Working-Class Masculinity and the All-Singing, All-Dancing Bo[d]y," *Studies in Musical Theatre* 1, no. 3 (2007): 275–292; Freshwater, "Consuming Authenticities: *Billy Elliot the Musical* and the Performing Child," *Lion and the Unicorn* 36, no. 2 (April 2012): 154–173; and Gordon, "*Billy Elliot* and Its Lineage: The Politics of Class and Sexual Identity in British Musicals since 1953," in *The Oxford Handbook of the British Musical*, ed. Robert Gordon and Olaf Jubin (New York: Oxford University Press, 2016), 419–444.

5. Jennifer Dunning, "Why Is Doris Humphrey a Lost Choreographer?" *New York Times*, April 30, 1991; and Marcia B. Siegel, *Days on Earth: The Dance of Doris Humphrey* (New Haven, CT: Yale University Press, 1987), xii.

6. This reading of Hon's dance was inspired not only by her work but also by Robin Bernstein's account of how the children's stories that she dubs "going-to-bed books" treat adult-child relations as an "intersubjective" process of identity formation in which "aggression and love cycle endlessly through each other" and "power swirls in multiple directions as adults and children—characters, readers, and performers—co-construct both childhood and adulthood and repeatedly renegotiate these categories together" (890). See Bernstein, "'You Do It!': Going-to-Bed Books and the Scripts of Children's Literature," *PMLA* 135, no. 5 (October 2020): 877–894.

7. Owen was director of the Limón Institute from 1988 through the early 2000s. He was responsible for licensing Limón repertory and overseeing educational programs and the Limón archives.

8. Ellen Robbins, personal interview, August 9, 2021.

9. According to the kinship model of childhood, children and adults are akin to one another—fundamentally similar, even if certain differences or deficiencies routinely attend certain parts of the aging process which might obligate older people to accord

younger ones special accommodation or assistance (or vice versa). See note 19 for more detail about the definition of kinship that informs this model.

10. Megan Drennan Meline, "Buddhist Nun Shares the Sound of Music," *Weekend Edition Sunday*, NPR, March 13, 2011, https://www.npr.org/2011/03/13/134455191/buddhist-nun-shares-the-sound-of-music. Neither Walcott nor Drolma were working alone when they composed these songs: Walcott's song "Awakening" on the album *Dawn Dance* (1981) was crafted in collaboration with Steve Eliovson, while Drolma's song "Tal" on the album *Chö* (1997) was cocreated with Steve Tibbetts.
11. Lingji Hon, personal interview, August 6, 2021.
12. Doris Humphrey, *The Art of Making Dances* (New York: Grove Press, 1959), 78.
13. Humphrey, *Art*, 119–123.
14. John Martin, "Humphrey Ballet Is Acclaimed Here," *New York Times*, December 24, 1949.
15. Hon, personal interview.
16. Bernstein, "'You Did It!,'" 879.
17. Children's literature critics Jacqueline Rose and Perry Nodelman use colonization as a metaphor for the adult-child relationship. Childhood studies scholars who align themselves "against agency" include Kristine Alexander and Karen Vallgårda et al. See Rose, *The Case of Peter Pan*, rev. ed. (Philadelphia: University of Pennsylvania Press, 1992); Nodelman, "The Other: Orientalism, Colonialism, and Children's Literature," *Children's Literature Association Quarterly* 17, no. 1 (Spring 1992): 29–35; Alexander, "Agency and Emotion Work," *Jeunesse* 7, no. 2 (Winter 2015): 120–128; Vallgårda, Kristine Alexander, and Stephanie Olsen, "Against Agency," Featured Commentary, Society for the History of Children and Youth, October 23, 2018, https://www.shcy.org/features/commentaries/against-agency/.
18. I find theoretical grounding for this way of thinking in philosopher Iris Marion Young's argument that morally respectful relationships between any two people are *inevitably* somewhat "asymmetrical" since "even when they find their relations defined by similarly socially structured differences of gender, race, class, nation, or religion"—and, I would add, age—"individuals usually also find many ways that they are strange to one another," divergences as well as commonalities that render "their positions irreversible" and thus never perfectly symmetrical (347). See Young, "Asymmetrical Reciprocity: On Moral Respect, Wonder, and Enlarged Thought," *Constellations* 3, no. 3 (1997): 340–363; and (eventually!) my work in progress *How to Think about Children*, in which I tweak Young's concept a bit by including age and renaming it asymmetrical mutuality.
19. Although the two adult-child pas de deux I'm discussing here both involve a parent-child pairing, other adult-child dance duets dramatize different kinds of kinship that are not based on consanguineous or familial ties. For example, Stanley Donen's 1974 film version of Antoine de Saint-Exupéry's children's book *The Little Prince* (1943) features an adult-child pas de deux between a little boy and a fox who he befriends on his travels. Crucially, the concept of kinship appeals to me because it, too, is elastic enough to encompass not just biological, familial, and romantic bonds but also endless other forms of affinity, similarity, and association, as anthropologists have recognized since Claude Lévi-Strauss reframed kinship as a cultural—and culturally diverse—phenomenon in the mid-twentieth century.
20. Humphrey, *Art*, 106.
21. William Wordsworth, "Ode: Intimations of Immortality from Recollections of Early Childhood," in *Poems, in Two Volumes, 1800–1807*, ed. Jared Curtis (Ithaca, NY: Cornell University Press, 1983), 269–277.

22. William Wordsworth, "To H. C.: Six Years Old," in *The Poetical Works of William Wordsworth: Poems Written in Youth; Poems Referring to the Period of Childhood*, ed. Ernest de Selincourt (Oxford: Oxford University Press, 1963), 247.

23. Marah Gubar, "Child," *Victorian Literature and Culture* 46, no. 3/4 (Fall/Winter 2018): 616–621.

24. William Wordsworth, "She dwelt among th' untrodden ways," in William Wordsworth and Samuel Taylor Coleridge, *Lyrical Ballads: 1798 and 1802*, ed. Fiona Stafford (New York: Oxford University Press, 2013), 224.

25. While I do not have time to delve into the intricacies of the "Lucy" poems here, I do want to register that Heather Glen makes a compelling case that we should not simply conflate Wordsworth with the narrator of these verses, but rather view the author as critically exposing the clueless "egocentricity" of his adult male character (47; see also 281–297). See Wordsworth, "A slumber did my spirit seal," in Wordsworth and Coleridge, *Lyrical Ballads*, 225, and Glen, *Vision and Disenchantment: Blake's* Songs *and Wordsworth's* Lyrical Ballads (Cambridge: Cambridge University Press, 1983).

26. See review of the Viennese Children, "Her Majesty's Theatre," *Morning Post* (UK), April 11, 1845; review of the Viennese Children, "Her Majesty's Theatre," *Morning Post* (UK), April 9, 1845; and review of the Viennese Children, "Her Majesty's Theatre," *Times* (UK), April 9, 1845.

27. Review of the Viennese Children, *Times*.

28. Thomas Ryan, *Recollections of an Old Musician* (New York: E. P. Dutton, 1899), 27–28.

29. Ryan, *Recollections*, 28, 29.

30. See review of the Viennese Children, "Theatres," *Satirist: or, The Censor of the Times*, April 13, 1845; review of the Viennese Children, "Her Majesty's Theatre," *Morning Post* (UK), April 21, 1845; and review of the Viennese Children, *Examiner* (UK), No. 1941, April 12, 1845.

31. J. M. Barrie, *Peter Pan and Other Plays*, ed. Peter Hollindale (New York: Oxford University Press, 1995), 1.1.394–1.1.395, 5.1.197–5.1.198.

32. Peter himself explicitly denies that he is an "ordinary" child in dialogue with Hook during the scene set in the mermaids' lagoon. See Barrie, *Peter Pan*, 3.1.129–3.1.130.

33. Julia Humphrey, Letter to May Walker, 1907, quoted in the New York Public Library's "Guide to the Doris Humphrey Collection," ix, https://archives.nypl.org/dan/19673.

34. Doris Humphrey, *Moment Musical*, in Mary Wood Hinman, *Gymnastic and Folk Dancing*, vol. 4 (New York: A.S. Barnes, 1916), 7.

35. See Wordsworth, "TO A YOUNG LADY, Who had been reproached for taking long Walks in the Country," in Curtis, *Poems*, 231.

36. Hinman, *Gymnastic*, vol. 3, rev. ed. 1922, 1.

37. Ashton Nichols, "Wordsworth as Environmental 'Nature' Writer," in *Nature and the Environment*, ed. Scott Slovic (Ipswich, MA: Salem Press, 2013), 109.

38. William Wordsworth, "I wandered lonely as a cloud," in Curtis, *Poems*, 207–209, 331.

39. Doris Humphrey, quoted in Selma Landen Odom, "Sharing the Dances of Many People: The Teaching Work of Mary Wood Hinman," in Society of Dance History Scholars, *Proceedings of the Tenth Annual Conference* (Riverside, CA: Dance History Scholars, 1987), 64.

40. Doris Humphrey, *Will o' the Wisp*, in Mary Wood Hinman, *Gymnastic and Folk Dancing*, vol. 3 (New York: A.S. Barnes, 1916), 65.

41. Doris Humphrey, *Daffodils*, in Mary Wood Hinman, *Gymnastic and Folk Dancing*, vol. 3 (New York: A.S. Barnes, 1916), 72.

42. Gina Marie Borden, "The Art of Making Children's Dances: A Look into Doris Humphrey's Early Choreography and Its Impact on Her Technique" (undergraduate thesis, Barnard College, 2014), 12.
43. Borden, "Art of Making," 19.
44. Siegel, *Days on Earth*, 239.
45. Jack Anderson, "Reviving the Work of a Modern Pioneer," *New York Times*, March 16, 1990.
46. Siegel, *Days on Earth*, 272.
47. Dunning, "Doris Humphrey?"
48. Susan Manning discusses and reproduces one of these photos in *Modern Dance, Negro Dance* (Minneapolis: University of Minnesota Press, 2004), 190–191.
49. Hon, personal interview.
50. Humphrey, *Art*, 106.
51. Humphrey, *Art*, 106, emphasis mine.
52. Humphrey, *Art*, 106–107.
53. Martin, "The Dance: Humphrey: Her 'Day on Earth' for Limon a Masterpiece," *New York Times*, January 4, 1948.
54. Martin, "Dance: Humphrey."
55. Martin, "Dance: Humphrey."
56. Martin, "Dance: Humphrey"; see also Siegel, *Days on Earth*, 243.
57. Doris Humphrey, quoted. in Siegel, *Days on Earth*, 243.
58. Martin, "Dance: Humphrey."
59. Dancer-choreographer Rebecca Rice, speaking in the 2009 documentary *A New Dance for America: The Choreography, Teachings and Legacy of Doris Humphrey 1895–1958*, directed by Ina Hahn (Rockport, MA: WW Films, 2010).
60. Siegel, *Days on Earth*, 181.
61. Notably, Humphrey dancer Eleanor King recalls that when she commented to Ruth St. Denis (one of the founders of Denishawn) that "the most vital and extraordinary dancing going on in New York these days [is] up at the Savoy in Harlem," St. Denis went on a racist rant in which she insisted that "'Africa has never contributed anything to world culture'" (King 179). In contrast, Humphrey publicly championed the work of Black dancers from the Bahamas, noting in a 1933 essay in *The American Dancer* that "in a dance-world infested with imitations and impressions of foreign and exotic dances, [their] genuineness . . . stands out like a beacon light." Although Humphrey's (positive) use of adjectives such as "primitive" to describe these dances may disturb readers today, it was in line with how Black dancer-choreographers such as Katherine Dunham were describing their own work during the interwar period, a moment when—as David Luis-Brown and Joanna Dee Das have noted—people of color "often used the discourse of primitivism to critique US empire and neocolonialism, even as, contradictorily, they ended up reinforcing problematic categories and romanticized notions of primitive life" (Das 31). See King, *Transformations* (New York: Dance Horizons, 1978); Doris Humphrey, "Dance, Little Chillun!" *American Dancer* 6, no. 10 (July 1933): 8; Luis-Brown, "Cuban *Negrismo*, Mexican *Indigenismo*: Contesting Neocolonialism in the New Negro Movement," in *Escape from New York*, ed. Davarian L. Baldwin and Minkah Makalani (Minneapolis: University of Minnesota Press, 2013), 53–75; and Das, *Katherine Dunham* (New York: Oxford University Press, 2017).
62. Siegel, *Days on Earth*, 7.

63. Glen, *Vision and Disenchantment*, 6.
64. Wordsworth and Coleridge, *Lyrical Ballads*, 63.
65. Leo Damrosch, *Eternity's Sunrise: The Imaginative World of William Blake* (New Haven, CT: Yale University Press, 2015), 160.
66. Siegel, *Days on Earth*, 153, 8.
67. Review of the Viennese Children, *Satirist.*
68. Ryan, *Recollections*, 29.
69. Reviews of the Viennese Children, *Morning Post*, April 9, 1845 and April 8, 1845.
70. Acocella, "Enchanting Children," 56.
71. London's *Morning Post* was not the only journal to describe the Viennese Children's performances as "unprecedented" events in which "the standard of excellence" for ensemble dancing had not only "risen, [but] utterly changed" (April 9, 1845; April 18, 1845); see also an 1868 journalistic account of the history of American theater and dance in *The Round Table*, which attributes the splash that the Viennese Children made in the United States to the fact that although American audiences had gotten used to seeing "single" European ballet dancers such as Fanny Elssler perform by the mid-1840s, "the sight of a full corps of trained *artistes* in America was an unprecedented one" ("Naughty Drama" 165). See "The Naughty Drama," *Round Table*, March 14, 1868.
72. For a description of how the Viennese Children differed in age and size, see the April 9, 1845 *Morning Post* review; for details about the *Montreal Transcript* review, see Crisp, "'Scandalous' and 'Delightful,'" 30–31.
73. Review of the Viennese Children, April 9, 1845.
74. Acocella, "Enchanting Children," 54.
75. The Viennese Children are described as "models of healthfulness" in a review that appeared in London's *Morning Post* (April 16, 1845). Many accounts of the formation of the troupe describe the children as having been raised in "the lowest class of society and in abject poverty" ("Madame Weiss"; see also the April 11, 1845 *Morning Post* review). See "Madame Weiss and the Viennese Children," clipping from an unidentified newspaper (ca. April 19, 1845), Dance Archives, L. E. Kirstein Collection, Jerome Robbins Dance Division, The New York Public Library for the Performing Arts. On their ability to embody "variety in unity," see John S. Dwight, "The Juvenile Choirs of Harmony," *Harbinger*, January 2, 1847, 61–62.
76. See Child (quoted in Dwight, "Juvenile Choirs," 61) and "The Viennese Children" in *Common School Journal* 9, no. 3 (February 1, 1847): 33. "Compared with these sylphs, according to all accounts," the latter source concludes, "our most agile and buoyant children" seem "maimed, and lame, and halt" (33).
77. See my essay "Who Watched *The Children's Pinafore*?" for an account of how all-child troupes, including the Viennese Children, were perceived as erotically enticing by both young and old theatergoers.
78. See "Observations on Men, Books, and Things," *Christian Observatory* 1, no. 2 (February 1847): 90–96.
79. See review of the Viennese Children, *Morning Post*, April 11, 1845.
80. Ryan, *Recollections*, 28, 27.
81. Dwight, "Juvenile," 61.
82. See John S. Dwight, "Integral Education—No. III," *Harbinger*, August 7, 1847, 143. On the Jena Set's symphilosophizing, see Andrea Wulf, *Magnificent Rebels* (New York: Knopf, 2022), 160–184. On the influence of Fourier in the United States, see Carl J. Guarneri, *The*

Utopian Alternative (Ithaca, NY: Cornell University Press, 1991) and John Michael Cooper's "Escape to—and from—Utopia," *American Music* 33, no. 2 (Summer 2013): 141–175.

83. Dwight, "Integral," 143.

84. Dwight, "Juvenile," 61.

85. Odom, "Sharing the Dances," 69.

86. Humphrey, *Art*, 19.

87. Ellen Robbins, quoted in Sara Jarrett, "Growing Dancers," *Dance Teacher*, September 2007, 113.

88. Robbins, personal interview.

11

Charli, Charlie, and Me

An Autoethnographic Study of TikTok Dance and Child/Adult Collaborations

TREVOR BOFFONE

> Charli D'Amelio is a famous TikToker. Her videos are really good. Mostly she dances. I really want to dance like her. There's not a lot of girls named Charlie. So it kind of makes me feel a little famous like her. Basically everyone at school calls me Charli D'Amelio. It's really funny.
>
> –Charlie, eight years old

When TikTok entered the U.S. market in 2018, it was quickly heralded as a space for teenagers. While millennials and Gen Xers might have flocked to malls, skating rinks, and arcades, Zoomers, or members of Gen Z, have used digital spaces as critical sites to develop and perform generational identity.[1] TikTok has been the de facto space for Zoomer cultural production in the United States. Yet, to this point, popular conversations and extant scholarship on TikTok have almost exclusively privileged culture produced by teenagers, excluding roughly half of Generation Z, specifically children and tweens.[2] Although famous TikTokers such as Charli D'Amelio, the app's second most followed creator, have transformed the platform into a definitive dance space, their dance moves, choreographies, and playlists permeate a much younger audience who then replicates and remixes their content, leading to a proliferation of child creators who use apps such as Zoomerang, Funimate, and Triller, in addition to TikTok.[3]

This is precisely where my eight-year-old niece, Charlie, encountered Charli D'Amelio, something that changed the course of her life. Inspired by the "Reigning Queen of TikTok" D'Amelio, my niece Charlie just wanted to dance. At the same time, I went viral by dancing with my high school students on TikTok, appearing on *Good Morning America*, *Inside Edition*, and *Access Hollywood*. I, too, just wanted to dance. Despite having a twenty-seven year age difference and living five hours apart, suddenly, Charlie and I had a commonality—digital dance cultures. When we would see each other, we traded in *Frozen* karaoke for TikTok dance. Knowing I was coming to town, Charlie would begin scrolling through videos of Charli D'Amelio on Zoomerang (the child-friendly alternative to TikTok) and YouTube (where TikTokers cross-share content) to find appropriate videos for us to dance to.[4] Throughout the process, Charlie was in the driver's seat, dictating what songs we danced to and teaching me the dances. Side by side, niece to uncle, our relationship transformed. We developed stronger bonds that were intrinsically tied to digital dance cultures, all through privileging Charlie's autonomy and creativity.

Using the child/adult collaborations between my niece and I, in this chapter, I engage in autoethnography to illustrate the relationship between TikTok, dance performance, and child-produced culture. Drawing from my work in dance studies as well as my experiences as a TikTok dancer, I analyze how TikTok dancing holds the power to forge stronger adult/child relationships and a more formidable sense of community by actualizing children as creators. Building off research from my first book, *Renegades: Digital Dance Cultures from Dubsmash to TikTok* (2021), this chapter analyzes child creation, specifically focusing on the role of unison movement and muscular bonding necessary to make TikTok videos. The chapter argues that children and adults dancing on TikTok creates an affective response that helps build stronger relationships and instills confidence in children, enabling them to construct and perform identity.

In "Children as Agents in Dance," dance scholar Eeva Anttila, questions, "To what extent is it possible to consider children as subjects, experts or active agents in researching dance education?"[5] My work, like Anttila's, views "children as experts and active agents in constructing their own culture."[6] Accordingly, I privilege child-produced culture and the creative processes of children rather than culture produced *for* children. I recognize that this chapter only includes one perspective, mine, and, therefore should be read in conversation with other scholarship on dance and child creativity.[7] My research in this chapter covers a two-year period from March 2019 to March 2021. During this time, Charlie and I saw each other every few months for one to seven days per visit. We engaged in cocreation—whether discussing TikTok dances, learning them, or performing them—every day, except on rare occasions. Furthermore, I interviewed Charlie in March 2021 about her experiences as a cultural producer and the role that TikTok dance plays in this work. Each section of this chapter begins with Charlie's words, creating a framework for writing about childhood agency and creativity that centers the thoughts of the child in question. In addition, my work draws from frequent conversations with Charlie over the same two-year period and informal chats well into the revision of this chapter. That is, at every turn, I have consulted with Charlie to ensure that her experiences were being ethically and intellectually represented in an accurate manner.[8] By shining an autoethnographic light on how Charlie and I use dance to cocreate, build confidence, and form stronger familial bonds, this chapter unpacks how young children engage with TikTok dance and what this experience means to them. Ultimately, I pose the following questions: How do children engage in TikTok dance? How does creativity influence their identity formation? And, what roles, if any, should adults play in child-produced culture on TikTok? In asking these questions, this chapter engages in a discussion of what it means for adults like me to write about child-produced culture.

TikTok: Or, What I, a Whole Grown-Ass Man, Learned from Gen Z

> TikTok is an app. You can film dances. You can sing. You can do a lot of things. Since I'm eight, I don't have TikTok. I have Zoomerang. My friends make TikToks. Well, basically everyone at school makes TikToks. We usually find TikTok dances on YouTube. We find one that we want to do and then we learn it and film it on Zoomerang. It takes some time to learn the dances. It doesn't matter how many tries it takes. You just have to try your best to get it right.
>
> –Charlie, eight years old

I still remember it like it was yesterday. I was sitting in fifth period one afternoon in fall 2018, waiting for the bell to ring. A group of girls in my class huddled together by a window. After some brief chatter and plenty of laughter, one of them placed their cell phone on the window ledge, pressed the circular button at the bottom of the screen, ran back to the group, and a countdown timer began. When the music started, the group performed an intricate dance in perfect unison. They did this without ever taking the time to learn the dance together or even rehearse the dance moves. This was my introduction to digital dance cultures. That day, my students had made a Dubsmash video, but the process of making videos on apps such as TikTok, Funimate, and Triller is comparable. I immediately asked my students what they were doing, how they all knew the dance, where they found the dances, and, most importantly, when could they teach me?

By summer 2019, TikTok had already entered what Zoomers lovingly refer to as "the golden age of TikTok." At this point, TikTok was *the* app of choice for young people in the United States. It would take nearly a year for the mainstream United States to catch up. By the time the COVID-19 pandemic began to wreak havoc through the country, TikTok had cemented itself as a critical site of generational identity, mindless entertainment, education, and activism. In my previous work, I have proposed that digital sites like TikTok allow young people the opportunity "to produce cultural content that, in turn, facilitates young people's participation in an increasingly inclusive and democratized media culture."[9] Thus, TikTok becomes a "digital playground," or what Sara A. Grimes refers to as a political space online where young people negotiate power alongside children, adults, and developers.[10] Naturally, digital playgrounds like TikTok are complicated matrixes in which young people make meaning and perform identity. Zoomers create a wide spectrum of TikTok videos that "present themselves not as random and short-lived entertainment but as complex, cultural artifacts."[11] A key facet of this work revolves around identity. TikTok, like other apps, is a site of identity formation and, as an extension, gives young people a blueprint for identity.[12] Virality leads to mimicry and, as more young people began to use TikTok's identity scripts, TikTok became more popular. As TikTok's cultural capital rose, so, too, did its influence on children. Although the app is not particularly known as a safe or appropriate place for those under the age of thirteen, TikTok culture nevertheless permeates far beyond the app itself. TikTok dance challenges are cross-shared on platforms such as YouTube and Zoomerang, where young people such as my niece are likely to encounter TikTok celebrities. This is precisely how Charlie learned about Charli.

I use the notion of the "D'Amelio Effect" to encompass the ways that Charli D'Amelio dictates not just TikTok culture but generational culture. As the app's second most followed creator (151.6 million followers as of January 2024) and, by extension, arguably the most famous Zoomer in the world, D'Amelio's aesthetic, sonic, and choreographic choices influence how other Zoomers create and perform identity.[13] Creators like D'Amelio and Addison Rae Easterling render the app a site of "silly, unashamed and unfiltered girlhood."[14] As cultural studies scholar Melanie Kennedy proposes, "TikTok celebrates girlhood and, thus, fashions girls' bedroom culture into a public space."[15] Teens such as D'Amelio draw spectators into their "private" lives and allow us to be a part of a shared digital space. This is why, when my niece scrolls through Zoomerang, she inevitably lands on D'Amelio's content and begins learning and creating the dance trends. Charlie, who once signed up for dance classes, went to one class, hated it, and abruptly quit, has largely become a dancer and identified as such by modeling herself after D'Amelio. Seeing D'Amelio create and produce culture inspired Charlie to create and produce culture. TikTok is an intrinsically creative space. Anyone who engages with TikTok is inevitably creating—meaning, virality, conversations, and trends. And, in the case of dancers, TikTokers create their own choreographed routines that inherently continue the TikTok creation loop. Anyone participating in TikTok culture, therefore, is creating. Even though viral dance trends may start with D'Amelio, they proliferate because of the passion and joy of young dancers like my niece.

Despite the unquestionable influence of TikTok's creative class, the app, as with other forms of youth culture, has been largely overlooked by adults. In "Leisure Is Hard Work: Digital Practices and Future Competences," Kirsten Drotner acknowledges, "We have also seen that adults tend to react to these explorations in rather normative ways, either by celebrating how creative, innovative and media savvy young users are or by ignoring their output as unimportant or trivial."[16] These critics inevitably consider children's digital culture as "inferior in cultural quality."[17] Dance scholars Karen E. Bond and Susan W. Stinson affirm this, stating that "work by children in every art form has been romanticized and criticized by adults."[18] In the case of TikTok, the app was mocked and ridiculed for nearly two years before the pandemic shifted the way we engage with entertainment. Even though the likes of Jennifer Lopez, Jason Derulo, and Lizzo—not to mention nearly every brand in the United States—may be commonplace on TikTok today, even in February 2020 this was not the case. It was still largely seen as an exclusively Zoomer space and, as a result, adults viewed it as a space to quickly disregard.[19] There was a failure to acknowledge the myriad ways that young people were strategically using the app as a critical site of identity formation and generational culture development and dissemination. The tendency to downplay or neglect TikTok as "child's play" inherently reflects an adult-centric perspective that views children's culture and children themselves as lesser. Even the expression "child's play" is used to denote something we should not take seriously, just like we should not take children seriously because they are not fully developed beings. Therefore, adults are not just dismissing children's creations as lesser, they are viewing children through the same lens. My work here reflects my efforts to resist adult-centric perspectives that erase children's culture and children themselves as seen but not heard. As my investigations down the TikTok rabbit hole and my autoethnographic work with my students and my niece have continually revealed, digital dance spaces serve as key sites to build self-esteem and community, not to mention their knack for enabling young people to become active producers of cultures as opposed to just passive receptors of culture.

Do You Wanna Make a TikTok?

> Once I find a dance I like, I start learning it by myself. I just watch the video. Normally it takes a lot of practice for me. Like I have to watch it a bunch of times to learn it. Sometimes it's hard but then it feels good to get it. Sometimes I teach people and sometimes someone else teaches me. I don't know if I like teaching them or someone else teaching me more. It's kind of a hard decision because they're both kind of good, but I like to teach people.
>
> –Charlie, eight years old

Immediately upon opening the app, TikTokers are met with a wave of content on their For You Page (FYP) that is tailor-made to their liking based on how users interact with the app's infamous algorithm.[20] In *Making it Personal: Algorithmic Personalization, Identity, and Everyday Life*, Tanya Kant proposes that the way digital spaces privilege personalization is a way for platforms to grant users an ideal online experience specifically catered to them.[21] Kant adds that social media platforms collect users' data in various ways and, as a result, "Your needs and interests can be algorithmically inferred and your experience 'conveniently'—and computationally—personalized on your behalf."[22] The more users interact with dance challenge videos, the more likely they are to see similar content on thc app.[23] With this in mind, media studies scholar Andrea Ruehlicke proposes that TikTok "represents a new development in how we think and talk about personalization in virtual spaces."[24] For young dancers, then, TikTok becomes not only a site of entertainment but also an educational space to learn about contemporary dance and music. Along the same vein, young readers will perhaps have a different TikTok experience on encountering the BookTok community. Slime enthusiasts may engage with Slime-Tok. And *Harry Potter* fans may spend time on DracoTok. All of these TikTok subcultures do fundamental community work, but for young dancers, there is no more desirable place to be than dance TikTok, which is the mainstream culture on the app and, therefore, does not have a catchy name.

Once young dancers begin to scroll TikTok, they attend a virtual dance recital in which they begin to take inventory of popular dance challenges and ones they might want to learn, remix, and recreate. Aspiring dancers first favorite or download videos and then begin learning the dance moves, using a variety of learning methods. Every digital dancer has a unique method for learning dance challenges. Usually, dancers will watch videos on autoplay, focusing on different parts of the dance until they learn the movements. In my case, I prefer to download videos and then replay them in slow motion to ease the learning process. In almost every case, dancers prefer to learn alongside others so they can teach each other the moves and help each other polish the dance.

Executing a TikTok video relies on a series of choreographed movements that lead to cultural identification. Naturally, young people come to depend on embodied consciousness such as this as it is intrinsically tied to socialization and fitting in with group culture. For social media dance apps, embodied consciousness takes the form of a series of dance moves that dancers must learn to become one with the group. I often refer to these viral dance moves as puzzle pieces. Although it may take a particular dancer time and patience to build out their tool kit, once each choreographic move is mastered, making a TikTok becomes a process of putting the puzzle pieces together. Having these puzzle pieces in your repertoire is essential to developing positive self-esteem and being able to feel a sense of group belonging. Even if someone is not a master dancer, knowing these dance moves allows individuals an entry point into the community. And, as this chapter reveals, there is power in making puzzles together, especially when children take on leadership roles and find agency in their creativity.

Charlie's Creativity, Creating with Charlie

> Dancing makes me feel creative. Whenever I don't know the dance, I just make it up and do what feels right. Being creative is important to me because I don't want to copy someone. I kind of want to make my own dance. When people copy my dances it makes me kinda happy. I like dancing with you because it lets us spend more time together. I feel creative. It makes me happy. And it makes me feel comfortable for some reason. We usually dance to the music I like and do dances that are popular with kids at school.
>
> –Charlie, eight years old

Dance scholars such as Jan Deans, Jeff Meiners, Adrienne Sansom, Wendy Schiller, and Sarah Young have advocated that dance is fundamental to young child development despite dance being often overlooked by early childhood education. For example, Deans proposes that dance allows children to "engage in embodied thinking, playful, imaginative problem solving and aesthetic decision making, while developing . . . a strong sense of self and collective agency."[25] In the case of creating with Charlie, her process of engaging with many of the positive effects that Deans claims begins with choice, which is a fundamental part of our child/adult collaborations and artistic practice. According to Susan Stinson, to push young dancers further, we must "give them choice, freedom, and a sense of control, so that they are motivating themselves, rather than depending on teachers to make it 'fun.'"[26] With Charlie in control, having made a series of choices, we begin to move as one.

TikTok's power as an incubator for child/adult cocreation lies in unison movement, a practice through which dancers construct feelings of community while recording a video with others. This forges a type of digital kinship, or, in cultural studies scholar Ashleigh Wade's words, "a relational practice through which familial ties—with both origin family and chosen family—are established and/or maintained through digital technologies."[27] Hence, there is power in making TikToks and engaging in unison dancing. There is power in group movement which is enhanced by learning as a group and gaining literacy in TikTok. Dancing in a collective holds transformative power to build community and (re)enforce a positive self of individual and group identity. And, as Kerry Chappell, Anna Craft, et al., suggest, co-creativity between young dancers and adults can energize young people's creativity.[28] Social media dance facilitates an embodied practice that positions the artistic and cultural contributions of young children as an act of resistance. Part of the resistance lies in the power of unison movement that transpires with children making artistic and executive decisions. Writing about this creative process and cultural production, therefore, becomes an act of resistance as well.

TikTok dance is a collective movement ritual that Charlie and I use to create group cohesion in our videos and beyond. In *Keeping Together in Time: Dance and Drill in Human History*, historian William Hardy McNeill uses his experience in the military to examine this phenomenon. As he details in his recollection about his time in the military, moving in unison with his fellow soldiers created a "strange sense of enlargement; a sort of swelling out, becoming bigger than life, thanks to participation in collective ritual."[29] It should come as no surprise that it is difficult to put words to what this feeling does to an individual; words can be limiting and, as was the case with me, for years I struggled with putting into words what Charlie and I felt while dancing together. In a sense it felt larger than life, like something that could not be contained to a brief description or theory. Creating a TikTok dance together is an act that triggers an emotional response which, to quote McNeill, constitutes "an indefinitely expansible basis for social cohesion among any and every group that keeps together in time, moving big muscles together and chanting, singing, or shouting rhythmically."[30] The experience of unison dancing was visceral and enabled us to develop (digital) kinship bonds between uncle and niece. Regardless of the dance challenge we rehearsed, a euphoric feeling swept over us. Indeed, there was magic in the air and a sense of joy at every turn.

In his journey to understanding his experiences of collective ritual in the military, McNeill introduces the theory of "muscular bonding" to explain how collective movement rituals lead to a positive feeling among participants. According to McNeill, this euphoric response is a leading reason that military troops are efficient, loyal, and equal.[31] Not to mention that veterans often continue to practice unison drills even when the movement has no practical use in their lives. It is something they just cannot shake off. Although military formations would seem a world away from the world of digital dance cultures, the focus on moving as one and the affective response it creates is not so different. By succumbing to group cohesion, the individual dancer increases their sense of self-worth. Unison dancing, therefore, is intrinsically linked to forming a positive self-value. And, as feelings of positive self-esteem grow, so do feelings of obligation to group identity. Dance leads to a situation in which harmony in the community is at a maximum and as a result can be felt by each individual member. This joint feeling and fusion of individual and collective identity becomes one of the primary functions of social media dance.

Mihály Csíkszentmihályi uses the term "flow" to encompass a similar feeling. Flow is the feeling of being completely immersed in an activity, somewhere "between boredom and anxiety."[32] According to Bond and Stinson, young people's experiences with dance are often linked to flow: "A number of elements that usually characterize flow experiences were present in young people's descriptions of dance, including merger of action and awareness (the mind is not 'somewhere else'), exclusion of distractions from one's consciousness, disappearance of self-consciousness, an altered sense of time, and autotelicity (experiences are intrinsically rewarding)."[33] In the case of TikTok, dance challenges such as Doja Cat's "Say So" and Megan Thee Stallion's "Savage" are difficult enough for children to push them while also being comfortable enough for them to successfully learn and execute the short dances.[34] As with flow experiences, young dancers must feel in control. If a dance is too difficult, the child can lose control and in turn, the experience turns sour, producing anxiety and negative self-esteem. Digital dance cultures, then, hold the potential to be a source of pleasure and enjoyment which builds up child dancers such as Charlie, becoming a satisfying experience and a way to use creativity to build confidence.

Choice is imperative to Charlie's cultural production, which facilitates flow. Stinson recognizes that in order to be engaged and to "flow," there must be "choice, freedom, a sense of control, intrinsic motivation, and appropriate levels of challenge."[35] When Charlie and I dance, she not only teaches the dances but she often chooses the material we work with and leads the process from idea to final product. Even if I already know a dance or learn it faster than she does, I keep this hidden, encouraging her to take agency and ownership of the process. The process, as with most art-making, outweighs the product. And, in this case, the process is dictated by an eight-year-old, not a thirty-five-year-old. Even if we do post our videos to my social media accounts, I am just a participant in Charlie's dance world.

This process of collaboratively creating a dance video creates a corporeal transference between Charlie and me. Put simply, doing complicated dances such as Jalaiah Harmon's Renegade Challenge to K-Camp's "Lottery" in unison fosters a level of synchronicity that releases endorphins. TikTok dance, then, creates a euphoric feeling, building an affective experience of "feeling together." Throughout the process, we strive to synchronize our movements with each other and to match our rhythm with the song's beat. Our goal is always to blend in together and move as "one singular sensation," to riff on the musical *A Chorus Line.*[36] When making a high-quality TikTok, it is imperative to be moving as one. Consequently, to make a TikTok is to become equal with fellow dancers and to engage in a form of culture sharing. In my case, uncles being on equal footing with their nieces is not a common occurrence. Even if the relationship dynamic is replicated, oftentimes adults dictate *how* culture is produced. In other words, even if a child chooses what culture will be produced, inevitably adults take on the role of facilitator or teacher, leading the process at every turn. To those adults, I suggest they let children take on a leadership role and dictate not just *what* is produced, but *how* it is produced. The process, not to mention the result, can be transformative and an integral component of how children experience creativity and reap all of the corresponding benefits from being active producers of culture.

Go, Go, Go . . . What's Next?

> I like teaching you and my mom TikTok dances. It's kind of good to have an uncle like you and my mom–two adults that will do the dances with me. I would like to teach other adults TikTok dances, too. I think adults can learn more about the actual kids they are around. They can learn about us.
>
> –Charlie, eight years old

Dance challenges come and go on TikTok, with each month featuring its own unique viral trend that dominates life on and off the app. In June 2020, there was arguably no bigger dance challenge than the "Who's Next" Challenge to Hip Hop Harry's song "Go Go Go Who's Next," a rap song featured on Hip Hop Harry's Emmy Award-winning after-school series (2006–2008) and resurrected in the middle of the pandemic. As with most popular TikTok challenges, the "Who's Next" Challenge's success lies in how easy it is to replicate. To do the challenge, dancers lean forward at the waist to their left side, placing both hands on their left knee. As the song continues "go go go," TikTokers pop their right knee out, on beat. The dance perfectly ties into the silliness of TikTok aesthetics and, consequently became a viral sensation.

This is precisely what Charlie and I found ourselves doing when I visited home in summer 2020, choosing to self-isolate with family for a bit and to benefit from interacting (re: dancing) with my family. After Charli D'Amelio hit the challenge, the dance became the obsession du jour of young Zoomers, including my niece. Once again, culture had passed from one Charli to another Charlie, with me serving as an interlocutor of sorts, fully participating but also always studying how this phenomenon of youth dance culture was transpiring.

So, as we did yet another dance challenge and our relationship grew stronger through the benefits of child/adult collaboration, Hip Hop Harry asked, "Who's next?" But a more apt question perhaps would have been "What's next?" I suggest that "what's next" is that we not just pay attention to the creativity of children, but listen and work to understand how child creative processes hold the potential to teach us about identity formation and community building. Doing this cultural and community-building work alongside children, with them in the driver's seat, can indeed be a transformative experience for everyone involved. TikTok is not a mindless app where Zoomers of all ages seek out entertainment and create short-form video content. Rather, it serves a fundamental role in childhood development in the digital age. As culture and creation are passed on from one Charli to another, children continue to exert agency to construct new cultures, ones that we should all be paying attention to.

NOTES

1. Crystal Abidin, "Mapping Internet Celebrity on TikTok: Exploring Attention Economies and Visibility Labours," *Cultural Science Journal* 12, no. 1 (2021): 77–103; Jing Zeng, Crystal Abidin, and Mike S. Schäfer, "Research Perspectives on TikTok and Its Legacy Apps," *International Journal of Communication* 15 (2021): 3161–3172; and Trevor Boffone, "The Rise of TikTok Cultures in the United States," in *TikTok Cultures in the United States*, ed. Trevor Boffone (Abingdon, UK: Routledge, 2022), 1–13.
2. See, for example, Sujatha Subramanian, "Bahujan Girls' Anti-Caste Activism on TikTok," *Feminist Media Studies* 21, no. 1 (2021): 154–156; Jing Zeng and Crystal Abidin, "'#OkBoomer, Time to Meet the Zoomers': Studying the Memefication of Intergenerational Politics on TikTok," *Information, Communication & Society* 24, no. 16 (2021): 2459–2481; Sarah Jerasa and Trevor Boffone, "BookTok 101: TikTok, Digital Literacies, and Out-of-School Reading Practices," *Journal of Adult & Adolescent Literacy* 65, no. 3 (2021): 219–226; and Trevor Boffone and Sarah Jerasa, "Toward a (Queer) Reading Community: BookTok, Teen Readers, and the Rise of TikTok Literacies," *Talking Points* 33, no. 1 (2021): 10–16.
3. Trevor Boffone, "'The D'Amelio Effect': TikTok, Charli D'Amelio, and the Construction of Whiteness," in Boffone, *TikTok Cultures*, 17–27. Like TikTok, Zoomerang, Funimate, and Triller are video-sharing social media platforms that operate on a much smaller scale than the behemoth that is TikTok. While each app targets a different demographic (for example: Zoomerang, children), these video-sharing platforms all hold the common goal of empowering young people and adults alike to become content creators as well as active audiences for each platform's microinfluencers.
4. Although Zoomerang is not created to be a child-friendly space—in terms of content (lyrics, for example)—the app skews younger than TikTok and therefore features a

higher percentage of PG-13 content. TikTok, especially in the post-2020 era, features an incredible range of content, which includes explicit language and humor about sex. While the app does not feature nudity, casual users will inevitably stumble upon content that is arguably inappropriate for children. As of this writing, apps like Zoomerang can fill gaps such as these.

5. Eeva Anttila, "Children as Agents in Dance: Implications of the Notion of Child Culture for Research and Practice in Dance Education," in *International Handbook of Research in Arts Education*, ed. Liora Bresler (New York: Springer 2007), 865.
6. Anttila, "Children as Agents in Dance," 865.
7. For more on dance and child creativity, see Shauna Pomerantz and Miriam Field, "A TikTok Assemblage: Girlhood, Radical Media Engagement, & Parent-Child Generativity," in *Visual & Cultural Identity Constructs of Global Youth: Situated, Embodied & Performed Ways of Being, Engaged & Belonging*, ed. Fiona Blaikie (Routledge, 2021), 139–157; and Wendyliz Martinez, "TikTok for Us by Us: Black Girlhood, Joy, and Self Care," in Boffone, *TikTok Cultures*, 39–46.
8. I have received consent to do this research from Charlie's parents (my sister and brother-in-law) given Charlie's age. Moreover, Charlie's parents have had access to drafts of this chapter and have offered feedback.
9. Trevor Boffone, *Renegades: Digital Dance Cultures from Dubsmash to TikTok* (New York: Oxford University Press, 2021), 12.
10. Sara A. Grimes, *Digital Playgrounds: The Hidden Politics of Children's Online Play Spaces, Virtual Worlds, and Connected Games* (Toronto, ON: University of Toronto Press, 2021), 10.
11. Andreas Schellewald, "Communicative Forms on TikTok: Perspectives from Digital Ethnography," *International Journal of Communication* 15 (2021): 1439.
12. Howard Gardner and Katie Davis, *The App Generation: How Today's Youth Navigate Identity, Intimacy, and Imagination in a Digital World* (New Haven, CT: Yale University Press, 2013), 32; Boffone, "Rise of TikTok Cultures," 1–13.
13. Boffone, "'D'Amelio Effect,'" 18–19.
14. Melanie Kennedy, "'If the Rise of the TikTok Dance and E-Girl Aesthetic Has Taught Us Anything, It's That Teenage Girls Rule the Internet Right Now': TikTok Celebrity, Girls and the Coronavirus Crisis," *European Journal of Cultural Studies* 23, no. 6 (2020): 1070.
15. Kennedy, "'If the Rise,'" 1070.
16. Kirsten Drotner, "Leisure Is Hard Work: Digital Practices and Future Competences," in *Youth, Identity, and Digital Media*, ed. David Buckingham (Cambridge, MA: MIT Press, 2008), 167.
17. Drotner, "Leisure Is Hard Work," 167.
18. Karen E. Bond and Susan W. Stinson, "'I Feel like I'm Going to Take Off!': Young People's Experiences of the Superordinary in Dance," *Dance Research Journal* 32, no 2 (Winter 2000/2001): 52.
19. Boffone, *Renegades*, 9–12.
20. The TikTok algorithm has been much criticized for how the app promotes Western beauty standards, whiteness, and normative bodies, for example. For more on the TikTok algorithm, see Boffone, *Renegades* and Jessica Sage Rauchberg, "TikTok's Digital Eugenics: Challenging Ableism and Algorithmic Erasure through Disability Activism," *Flow Journal* 27, no. 1 (2020), http://www.flowjournal.org/2020/09/tiktok-digital-eugenics/. For more on the oppressive nature of algorithms, see Safiya Umoja Noble, *Algorithms of Oppression: How Search Engines Reinforce Racism* (New York: NYU Press, 2018) and Ruha Benjamin, *Race After Technology: Abolitionist Tools for the New Jim Code* (Cambridge, UK: Polity Press, 2019).

21. Tanya Kant, *Making It Personal: Algorithmic Personalization, Identity, and Everyday Life* (Oxford Scholarship Online, 2020).
22. Kant, *Making it Personal.*
23. TikTok has also drawn criticisms for how the platform potentially collects users' data. While a political economy critique is beyond the scope of this chapter, I do not want to dismiss the intersections between child safety, autonomy, and predatory data collection.
24. Andrea Ruehlicke, "All the Content, Just for You: TikTok and Personalization," *Flow Journal* 27, no. 1 (2020), http://www.flowjournal.org/2020/10/content-just-for-you/.
25. Jan Deans, "Thinking, Feeling and Relating: Young Children Learning through Dance," *Australasian Journal of Early Childhood* 41, no. 3 (2016): 46.
26. Susan Stinson, "A Question of Fun: Adolescent Engagement in Dance Education," *Dance Research Journal* 29, no. 2 (1997): 65.
27. Ashleigh Wade, "When Social Media Yields More than 'Likes': Black Girls' Digital Kingship Formations," *Women, Gender, and Families of Color* 7, no. 1 (2019): 81.
28. Kerry Chappell, Anna Craft, Linda Rolfe, and Veronica Jobbins, "Dance Partners for Creativity: Choreographing Space for Co-Participative Research into Creativity and Partnership in Dance Education," *Research in Dance Education* 10, no. 3 (2009): 177–197.
29. William Hardy McNeill, *Keeping Together in Time: Dance and Drill in Human History* (Cambridge, MA: Harvard University Press, 1995), 2.
30. McNeill, *Keeping Together in Time*, 2.
31. McNeill, 2–3.
32. Mihály Csíkszentmihályi, *Beyond Boredom and Anxiety* (San Francisco: Jossey-Bass, 1975), 47.
33. Bond and Stinson, "'I Feel Like!,'" 73. See also Csíkszentmihályi, *Beyond Boredom and Anxiety*, 38–50.
34. Whether these songs are appropriate songs for children to dance to is beyond the scope of this chapter.
35. Stinson, "Question of Fun," 63.
36. Dance scholar Adrienne Oehlers has investigated the relationship between Michael Bennett's choreography in *A Chorus Line*, muscular bonding, and audience reception.

NOTES ON CONTRIBUTORS

BRIANNA ANDERSON is an assistant professor of English at the University of Texas at El Paso. Her research examines representations of environmental issues and youth agency in children's visual media. She is currently working on a monograph about the history of children's environmental comics. Her work has recently appeared in *Alt Kid Lit*, *Gothic Nature*, *Children's Literature in Education*, and *International Research in Children's Literature*.

TREVOR BOFFONE is a lecturer in the Women's, Gender & Sexuality Studies Program at the University of Houston. His work using TikTok with his students has been featured on *Good Morning America*, *ABC News*, *Inside Edition*, and *Access Hollywood*, among numerous national and local media platforms. He is the author of *Renegades: Digital Dance Cultures from Dubsmash to TikTok*, *TikTok Broadway: Musical Theatre Fandom in the Digital Age*, *Social Media in Musical Theatre*, and the coauthor of *Latinx Teens: U.S. Popular Culture on the Page, Stage, and Screen*. He is the coeditor of *Encuentro: Latinx Performance for the New American Theater*; *Nerds, Goths, Geeks, and Freaks: Outsiders in Chicanx and Latinx Young Adult Literature*; and *Shakespeare and Latinidad*, among other collections.

RACHEL CONRAD is a professor of childhood studies at Hampshire College in Amherst, Massachusetts, where she teaches courses on youth-authored texts and critical childhood studies. She is the author of *Time for Childhoods: Young Poets and Questions of Agency* and coeditor of *Literary Cultures and Twentieth-Century Childhoods*, which won the Children's Literature Association Edited Book Honor Award. Her articles on young poets, African American poetry, and young climate activists have appeared in the *Lion and the Unicorn*, *Children's Literature Association Quarterly*, *Childhood*, *Jeunesse*, *Callaloo*, and *International Research in Children's Literature*.

BRIGITTE FIELDER is an associate professor at the University of Wisconsin-Madison and the author of *Relative Races: Genealogies of Interracial Kinship in Nineteenth-Century America* and coeditor of *Against a Sharp, White Background: Infrastructures of African American Print*. She is a cofounder of Taught by Literature, a collaborative digital humanities project honoring Black author and activist

Alice Dunbar-Nelson's lifelong commitment to education and making work by other early Black women intellectuals available to readers of all ages.

MARAH GUBAR, associate professor of comparative media studies/writing at MIT, is the author of *Artful Dodgers: Reconceiving the Golden Age of Children's Literature*, which won the Children's Literature Association Book Award. A through line that connects her past and present work is her appreciative recognition of how creative writers and other artists whose audience includes young people have paved the way for critical theorists by generating nuanced accounts of youth agency that acknowledge the existence of age-related asymmetries of ability, experience, and power without essentializing them. Building on their work, her scholarship addresses philosophical questions such as what it means to be a child; what children's literature is and how to teach it; whether a critically ambivalent form of paternalism might sometimes be justified; and why elaborating a positive vision of the concept of innocence might be beneficial.

PETER C. KUNZE is assistant professor of communication at Tulane University. In 2023, Rutgers University Press published his first book, *Staging a Comeback: Broadway, Hollywood, and the Disney Renaissance.*

MAGGIE E. MORRIS DAVIS is an assistant professor in the Department of English at Illinois State University in Normal, Illinois. Her research focuses on class and childhood/youth and how, as social constructions, representations of these concepts not only enter our language, culture, and literatures, but also shape our classrooms, curriculums, and pedagogy. Most recently her work has been published in the journals *Children's Literature* and *Resources for American Literary Study* and the edited collection *Adaptation Before Cinema.*

CRISTINA RHODES is an associate professor of English at Shippensburg University, where she also teaches courses in ethnic studies and women's and gender studies. Her forthcoming book project, *Facing Uncertain Futures: The Transformative Possibilities of Latinx Youth Literatures*, considers Latinx futurities and the positionality of young Latinxs to be drivers of progress. Cris's research on Latinx youth, activism, and diverse children's and young adult literature can be found in journals such as *Women's Studies, Latino Studies, Children's Literature Association Quarterly*, and *Research on Diversity in Youth Literature*, and the edited collections *Companion to the Multi-Ethnic Literature of the United States, Alt Kid Lit: What Children's Literature Might Be*, and *Atravesados: Essays on Queer Latinx Young Adult Literature.* She is also the book review coeditor for the open-access journal *Research on Diversity in Youth Literature.*

KATHARINE SLATER is an associate professor of English at Rowan University in Glassboro, New Jersey; there, she teaches children's and young adult literature. In her current book project, she explores the queer mobilities of sapphic YA literature, arguing that girls in these texts move in ways that disturb dominant narratives around linear development. Her publications include articles on race, queerness, and geographies of childhood in the *Lion and the Unicorn*, *Children's Literature Association Quarterly*, *Research on Diversity in Youth Literature*, and *Children's Literature in Education*, as well as essays in the book collections *Children's Literature in Place* and *L. M. Montgomery's Emily of New Moon: A Children's Classic at 100*.

VICTORIA FORD SMITH is an associate professor of English at the University of Connecticut, where she specializes in childhood studies and nineteenth-century British literature and culture. Her book *Between Generations: Collaborative Authorship in the Golden Age of Children's Literature* won the Children's Literature Association Book Award. Her work has appeared in *Children's Literature*, *Children's Literature Association Quarterly*, *Dickens Studies Annual*, the *Lion and the Unicorn*, and *Victorian Poetry*.

IVY LINTON STABELL is an associate professor of English at Iona University in New Rochelle, New York, where she teaches children's, young adult, and early American literature. Her work has appeared in *Children's Literature*, the *Lion and the Unicorn*, and numerous scholarly collections. Her research focuses on children's nonfiction, especially biography, history, and food writing and culture.

INDEX

Available titles in the Rutgers Series in Childhood Studies:

Peter C. Kunze and Victoria Ford Smith, eds., *Producing Children: Critical Studies in Childhood Creativity*

Amanda E. Lewis, *Race in the Schoolyard: Negotiating the Color Line in Classrooms and Communities*

Donna M. Lanclos, *At Play in Belfast: Children's Folklore and Identities in Northern Ireland*

Cindy Dell Clark, *In Sickness and in Play: Children Coping with Chronic Illness*

Peter B. Pufall and Richard P. Unsworth, eds., *Rethinking Childhood*

David M. Rosen, *Armies of the Young: Child Soldiers in War and Terrorism*

Lydia Murdoch, *Imagined Orphans: Poor Families, Child Welfare, and Contested Citizenship in London*

Rachel Burr, *Vietnam's Children in a Changing World*

Laurie Schaffner, *Girls in Trouble with the Law*

Susan A. Miller, *Growing Girls: The Natural Origins of Girls' Organizations in America*

Marta Gutman and Ning de Coninck-Smith, eds., *Designing Modern Childhoods: History, Space, and the Material Culture of Children*

Jessica Fields, *Risky Lessons: Sex Education and Social Inequality*

Sarah E. Chinn, *Inventing Modern Adolescence: The Children of Immigrants in Turn-of-the-Century America*

Debra Curtis, *Pleasures and Perils: Girls' Sexuality in a Caribbean Consumer Culture*

Don S. Browning and Bonnie J. Miller-McLemore, eds., *Children and Childhood in American Religions*

Marjorie Faulstich Orellana, *Translating Childhoods: Immigrant Youth, Language, and Culture* Don S. Browning and Marcia J. Bunge, eds., *Children and Childhood in World Religions*

Hava Rachel Gordon, *We Fight to Win: Inequality and the Politics of Youth Activism*

Nikki Jones, *Between Good and Ghetto: African American Girls and Inner-City Violence*

Kate Douglas, *Contesting Childhood: Autobiography, Trauma, and Memory*

Jennifer Helgren and Colleen A. Vasconcellos, eds., *Girlhood: A Global History*

Karen Lury, *The Child in Film: Tears, Fears, and Fairy Tales*

Michelle Ann Abate, *Raising Your Kids Right: Children's Literature and American Political Conservatism*

Michael Bourdillon, Deborah Levison, William Myers, and Ben White, *Rights and Wrongs of Children's Work*

Jane A. Siegel, *Disrupted Childhoods: Children of Women in Prison*

Valerie Leiter, *Their Time Has Come: Youth with Disabilities on the Cusp of Adulthood*

Edward W. Morris, *Learning the Hard Way: Masculinity, Place, and the Gender Gap in Education*

Erin N. Winkler, *Learning Race, Learning Place: Shaping Racial Identities and Ideas in African American Childhoods*

Jenny Huberman, *Ambivalent Encounters: Childhood, Tourism, and Social Change in Banaras, India*

Walter Hamilton, *Children of the Occupation: Japan's Untold Story*

Jon M. Wolseth, *Life on the Malecón: Children and Youth on the Streets of Santo Domingo*

Lisa M. Nunn, *Defining Student Success: The Role of School and Culture*

Vikki S. Katz, *Kids in the Middle: How Children of Immigrants Negotiate Community Interactions for Their Families*

Bambi L. Chapin, *Childhood in a Sri Lankan Village: Shaping Hierarchy and Desire*

David M. Rosen, *Child Soldiers in the Western Imagination: From Patriots to Victims*

Marianne Modica, *Race among Friends: Exploring Race at a Suburban School*

Elzbieta M. Gozdziak, *Trafficked Children and Youth in the United States: Reimagining Survivors*

Pamela Robertson Wojcik, *Fantasies of Neglect: Imagining the Urban Child in American Film and Fiction*

Maria Kromidas, *City Kids: Transforming Racial Baggage*

Ingred A. Nelson, *Why Afterschool Matters*

Jean Marie Hunleth, *Children as Caregivers: The Global Fight against Tuberculosis and HIV in Zambia*

Abby Hardgrove, *Life after Guns: Reciprocity and Respect among Young Men in Liberia*

Michelle J. Bellino, *Youth in Postwar Guatemala: Education and Civic Identity in Transition*

Vera Lopez, *Complicated Lives: Girls, Parents, Drugs, and Juvenile Justice*

Rachel E. Dunifon, *You've Always Been There for Me: Understanding the Lives of Grandchildren Raised by Grandparents*

Cindy Dell Clark, *All Together Now: American Holiday Symbolism among Children and Adults*

Laura Moran, *Belonging and Becoming in a Multicultural World: Refugee Youth and the Pursuit of Identity*

Hannah Dyer, *The Queer Aesthetics of Childhood: Asymmetries of Innocence and the Cultural Politics of Child Development*

Julie Spray, *The Children in Child Health: Negotiating Young Lives and Health in New Zealand*

Franziska Fay, *Disputing Discipline: Child Protection, Punishment, and Piety in Zanzibar Schools*

Kathie Carpenter, *Life in a Cambodian Orphanage: A Childhood Journey for New Opportunities*

Norbert Ross, *A World of Many: Ontology and Child Development among the Maya of Southern Mexico*

Camilla Morelli, *Children of the Rainforest: Shaping the Future in Amazonia*

Junehui Ahn, *Between Self and Community: Children's Personhood in a Globalized South Korea*

Francesca Meloni, *Ways of Belonging: Undocumented Youth in the Shadow of Illegality*

Xiaojin Chen, *China's Left-Behind Children: Caretaking, Parenting, and Struggles*

Jeanine Anderson and Jessaca B. Leinaweaver, *Care and Agency: The Andean Community through the Eyes of Children*

Ursina Jaeger, *Children as Social Butterflies: Navigating Belonging in a Diverse Swiss Kindergarten*